## RECIPE FOR JOY

Take one man and one woman deeply inlove;
    marry them.
Add one bundle of children in assorted sizes—
    mix together in a family -sized house.
Fold in generous measures of thoughtfulness,
    patience, goodwill and self-sacrifice
    and carefully  shape them by the disciplines
    of responsibility and good personal
    habits.
Prepare a sauce of personal example and stir in.
Steep the mixture in a constant temperature of
    Christian faith kept warm by regular
    worship, study and prayer.
When all parts of the mixture  are thoroughly
    heated, share with others so that their
    lives may be enriched and your joy be
    complete.

(Note: Persons not married should reduce the
    number of original ingredients to
    suit the taste.)

                R.W. Fribley

# Easy-on-the-Cook
# BOOK

*Chicago Home Economists in Business*

Members, American Home Economics Association

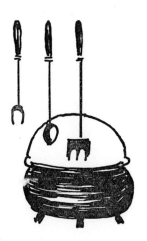

THE IOWA STATE UNIVERSITY PRESS, *Ames,* IOWA

# About this COOK BOOK

You're sure to enjoy eating these favorite dishes—and we hope you have fun preparing them. You'll find choice recipes for all your whims and occasions—from appetizers and party nibblers to main dishes and elegant desserts. We've titled this outstanding collection of recipes "easy-on-the-cook" because they take away all the worry about success. They are all presented in an easy to use form, with good results assured when directions are followed. It is our hope that meals with family and friends will be transformed into special occasions as a result of your efforts . . . and ours.

The creation of new recipes and food ideas is the chief responsibility of many members of the Chicago Home Economists in Business group. These "food professionals" are found in major food companies, trade associations, restaurants, advertising agencies, equipment and utility companies, on newspaper staffs and in many related types of work. Joining them for this venture have been other home economists for whom food preparation is a favorite "pastime," with a total of some 200 individuals playing a part with good food and *you* in mind. Copy has been edited by Miss Nellie Fredeen; layout and art work is by Arch MacDonald.

A special word of appreciation goes to the following for permitting use of striking illustrations:

| | |
|---|---|
| American Dairy Association | Corn Products Company |
| California Packing Corporation (Del Monte Products) | General Mills, Inc. |
| | Pillsbury Mills, Inc. |
| The Nestle Company, Inc. | |

# Recipes have been contributed by:

Accent — International

American Dairy Association

American Dry Milk Institute

American Institute of Baking

American Lamb Council

American Meat Institute

Armour and Company

Beatrice Foods Company

California Packing Corporation
(Del Monte Products)

Campbell, Thora Hegstad —
*Consultant*

Carroll, Leone Rutledge —
*Consultant*

Central Illinois Electric & Gas
Company

Cereal Institute, Inc.

Chicago American

Chicago Daily News

Chicago Printed String Company

Chicago Sun - Times

Chicago Tribune

Club Aluminum Products Company

Commonwealth Edison Company

Corn Products Company

Culinary Arts Institute & Family
Weekly Magazine

Fredeen, Nellie A.

Evaporated Milk Association

General Electric Company

General Mills, Inc.

Glick and Lorwin

The Grace Kent Corporation

Harding's Restaurant

Harper Wyman Company

Henry, M. Frances — *Consultant*

Holst, Elsie D. — *Consultant*

Hotpoint Company

Household Finance Corporation

Hyde Park Cooperative Society

John Sexton and Company

Johnson Publishing Company

J. Walter Thompson Company

Kraft Foods Company

Lawrence H. Selz Organization,
Inc.

Leo Burnett Company, Inc.

Libby, McNeill, Libby

Marshall Field & Company

McCann - Erickson, Inc.

Mettenet, Elizabeth L.

National Dairy Council

National Live Stock and Meat
Board

The Nestle Company, Inc.

The Peoples Gas Light and Coke
Company

Poultry & Egg National Board

The Quaker Oats Company

Sears Roebuck and Company

Swift and Company

Western Beet Sugar Products, Inc.

Wheat Flour Institute

Wilson and Company

What's New in Home Economics
Experimental Kitchens

Wright, Mary Lawton —
*Consultant*

# CONTENTS

|   |   | Page |
|---|---|---|
| 1 | Menus . . . . . . . . . . | 7 |
| 2 | Appetizers and Beverages . . . . . | 17 |
| 3 | Breads (Quick, Yeast and Ways with Bread) . . . . . . | 31 |
| 4 | Cakes, Cookies and Pies . . . . . | 47 |
| 5 | Desserts – Candies and Confections . . . | 79 |
| 6 | Main Dishes . . . . . . . . . | 93 |
| 7 | Salads and Salad Dressings . . . . . | 133 |
| 8 | Sandwiches and Soups . . . . . . | 145 |
| 9 | Vegetables . . . . . . . . | 151 |
| 10 | Over-the-Coals Cookery . . . . . | 161 |
| 11 | Quantity Cookery for Fifty . . . . . | 169 |
|   | Index . . . . . . . . . . | 183 |

Favored dishes rate top enjoyment when they're accented by just the right accompaniments. Here are some proven "go-togethers". (Asterisks indicate recipes are included.) As you build menus around other recipes in this book, why not make a note in the margin when you've served an especially pleasing combination? You'll have a valuable timesaving reference for repeat success.

## Morning Call

**Orange Juice**

**Beef Helene\***    on    **Corn Bread\***

**Herb Baked Tomatoes\***      **Preserved Watermelon Rind**

**Cheese and Fruit\***

**Coffee**

\* Asterisks indicate recipes are included

Fresh Fruit Cup Topped with Raspberry Sherbet

Poached Eggs on Wild Rice—Western Sauce*

Toast          Marmalade          Butter Rolls

Cafe au Lait
(Half Hot Milk and Half Triple Strength Hot Coffee)

———————

Hot Buttered Tomato Juice*

Baked Eggs au Gratin with Nippy Cheese Sauce*

Bacon Curls

Fruit Filled Coffee Cake*          Butter

Milk          Coffee

———————

# Hunches for Lunches
## Especially for the Ladies

Bouillon

Tuna Suey*          Chilled Tomato Slices

Hot Biscuits          Butter

Creamy Cheese Cake*

Milk          Coffee

———————

Southern Baked Jambalaya Salad*

Corn Sticks*          Butter

Fresh Fruit Salad

Ice Cream Parfait          Butter Cookies

Coffee New Orleans Style
(Half Milk—Half Chickory Coffee)

* Asterisks indicate recipes are included

Lobster and Crab Meat Casserole*

French Peas*

Tiny Corn Muffins*

Orange Avocado Salad

Apple Caramel*

Coffee

————————

Shrimp and Pineapple Salad*

Currant Scones*                    Butter

Coffee                    Tea

————————

Chilled Consomme

Individual Crab Meat Souffles*

Tomato Artichoke Salad*

Hot Rolls*

Honeydew Melon

Coffee

————————

Chicken Grape Salad*

Potato Chips                    Hot Buttered Peas

Party Cake* with Fluffy Icing*

Coffee                    Tea

* Asterisks indicate recipes are included

# Dessert Bridge

**Walnut Honey Cake***

**Coffee**                              **Tea**

---

**Ice Cream Party Loaf***

**Mints**                    **Nuts**

**Coffee**

---

# Lunch Basket

**Beefeater Sandwich***

**Shoestring Potatoes**          **Relishes**

**Fudge-Topped Brownies* with Fudge Frosting***

**Milk**                    **Lemonade**

---

# Five to Seven Menu

**Cocktails**

**or**

**Hot Beef Consomme or Cranberry-Pineapple Juices Blended**

**Party Cheese Ball***          **or**          **Sesame Cheese Log***

**Appetizing Cucumber Dip***

**French Fried Liver***

**Crisp Vegetable Relishes**

**Marinated Meat***

**Do-Ahead Cheese Appetizer Puffs***

**Deviled Eggs***

* Asterisks indicate recipes are included

# Winners for Dinner
## Quick Meals

**Lobster Thermidor***

**Green Rice Casserole***

**Baked Tomatoes**          **Green Beans and Mushrooms***

**Sherbet Ring with Strawberries***

**Milk**          **Coffee**

---

**South Sea Island Treat***          **Steamed Rice**

**Tossed Green Salad**

**Curried Fruit***          **Coconut Kisses***

**Milk**          **Tea**

---

# Winners for Dinner
## Family Fare

**Barbecued Lamb Shanks***

**Fluffy Buttered Rice**          **Buttered Lima Beans**

**Grapefruit Salad***

**Hot Rolls***          **Butter**

**Pineapple Sherbet**

**Milk**          **Coffee**

---

**Tomato-Corn Chowder***

**Savory Baked Fish***

**Oven-Baked Potatoes***          **Buttered Zucchini***

**Mixed Green Salad**          **Blue Cheese Dressing**

**Bread Sticks**          **Butter**

**Cream Puffs with Chocolate Chip Cream Filling***

**Milk**          **Coffee**

* Asterisks indicate recipes are included

Veal Paprika with Buttered Noodles*

Spinach

Dark Sweet Cherry Mold*                    Sour Cream Dressing*

Sweet Coffee Cake*

Milk                    Coffee

---

Sweet Sour Pot Roast*

Parsley Buttered Potatoes            Julienne Carrots

Tossed Salad*

Bread            Butter            Jelly

Ice Cream                    Crisp Molasses Cookies*

Milk                    Coffee

---

Glazed Ham Balls in Noodle Ring*

Buttered Broccoli

Celery Sticks            Carrot Curls            Radish Roses

Lime or Lemon Sherbet*

Chocolate Chip Oatmeal Cookies*

Milk                    Coffee

---

Beef Stroganoff*

Avocado and Citrus Fruit Salad*                    Celery Seed Dressing*

Relish Tray

Carrot Sticks            Celery Hearts            Black Olives            Stuffed Olives

Hot Parker House Rolls                    Butter

Creme de Cacao Bavarian*

Milk                    Coffee

* Asterisks indicate recipes are included

# Winners for Dinner
## Entertaining Company

**Appetizer Tray**

**Standing Rib Roast of Beef***

**Baked Potatoes**     **Sour Cream Bacon Topping***

**Corn Casserole***

**Tossed Green Salad**     **Gourmet Sour Cream Dressing***

**Ice Cream and Fruit Compote***

**Coffee**

———————

**Sausage-Stuffed Beef Birds in Barbecue Sauce***

**Wild Rice and Mushroom Casserole***

**Broccoli with Lemon Butter**

**Pears Molded in Apple Gelatin**     **Sour Cream Dressing***

**Rolls**     **Butter**     **Jelly**

**Pineapple Sherbet**     **Two-Tone Brownies***

**Coffee**     **Tea**

———————

**Red-Rock Shrimp Cocktail***

**Roast Turkey***

**Wild Rice**

**Crisp-Top Corn with Herbs***     **Harvest-Style Green Beans***

**Minted Pineapple Salad with Lemon Dressing***

**Relish Tray**

**Ripe and Stuffed Olives**     **Sliced Pickled Beets**

**Hot Rolls***     **Butter**

**Frozen Pumpkin "Peace-Pipe" Pie***

**Coffee**

* Asterisks indicate recipes are included

Tomato Cream Frosty*

Celestial Chicken*

Julienne Green Beans

Tossed Salad*

Hot Rolls*                    Butter

Assorted Cheese and Crackers with Fresh Fruit

Coffee

———————

Rotisserie Rolled Leg of Lamb*

Minted Pineapple Garnish

Baked Creamed Potatoes*                    Baked Carrot Sticks*

Tray of Relishes

Spiced Peach Salad*

Herb or Garlic French Bread*

Coconut Tart Shells with Strawberry Parfait Filling*

Coffee

———————

Baked Ham with Cumberland Sauce*

Argante Potatoes*

Green Beans Amandine*

Golden Salad Ring*                    Whipped Fruit Dressing*

Crescents                    Butter

Cherries Jubilee*

Coffee

* Asterisks indicate recipes are included

# Five-Bowl Hawaiian Menu

Passion Punch*

Avocado Ham Dip*

Maikai Spareribs*         One Bowl Chicken and Curried Rice*

Fruit Salad            Tropical Salad Dressing*

Almond Tea Cakes*

Coffee

---

# Teenage Parties

Jumbo Pizza Sandwich*

Crisp Relishes

Pecan Brownies*

Milk Shake

---

Cinnamon Sparkle Punch*

Gumdrop Oatmeal Cookies*

Nuts            Mints

# Midnight Snack

Beef-Rye Sandwich Specialty*

Potato Chips

Carrot Curls      Celery Sticks

Ripe Olives

Applesauce Cake*

Milk         Coffee

\* Asterisks indicate recipes are included

# Over-the-Coals Cookery

**Dilly Barbecued Chicken***

**Grilled Potatoes***        **Corn on the Cob***

**Tossed Mixed Green Salad**

**Herb Buttered Bread in Foil***

**Watermelon**

**Milk**        **Coffee**

---

**Chilled Melon or Fresh Berries**

**Grilled French Toast with Bacon***
**OR**
**Grilled Bacon and Egg Sandwiches***

**Assorted Doughnuts**

**Milk**        **Coffee**

---

**Skewered Fish Steaks***

**Cheese Tomatoes***        **Tossed Salad**

**French Bread**

**Angels on Wings***

**Milk**        **Coffee**

\* Asterisks indicate recipes are included

# APPETIZERS and BEVERAGES

RED-ROCK SHRIMP
  COCKTAIL
BAMBINOS
PASTRY BOATS
DO-AHEAD CHEESE
  APPETIZER PUFFS
SHRIMP PUFFS
DEVILED EGGS
CRAB MEAT SPREAD
SHARP CHEDDAR SPREAD
SESAME CHEESE LOG
CHEESE SWIRLS
CHEESE PARTY TRAY
PARTY CHEESE BALL
ARTICHOKE ANTIPASTO
FRESH ORANGE CUP
SNOW CAP MOLD
EGG FOO YUNG
MARINATED MEAT
ORIENTAL-STYLE MEAT
  BALLS
COCK KABOBS
HAM-OLIVE DIP

WEST INDIES DIP
RUMAKI
FRENCH FRIED LIVER
SMOKED EGG DIP
APPETIZING CUCUMBER DIP
FRUIT CURRY DIP
HERB DIP
AVOCADO HAM DIP
FRUIT JUICE SHRUB
CINNAMON SPARKLE PUNCH
RHUBARB SHRUB
HOT BUTTERED TOMATO
  JUICE
HOT MULLED PINEAPPLE
  JUICE
ORANGE-PINEAPPLE PUNCH
PASSION PUNCH
HEAVENLY NECTAR PUNCH
MILK PUNCH
PARTY PUNCH
TEENAGERS SWINGIN'
  SWIZZLE PUNCH
TOMATO CREAM FROSTY

*Illustration:* Cheese Party Tray (page 22).

# Appetizers and Beverages

Some say that it scarcely seems necessary to whet the appetites of hearty-eating Americans. Nevertheless there is a growing tradition of serving a "little something to start with" . . . particularly when the occasion is a special one.

## Red-Rock Shrimp Cocktail

3 tablespoons prepared
  horseradish
Dash Tabasco
2 teaspoons Worcestershire
  sauce

1 1-pint 2-ounce can (2¼ cups)
  tomato juice
2 cups cooked and cleaned
  shrimp, chilled
Lemon wedges
Lettuce

Stir seasonings into tomato juice, mixing well to blend. Pour into refrigerator freezing tray. Freeze to sherbet consistency, about 1½ hours. Spoon lightly into chilled appetizer dishes. Top with shrimp. Garnish with lemon and a frill of lettuce.     6 *servings.*

# Bambinos

2 cups sifted flour
1 teaspoon salt
⅔ cup shortening
¼ cup water
TOPPING:
1 6-ounce can tomato paste
1 teaspoon garlic salt

¼ teaspoon oregano
¼ pound American or
  Mozzarella cheese, cubed
⅛ pound salami or pepperoni,
  cubed
Oregano

Mix flour and salt. Cut in shortening. Sprinkle with water; mix with fork. Round into ball; divide in half. Roll each half ¼ inch thick. Cut in 1½- or 2-inch circles. Place on foil-covered baking sheet, prick 2 or 3 times. Bake in 475° oven 8 to 10 minutes.

Topping: Combine tomato paste, garlic salt, oregano; spoon small amount on baked pastry round. Top with cheese and meat. Sprinkle with oregano. Bake 3 to 5 minutes or until cheese melts. Serve hot.

*Makes* 10 *dozen* 1½-*inch rounds or* 5 *dozen* 2-*inch rounds.*

# Pastry Boats

2 cups sifted flour
1 teaspoon salt
⅔ cup shortening
¼ cup water
SEA FOOD SALAD FILLING:
1 cup flaked cooked sea food
1 teaspoon lemon juice
1 teaspoon finely minced onion
Salt
Paprika
1 cup diced celery
Mayonnaise
Pimiento strips
Parsley

CRAB MEAT FILLING:
1 6½-ounce can crab meat,
  flaked
¼ cup mayonnaise
1 teaspoon Worcestershire
  sauce
½ teaspoon salt
½ teaspoon dry minced onion
¼ cup finely diced celery
1 dill pickle, finely diced
Cheddar cheese strips

Mix flour and salt. Cut in shortening. Sprinkle with water; mix with fork. Round into ball; divide in half. Roll each ⅛ inch thick on heavy-duty foil with lightly floured cloth-covered rolling pin. Cut foil and pastry in 5 x 2 inch rectangles; perforate with fork. To form boats: Bring long side of rectangle up, moisten and pinch ends firmly together. Place on baking sheet. Spread sides out like a canoe and balance to stand by themselves. Bake in 475° oven 10 to 12 minutes. Fill.

Sea Food Salad Filling: Mix together first 6 ingredients lightly. Chill. Just before serving, add mayonnaise to moisten. Spoon into pastry boats. Garnish with pimiento strips and parsley.

Crab Meat Filling: Mix together all ingredients except cheese. Fill boats; top with cheese. Broil 5 inches from heat until cheese melts.

# Do-Ahead Cheese Appetizer Puffs

**CREAM PUFFS:**
½ cup butter
1 cup boiling water
1 cup sifted flour
¼ teaspoon salt
4 eggs
**CHEESE FILLINGS:**
**CHEDDAR**
¾ cup shredded Cheddar
cheese
¼ cup finely chopped pimiento
stuffed olives
⅛ teaspoon garlic salt

**PARMESAN**
⅓ cup grated Parmesan cheese
¼ cup finely chopped ripe
olives
½ teaspoon chili powder
**BLUE**
¼ cup crumbled blue cheese
¼ cup cottage cheese
2 teaspoons red wine vinegar
**PROVOLONE**
½ cup shredded Provolone
cheese
⅓ cup pureed peas, or strained
peas (baby food)
½ teaspoon chervil

Cream Puffs: Melt butter in saucepan and add water; bring to a boil. Lower heat, add flour and salt and stir constantly until mixture leaves sides of pan in a compact mass. Remove from heat; cool slightly. Add eggs, one at a time, beating well after each addition, and until batter is smooth and shiny. Drop by teaspoon onto well greased cooky sheet about 2 inches apart. Bake in 425° oven 18 to 20 minutes. Remove from oven. Cut small slit in side of each puff. When cool, fill with cheese mixtures. *Makes 48 tiny puffs.*
To freeze puffs: bake about 15 minutes; cool; fill; freeze. For serving, bake 6 to 7 minutes if thawed; 12 minutes if frozen.

**For Desired Cheese Filling:** Stir ingredients to uniform consistency. *Makes filling for 12 puffs.*

# Shrimp Puffs

16 small round crackers
16 cooked shrimp, well drained

1 cup mayonnaise
Grated Parmesan cheese

Place crackers on cooky sheet and top each with a shrimp. Cover shrimp with 1 tablespoon mayonnaise. Sprinkle with cheese. Broil until lightly browned and puffy. Serve hot.

*Makes 16.*

# Deviled Eggs

6 hard cooked eggs
½ teaspoon salt
¼ teaspoon pepper
½ teaspoon dry mustard

3 tablespoons salad dressing
(about)
Pimiento, diced

Cut eggs in halves. Slip out yolks, mash with fork. Mix in remaining ingredients. Refill whites with yolk mixture, heaping it up lightly. Dot with pimiento. *Makes 12 deviled eggs.*

# Crab Meat Spread

1 8-ounce package cream cheese
¼ cup butter, melted
1 tablespoon lemon juice
2 tablespoons milk
¼ teaspoon garlic salt

3 small green onions (white part minced, green stalks cut in small rings)
1 6½-ounce can (1 cup) crab meat, rinsed, drained and shredded
Potato chips OR Crackers

Cream cheese with a fork. Slowly add butter. Add other ingredients in order given. Cover and refrigerate to mellow. Remove from refrigerator 1 hour before serving. Serve on potato chips or crackers.

Note: Spread will keep under refrigeration for 3 to 4 days.

# Sharp Cheddar Spread

½ pound sharp Cheddar cheese, finely shredded
2 ounces blue cheese, crumbled
2 teaspoons prepared mustard
¼ cup soft butter
Dash Tabasco

2 teaspoons minced onion
1 tablespoon chopped green olives
Dash salt
½ cup light beer
Crackers

Place all ingredients except beer and crackers in mixing bowl. Let stand about 30 minutes to soften. Add beer gradually, beating until light and fluffy. Store in tightly covered jar in refrigerator. Serve with crackers. *Makes about 2 cups.*

# Sesame Cheese Log

1 3-ounce package cream cheese
¼ cup (2 ounces) blue cheese
¼ cup minced dried beef

Dash Tabasco OR cayenne
   pepper
½ cup toasted sesame seeds
Crackers

Let cheeses soften at room temperature; blend with dried beef and seasoning. Form in a long roll or small balls the size of marbles. Chill. Roll in toasted sesame seeds.

*Makes 20 to 30 balls or one roll 4 x 1½ inches.*

# Cheese Swirls

6 egg whites
½ teaspoon salt
6 egg yolks
2 teaspoons lemon juice
2 tablespoons water
½ cup sifted flour

¼ cup butter or margarine,
   melted
1½ cups shredded sharp
   Cheddar cheese (about ⅓
   pound or 6 ounces)
1 teaspoon paprika
1 teaspoon cayenne pepper
2 teaspoons minced onion

Beat egg whites with salt until stiff but not dry. Beat egg yolks until thick and lemon-colored. Gradually beat in lemon juice and water. Fold yolk mixture into egg whites, then fold in flour. Spread in a greased and floured jelly roll pan, 15 x 10 x 1 inches. Bake in 350° oven about 15 minutes or until sponge roll springs back when touched lightly with the finger tip. Turn out immediately onto a clean towel. Roll, from the long side, jelly roll fashion. Unroll and brush with melted butter. Combine cheese, paprika, cayenne pepper and onion. Spread evenly over the roll. Reroll tightly. Wrap in foil and heat in 350° oven 10 minutes. Serve hot. Cut into ½-inch slices. This roll may be prepared in advance. When ready to serve, heat and slice as above.

*Makes about 24 slices.*

# Party Cheese Ball

2 8-ounce packages cream
  cheese
½ pound sharp Cheddar cheese,
  shredded
1 tablespoon chopped pimiento
1 tablespoon chopped green
  pepper
1 teaspoon minced onion

2 teaspoons Worcestershire
  sauce
1 teaspoon lemon juice
Dash cayenne pepper
Dash salt
Finely chopped pecans
Assorted crackers
Ice box rye bread, sliced

Combine cream and Cheddar cheeses; mix until well blended. Add pimiento, green pepper, onion, Worcestershire sauce, lemon juice and seasonings; blend well. Chill. Shape into a ball. Roll in pecans. Serve with crackers and bread.

*Spreads about 8 dozen crackers.*

# Cheese Party Tray

Cheddar Cheese
Crackers
Pimiento strips
Anchovies
Brick cheese, sliced
Gouda slices
Aged Cheddar

Baby Gouda, cubed
Camembert wedges
2 eating apples, sliced
Endive
Pimiento stuffed olives
Ripe olives
Grapes

Spread Cheddar cheese on crackers. Top each cracker with pimiento and anchovy to make appetizers. Arrange remaining cheeses and apple slices on tray. Garnish with endive, olives and grapes.

# Artichoke Antipasto

½ cup salad oil
⅓ cup wine vinegar
2 tablespoons water
½ clove garlic
⅛ teaspoon seasoned salt
⅛ teaspoon pepper
2 9-ounce packages frozen
   halved artichoke hearts
1 medium head lettuce
3 heads bibb lettuce

4 hard cooked eggs, sliced
Slices of Provolone, Scamozza,
   Mozzarella OR Gorgonzola
   cheese
1 3-ounce bottle anchovy
   stuffed olives
1 9-ounce can ripe olives
5 pimiento strips
1 tablespoon chopped chives

Combine oil, vinegar, water, garlic and seasonings in jar. Cover, shake well, chill. Cook artichokes according to package directions; cool. Remove garlic and pour dressing over artichokes; chill. On a large platter arrange outer leaves of head and bibb lettuce. Break small inner leaves and fill in center of platter. Remove artichokes from dressing; center on lettuce. Pour dressing over lettuce. Arrange eggs, cheese and olives around artichokes. Garnish with pimiento. Sprinkle chives over antipasto.

*6 servings.*

# Fresh Orange Cup

2 naval oranges
1 grapefruit

1 tablespoon strained honey
½ teaspoon Grenadine syrup

Cut fruit in half crosswise. Remove sections of fruit from membranes. Smooth out interiors of orange cups. Add honey and syrup to fruit sections; let stand ½ hour. Fill orange cups with fruit. Chill well before serving.

*4 servings.*

# Snow Cap Mold

½ pound liver sausage
3 tablespoons mayonnaise
2 tablespoons lemon juice
½ teaspoon salt
⅛ teaspoon pepper
2 tablespoons minced onion

Dash Tabasco
2 3-ounce packages cream
   cheese
2 or 3 tablespoons cream
Crackers OR
Party rye bread

Blend together liver sausage, mayonnaise, lemon juice, salt, pepper, onion and Tabasco. Pack into small round bowl; cover. Chill until firm. Unmold on plate. Soften cream cheese and blend to spreading consistency with cream or milk. Spread over meat mold as "frosting." Chill again until firm. Serve with crackers or party rye bread.

*Makes about 2 cups.*

# Egg Foo Yung

3 eggs
½ cup well drained, mixed
  Chinese vegetables (canned)
½ cup diced cooked chicken or
  pork
¾ teaspoon salt
2 tablespoons salad oil

SOY SAUCE:
2 teaspoons cornstarch
1½ teaspoons sugar
1 tablespoon soy sauce
1 cup water

Heat griddle. Break eggs into mixing bowl. Beat until yolks and whites are well blended. Add vegetables, chicken or pork and salt. Mix ingredients thoroughly. Brush griddle with oil. Pour mixture by tablespoonfuls onto griddle. Brown on each side, about a minute. *Makes 16 patties.*

**Sauce:** Mix cornstarch and sugar in small saucepan. Stir in soy sauce and water. Cook, stirring constantly, until sauce thickens. Reduce heat to very low; cook 10 minutes. Serve on Egg Foo Yung. *Makes 1 cup sauce.*

# Marinated Meat

1 pound cooked beef or lamb,
  sliced ⅛ inch thick
6 green onions and tops
1 teaspoon salt
⅛ teaspoon pepper

1 tablespoon lemon juice
1 cup dairy sour cream
Buttered crackers
Toast rounds

Cut beef or lamb slices in matchlike strips. Slice green onions and tops thinly; mix with salt, pepper, lemon juice and sour cream. Pour cream mixture over meat. Chill 1 hour. Place chilled mixture on buttered crackers or toast rounds.

*14 to 16 servings.*

# Oriental-Style Meat Balls

MEAT BALLS:
1 pound ground beef
¼ teaspoon salt
⅛ teaspoon garlic powder
⅛ teaspoon pepper
1 tablespoon onion juice
½ cup chow mein noodles,
  finely crushed
½ cup milk

MARINADE SAUCE:
½ cup soy sauce
¼ cup water
1 clove garlic, crushed
1 tablespoon sugar
½ teaspoon ground ginger

Mix together ingredients for meat balls. Shape in balls 1 inch in diameter. Place in shallow 1¼-quart baking pan. Blend together ingredients for sauce. Pour sauce over meat balls. Let stand in refrigerator about an hour. Bake in Marinade Sauce, uncovered, in 350° oven 25 to 30 minutes. Serve hot, inserting wooden pick in each ball.                          *Makes about* 30 *meat balls.*

# Cock Kabobs

1 cup sifted flour
½ teaspoon salt
⅓ cup shortening
¼ cup finely shredded
   American cheese
2 tablespoons water
1-inch cubes sausage (Vienna,
   salami, bologna)
Stuffed olives

HOT COCKTAIL SAUCE:
½ cup chili sauce
⅓ cup catsup
3 tablespoons prepared horseradish
1½ teaspoons Worcestershire
   sauce

Mix flour and salt. Cut in shortening. Blend in cheese. Sprinkle with water; mix with fork. Round into ball. Roll ⅛ inch thick on lightly floured pastry cloth. Cut in 1-inch rounds. Alternate with sausage cubes and olives on wooden pick, kabob style. Place on foil-covered baking sheet; bake in 475° oven 10 to 12 minutes. Serve with Hot Cocktail Sauce.                          3 *dozen.*

**Hot Cocktail Sauce:** Combine ingredients. Heat.

# Ham-Olive Dip

1 3½-ounce jar (½ cup)
   chopped ham
1 8-ounce package cream cheese
4 pimiento stuffed olives,
   sliced
½ teaspoon Worcestershire
   sauce

¼ teaspoon onion salt
Dash Tabasco
Crackers
Potato chips

Combine ham, cheese, olives and seasonings. Serve with crackers and chips.                          *Makes* 1½ *cups.*

# West Indies Dip

1 3-ounce package cream
   cheese, softened
1 tablespoon finely chopped
   chutney
¾ teaspoon curry powder
1 teaspoon lemon juice

½ teaspoon grated onion
2 to 3 tablespoons cream
Potato chips OR
Corn chips OR
Pretzel sticks

Combine cheese, chutney, curry powder, lemon juice and onion; blend well. Add enough cream to thin mixture to dipping consistency. Serve with potato chips, corn chips or pretzel sticks.
*Makes about* ½ *cup.*

Note: For a more pronounced curry flavor add additional curry to taste.

# Rumaki

½ pound chicken livers      ½ pound sliced bacon
1 8-ounce can water chestnuts

Drain chicken livers and water chestnuts; dry thoroughly between paper towels. Cut chicken livers in ¾-inch pieces. Cut chestnuts and bacon in half crosswise. Place a chicken liver and a chestnut half on each piece of bacon. Roll up and fasten with a wooden pick. Bake in 425° oven 15 to 20 minutes. Serve hot.

*Makes 3 dozen.*

# French Fried Liver

1 pound beef liver      Dash pepper
¼ cup flour      Lard for frying
½ teaspoon salt

Have liver sliced about ½ inch thick. Cut in strips about ⅜ inch wide, using sharp knife or kitchen shears. Roll liver in flour seasoned with salt and pepper or shake liver and seasoned flour together in a paper bag. Drop into kettle of deep lard heated to 350°. Cook until brown. Drain on absorbent paper. 10 *servings*.

# Smoked Egg Dip

12 hard cooked eggs, riced or sieved
2 tablespoons soft butter or margarine
1½ teaspoons liquid smoke seasoning
1 tablespoon lemon juice or vinegar
2 teaspoons prepared mustard
2 teaspoons Worcestershire sauce
2 drops Tabasco
1 teaspoon salt
¼ teaspoon ground pepper
¾ cup mayonnaise or salad dressing
Radish slices
Potato chips
Tiny rolls

Combine all ingredients except radishes, potato chips and rolls. Beat until smooth. If desired, add more seasonings. Have consistency soft enough to permit potato chips to be dipped into it easily. Refrigerate until ready to serve. About 30 minutes before serving, remove from refrigerator and beat dip to fluff and soften it. Garnish with radish slices. Serve with potato chips and tiny rolls. Dip can be prepared the day before serving.

*Makes 1 quart.*

Note: Smoked Egg Dip makes an excellent sandwich filling.

# Appetizing Cucumber Dip

1 8-ounce package cream cheese
¼ cup well drained, finely
   shredded unpared cucumber
¼ teaspoon Worcestershire
   sauce
Dash garlic salt
Potato chips

Combine cream cheese and cucumber, blending until smooth. Add Worcestershire sauce and garlic salt; mix well. Serve with potato chips. *Makes about 1 cup.*

# Fruit Curry Dip

1 pint dairy sour cream
¾ cup drained, crushed
   pineapple
⅔ cup chopped, cored, unpared
   apple
1 teaspoon curry powder
½ teaspoon garlic salt
Sliced apples
Corn chips
Shredded wheat wafers

Blend sour cream with pineapple, apple, curry powder and garlic salt. Chill several hours. Garnish with sliced apples. Serve with corn chips and shredded wheat wafers.

*Makes about 3 cups.*

# Herb Dip

1 cup dairy sour cream
1 cup mayonnaise
2 tablespoons chopped chives
2 teaspoons prepared
   horseradish
½ teaspoon marjoram
½ teaspoon basil
Potato chips OR
Crackers

Mix together sour cream, mayonnaise, chives, horseradish, marjoram and basil. Allow to season in refrigerator at least one hour or overnight. Serve with potato chips or crackers.

*Makes about 2 cups.*

# Avocado Ham Dip

1 3-ounce can deviled ham
1 ripe avocado
¼ teaspoon salt
¼ teaspoon paprika
½ teaspoon lemon juice
1 teaspoon finely chopped onion

Place ham in bowl. Pare avocado; remove pit. Mash avocado with deviled ham. Blend in salt, paprika, lemon juice and onion. Serve in a coconut shell. May be prepared in advance and chilled. *Makes about 1 cup.*

# Fruit Juice Shrub

1 1-pint 2-fluid ounce can
  (2¼ cups) pineapple juice,
  chilled
1 6-ounce can frozen orange
  juice

1½ cups cold water
2 7-ounce bottles ginger ale,
  chilled
1 pint orange sherbet
1 orange cut in slices

Combine pineapple and orange juices and water. Mix well. Add ginger ale. Spoon sherbet into 6 tall glasses. Fill with fruit ginger ale mixture. Garnish with orange slices.   *Makes 6 tall glasses.*

# Cinnamon Sparkle Punch

3 cinnamon sticks
¼ cup sugar
2 cups water
2 cups pineapple juice

1 cup orange juice
¼ cup lemon juice
4 7-ounce bottles lemon-lime
  carbonated beverage

Simmer cinnamon sticks and sugar in water 10 minutes. Cool; discard cinnamon sticks. Chill remaining ingredients. Combine fruit juices with cinnamon syrup in large punch bowl. Slowly pour in carbonated beverage. Add ice to cool.

18 *4-ounce servings.*

# Rhubarb Shrub

2 pounds fresh rhubarb
3 cups water
⅔ cup sugar

Few drops red food coloring,
  optional
1 pint lime sherbet

Clean and cut rhubarb in 1-inch pieces. Cook in water until tender. Strain well through sieve but do not push pulp through. Add sugar to juice; stir until sugar is dissolved. Cool to room temperature; add few drops food coloring, if desired. Cover; chill. Serve in cocktail glasses, topping each with small scoop of sherbet.   8 *servings.*

# Hot Buttered Tomato Juice

1 1-quart 14-ounce can (5¾
  cups) tomato juice
1 teaspoon Worcestershire
  sauce

½ teaspoon salt
½ teaspoon oregano
4 cloves
¼ cup butter

Combine ingredients in 2-quart saucepan. Heat slowly until butter is melted. Do not boil. Serve immediately.   8 *servings.*

# Hot Mulled Pineapple Juice

1 1-pint 2-ounce can (2¼ cups)       4 sticks cinnamon
   pineapple juice       1 teaspoon whole cloves
½ cup sugar       ¼ cup lemon juice

Simmer first 4 ingredients together for about 10 minutes. Add lemon juice; strain. Serve in mugs with a stick of cinnamon for a stirrer.       *4 servings.*

# Orange-Pineapple Punch

½ cup sugar       1½ cups orange juice
1½ cups water       ½ cup lemon juice
4 sticks cinnamon       Ice cubes OR
12 cloves       Frozen pineapple juice cubes
1 46-ounce can (5¾ cups)
   pineapple juice

Simmer first 4 ingredients about 30 minutes. Strain; add to fruit juices. Pour over ice or frozen pineapple juice cubes.       *Makes 2 quarts.*

# Passion Punch

1 46-ounce can (5¾ cups)       1 8-ounce bottle lime juice
   fruit punch       1 quart ginger ale
1 6-ounce can frozen       Fresh flowers
   concentrated pineapple juice

Combine chilled juices; pour into a punch bowl. Add ginger ale just before serving. Garnish by floating fresh flowers on the punch.       *Makes about 3 quarts.*

# Heavenly Nectar Punch

1 46-ounce can (5¾ cups)       1 quart ginger ale
   apricot, peach OR pear       Ice cubes
   nectar       Food coloring
¾ cup lemon juice

Pour nectar, lemon juice and ginger ale over ice in punch bowl. Tint with a small amount of food coloring, red for peach or apricot nectar punch, green for pear.       *Makes 2½ quarts.*

# Milk Punch

¾ cup rum, brandy, whisky OR
   sherry
1 quart milk OR milk and cream
4 eggs

5 tablespoons sifted
   confectioners' sugar
Nutmeg

Pour all ingredients except nutmeg into blender; blend just a few seconds. Pour into glasses. Top with a sprinkling of nutmeg.

*4 servings.*

# Party Punch ✓

2 6-ounce cans frozen orange
   juice
1 6-ounce can frozen grapefruit
   juice

1 1-pint 12-ounce bottle ginger
   ale
1 pint orange sherbet
½ orange, thinly sliced
2 maraschino cherries, sliced

Dilute frozen juices as directed on each can. Combine juices and chilled ginger ale. Cut orange sherbet in 16 pieces and float on top of punch. Garnish with orange and cherry slices.
*Makes 3½ quarts punch or sufficient for 28 to 30 servings in ½ cup punch glasses.*

# Teenagers Swingin' Swizzle Punch

1 46-ounce can (5¾ cups)
   pineapple juice
3 cups grapefruit juice
3 pints cranberry juice cocktail
6 7-ounce bottles lemon-lime
   carbonated beverage

1 cup whole fresh or frozen
   cranberries
1 cup drained pineapple chunks

Chill ingredients. Mix pineapple, grapefruit and cranberry juices in punch bowl. Slowly pour in carbonated beverage. Skewer cranberries and pineapple on swizzle sticks for garnish. Serve punch in tall glasses with garnish. *20 1-cup servings.*

# Tomato Cream Frosty

4 cups milk, chilled
2 cups tomato juice, chilled
½ teaspoon celery salt
2 teaspoons onion salt

2 teaspoons Worcestershire
   sauce
Dash salt
Minced chives OR
   Parsley

Combine ingredients, except chives; blend thoroughly. Pour into glasses. Garnish with chives or parsley. *8 servings.*

# BREADS

POPOVERS
CHEESE BISCUITS
CRANBERRY MUFFINS
MOLASSES BRAN MUFFINS
SPOONBREAD MUFFINS
TINY CORN MUFFINS
CORN BREAD OR STICKS
FLAT BREAD
CURRANT SCONES
BANANA-NUT BREAD
PECAN WAFFLES WITH
  PEACH SAUCE
BRUNCH CAKE
YUM YUM COFFEE CAKE
LAYERED COFFEE CAKE
SWEET COFFEE CAKE
FRUIT FILLED COFFEE CAKE
CHERRY ORANGE COFFEE
  CAKE
SAUSAGE-APPLE COFFEE
  CAKE
CEREAL FLAKE BLUEBERRY
  KUCHEN

PEACH KUCHEN
MINIATURE PAN ROLLS
HOT ROLLS (Standard Sweet
  Dough)
HOW TO SHAPE ROLLS
ROLL GLAZES
CORN MEAL ROLLS
COTTAGE CHEESE SPIRALS
COFFEE CRESCENTS
ITALIAN BREAD
HOLIDAY FRUIT BREAD
CINNAMON "WHIZZES"
BASIC COFFEE CAKE DOUGH
SWEDISH TEA RING
PECAN ROLLS
BROILED GARLIC BREAD
  SLICES
HERB OR GARLIC FRENCH
  BREAD
MUSTARD BREAD
WINE FRENCH TOAST

*Illustrations:* Swedish Tea Ring (page 45), Pecan Rolls (page 45).

# Breads

Few aromas from the kitchen can equal that of bread baking in the oven. It spells a happy home and a happy meal. In busy America, few women have the time to bake breads regularly . . . and thanks to modern food processors, such home baking isn't required. But occasionally it's fun for the cook and fun for the family to feature home-baked specialties. Here are some outstanding selections, with results assured . . . when directions are followed.

## Popovers

2 eggs
1 cup milk
1 cup sifted flour

½ teaspoon salt
1 tablespoon salad oil

Beat eggs slightly; add milk. Sift flour and salt together and add to egg mixture. Beat together for 1 minute or until smooth. Add oil and beat until blended. Grease 10 (⅔ cup) heat-proof glass custard cups very lightly on bottom and half way up the sides. Pour batter into cups. Place cups on rack in 400° oven. Bake 30 minutes. Pierce each one with a sharp knife and bake 5 minutes longer. Serve at once. *Makes* 10.

# Cheese Biscuits

2 cups sifted flour
3 teaspoons baking powder
½ teaspoon salt
¼ cup lard

1 cup (4 ounces) shredded
   sharp Cheddar cheese
⅔ cup milk (approximately)

Sift together flour, baking powder and salt. Using pastry blender or 2 knives, cut in lard and grated cheese until a crumbly mixture resembling corn meal is formed. Make a hole in the center of dry ingredients. Pour in milk, adding almost all at once. Use a fork to gently and quickly stir the mixture. Add rest of milk if necessary until dough is soft, sticky to the touch and leaves sides of bowl. Mix only enough to moisten. Turn mixture from bowl onto lightly floured bread board or pastry cloth. Knead gently with lightly floured hands only 30 seconds. Pat out dough or roll lightly with rolling pin dusted with flour to ¾ inch or desired thickness. Cut dough with biscuit cutter. Bake in 425° oven 10 to 12 minutes.

*Makes about 1½ dozen biscuits, 2 inches in diameter.*

# Cranberry Muffins

1 cup cranberries, halved or
   chopped
¼ cup sugar
2 cups sifted flour
⅓ cup sugar
1 tablespoon baking powder

½ teaspoon salt
⅓ cup margarine
1 egg, slightly beaten
¾ cup milk
1 teaspoon vanilla

Combine cranberries and ¼ cup sugar. Sift together flour, ⅓ cup sugar, baking powder and salt. Cut in margarine until mixture resembles coarse crumbs. Add the combined egg, milk and vanilla. Stir just until ingredients are blended. Fold in cranberry mixture. Fill greased 2½-inch muffin cups ⅔ full. Bake in 400° oven 15 to 20 minutes. *Makes 1½ dozen.*

# Molasses Bran Muffins

2 cups whole bran cereal
½ cup molasses
1½ cups milk
1 egg, slightly beaten

1 cup sifted flour
½ teaspoon salt
1 teaspoon baking soda

Soften whole bran cereal in molasses and milk (5 to 15 minutes). Add egg. Sift together flour, salt and baking soda. Combine with bran mixture. Fill greased 2½-inch muffin cups ⅔ full. Bake in 400° oven about 20 minutes. *Makes 1 dozen.*

# Spoonbread Muffins

3/4 cup sifted flour
1/2 teaspoon baking soda
1 1/2 teaspoons sugar
1 cup water
1/2 cup yellow corn meal

1/2 teaspoon salt
1 tablespoon butter or
margarine
1 cup buttermilk
2 eggs, separated

Sift together flour, baking soda and sugar. In a 1 1/2-quart saucepan heat water to boiling point; slowly add corn meal to the boiling water, stirring constantly. Boil mixture until thick and smooth; remove from heat and add salt and butter. Beat together buttermilk and egg yolks until thoroughly blended; stir into corn meal mixture. Stir in dry ingredients. Beat egg whites until stiff but not dry; fold into batter. Spoon batter into greased and floured 2 1/2-inch muffin cups. Bake in 400° oven 25 minutes. Serve immediately. *Makes 1 1/2 dozen.*

# Tiny Corn Muffins

1 cup corn meal
1 cup sifted flour
1/4 cup sugar
1/2 teaspoon salt
4 teaspoons baking powder

1/2 teaspoon onion salt
1 tablespoon caraway seeds
1 egg
1 cup milk
1/4 cup soft shortening

Sift dry ingredients (except caraway seeds) together into a bowl. Add caraway seeds, egg, milk and shortening. Beat with rotary beater until smooth, about 1 minute. (Do not overbeat!) Fill small greased muffin cups 2/3 full. Bake in 425° oven about 15 minutes. *Makes 2 dozen.*

# Corn Bread or Sticks

1 cup sifted flour
1/3 cup sugar
2 teaspoons baking powder
3/4 teaspoon salt
1/2 teaspoon baking soda

1 cup yellow corn meal
1 egg
1 cup buttermilk
2 tablespoons butter, melted

Sift together into mixing bowl flour, sugar, baking powder, salt and baking soda. Mix in corn meal. Make a well in center of dry ingredients. Add egg, buttermilk and butter. Stir together quickly until dry ingredients are moistened. Pour immediately into buttered 8-inch square pan, or corn stick pans. Bake in 425° oven 15 to 20 minutes.

*Makes 4 4-inch squares or 12 corn bread sticks.*

# Flat Bread

1 cup sifted flour
¼ teaspoon baking soda
¼ teaspoon salt
1 tablespoon sugar
¼ cup yellow corn meal

2 tablespoons butter or
  margarine
¼ cup water
1 tablespoon vinegar

Sift together flour, baking soda, salt and sugar. Blend in corn meal. Cut in butter until mixture is fine. Combine water and vinegar; add all at once to flour mixture. Stir until just blended. Chill. Form dough into ¾-inch balls. Roll each into paper thin rounds, about 4 inches in diameter, on lightly floured board or pastry cloth. Place rounds on ungreased cooky sheet. Bake in 375° oven about 6 minutes. Cool. Store in tightly covered can or jar. Serve as accompaniment to salads, soups or cheese dips.

*Makes* 4 *dozen.*

# Currant Scones

2 cups sifted flour
½ teaspoon salt
2½ teaspoons baking powder
2 tablespoons sugar
⅓ cup shortening

⅓ cup currants
1 egg
½ cup milk
Milk
Sugar

Sift together flour, salt, baking powder and 2 tablespoons sugar. Cut in shortening. Stir in currants. Combine egg and ½ cup milk; beat until blended. Add all at once to dry mixture. Stir lightly with fork, just enough to moisten all flour. Knead gently about ½ minute on floured board or pastry cloth. Divide dough in half. Form each into a round ball; roll each into a ¼-inch thick round. Place on greased baking sheet. Cut each round with a sharp knife into 6 wedges. Brush with milk and sprinkle with sugar. Bake in 450° oven 10 to 12 minutes. Serve hot. 6 *servings.*

# Banana-Nut Bread

1½ cups sifted flour
1 teaspoon salt
2 teaspoons baking powder
½ teaspoon baking soda
½ cup sugar
¾ cup rolled oats (quick or old
  fashioned, uncooked)

⅓ cup salad oil
2 eggs, slightly beaten
⅓ cup buttermilk
⅔ cup mashed bananas
½ cup chopped nuts

Sift together flour, salt, baking powder, baking soda and sugar into bowl. Stir in oats. Mix together salad oil, eggs and buttermilk. Add to dry ingredients with bananas and nuts; stir only until blended. Pour into greased 1-pound loaf pan. Bake in 350° oven 50 to 60 minutes.

# Pecan Waffles with Peach Sauce

| | |
|---|---|
| 1 cup milk | PEACH SAUCE: |
| 1 egg | ½ cup sugar |
| 3 tablespoons salad oil or | 1 tablespoon cornstarch |
| melted shortening | 1 cup cold water |
| 1 cup prepared pancake mix | 2 tablespoons lemon juice |
| ½ cup nuts, chopped | 1 cup sliced peaches |

Place milk, egg and shortening in a shaker or glass jar. (If melted shortening is used, add after pancake mix.) Add pancake mix and nuts. Shake vigorously 10 to 15 times or until batter is fairly smooth. Bake in a hot waffle baker until steaming stops.

Peach Sauce: Combine sugar and cornstarch. Stir into water; bring to boil, stirring constantly. Add lemon juice and peaches. Simmer 10 minutes, stirring occasionally. Serve over hot waffles.

*3 servings.*

Note: If canned or frozen peaches are used, decrease sugar slightly.

# Brunch Cake

| | |
|---|---|
| ½ cup margarine | ¼ teaspoon salt |
| 1 8-ounce package cream cheese | ¼ cup milk |
| 1¼ cups sugar | TOPPING: |
| 2 eggs | ⅓ cup firmly packed brown |
| 1 teaspoon vanilla | sugar |
| 2 cups sifted cake flour | ⅓ cup sifted cake flour |
| 1 teaspoon baking powder | ½ teaspoon cinnamon |
| ½ teaspoon baking soda | 2 tablespoons margarine |

Cream margarine, cream cheese and sugar. Add eggs and vanilla; beat well. Sift together flour, baking powder, baking soda and salt. Add to creamed mixture alternately with milk, mixing well after each addition. Pour into greased and floured 13 x 9-inch pan.

Topping: Combine brown sugar, flour, cinnamon and margarine; mix until crumbly; sprinkle over batter. Bake in 350° oven 35 to 40 minutes. *12 to 16 servings.*

# Yum Yum Coffee Cake

½ cup butter
1 cup sugar
2 eggs
2 cups sifted flour
1 teaspoon baking soda
1 teaspoon baking powder
½ teaspoon salt
1 cup dairy sour cream
1 teaspoon vanilla

CINNAMON-NUT TOPPING
AND FILLING:
⅓ cup firmly packed brown
  sugar
¼ cup white sugar
1 teaspoon cinnamon
1 cup finely chopped pecans

Cream butter. Add sugar; cream until light and fluffy. Add eggs one at a time, beating well after each addition. Sift together flour, baking soda, baking powder and salt. Add dry ingredients alternately with sour cream, beginning and ending with flour mixture. Stir in vanilla. Pour half of batter into a lightly greased 9-inch square baking pan. Cover with half of Cinnamon-Nut Topping and Filling. Pour remaining batter over nut mixture. Top with rest of nut mixture. Bake in 325° oven about 40 to 45 minutes.                    *Makes 1 coffee cake.*

**Cinnamon-Nut Topping and Filling:** Combine all ingredients; mix well. Use as filling and topping for coffee cake.

# Layered Coffee Cake

1¾ cups sifted cake flour
1½ teaspoons baking powder
½ teaspoon baking soda
½ teaspoon salt
½ cup butter or other
  shortening
¾ cup sugar

2 eggs
1 teaspoon vanilla
1 cup dairy sour cream
¼ cup sugar
2 teaspoons cinnamon
½ cup finely chopped nuts

Sift together flour, baking powder, baking soda and salt. Cream butter with ¾ cup sugar until light and fluffy. Add eggs, one at a time, beating well after each addition. Beat in vanilla. Add dry ingredients alternately with sour cream, beating until smooth after each addition. Pour half of batter into a well greased 9 x 9 x 2-inch pan. Mix ¼ cup sugar with cinnamon and nuts; sprinkle half of mixture over batter in pan. Cover with remaining batter; top with remaining sugar mixture. Bake in a 350° oven 40 to 45 minutes. Serve warm.          *9 to 12 servings.*

# Sweet Coffee Cake

¾ cup pecans, coarsely chopped
6 tablespoons shortening
2 tablespoons butter
1 cup sugar
2 eggs
2 teaspoons vanilla

2 cups sifted cake flour
2½ teaspoons baking powder
½ teaspoon salt
⅔ cup milk
Confectioners' sugar

Grease or butter, and flour a 9-inch turk's head or spring form pan, 9 x 2½ inches. Sprinkle with pecans. Cream shortening and butter together. Add sugar and cream until light. Beat in eggs, one at a time, beating well after each addition. Add vanilla. Sift together flour, baking powder and salt. Fold into first mixture alternately with milk, adding flour first and last. Carefully pour batter into prepared pan. Bake in 350° oven 45 to 50 minutes. Remove from oven and let stand in pan 1 or 2 minutes. Turn out on cooling rack. Sprinkle with confectioners' sugar.

*Makes 1 coffee cake.*

# Fruit Filled Coffee Cake

BATTER:
⅓ cup butter
½ cup sugar
2 eggs
2 cups sifted flour
3 teaspoons baking powder
1 teaspoon salt
½ teaspoon mace
½ teaspoon cinnamon
1 cup milk
FRUIT AND NUT FILLING:
½ cup chopped cooked prunes
½ cup chopped dates

½ cup chopped nuts
¼ cup sugar
TOPPING:
¼ cup flour
⅔ cup firmly packed brown
  sugar
Dash salt
⅛ teaspoon mace
⅛ teaspoon cinnamon
3 tablespoons butter
⅓ cup blanched almonds,
  chopped

Batter: Cream butter; add sugar and cream again. Beat in eggs, one at a time, beating well after each addition. Sift together dry ingredients. Add alternately with milk to first mixture; mix well. Pour ½ of batter into an 8 x 8-inch greased baking pan. Cover evenly with fruit and nut filling. Spoon remaining batter evenly over filling. Sprinkle with topping and then with almonds. Bake in 350° oven about 1 hour. Serve warm.          *8 or 9 servings.*

Fruit and Nut Filling: Combine prunes, dates and nuts. Add sugar and mix well.

Topping: Mix flour, sugar, salt, mace and cinnamon. Cut in butter.

# Cherry Orange Coffee Cake

1 14-ounce package orange muffin mix
1 16- to 17-ounce can (2 cups) tart red pitted cherries
⅓ cup firmly packed brown sugar
⅓ cup flour
¼ cup butter
1 teaspoon cinnamon

Mix muffin mix according to directions on package. Pour mixture into 9 x 9 x 2-inch greased baking pan or dish. Drain cherries thoroughly and arrange over batter. Mix remaining ingredients together with fork or pastry blender. Sprinkle over top. Bake in 400° oven 20 to 25 minutes. Serve warm.

*Makes 9 3-inch squares.*

# Sausage-Apple Coffee Cake

1 8-ounce package brown 'n serve sausage
12 thin apple slices, pared
½ cup finely chopped apple
¼ teaspoon cinnamon
3 tablespoons sugar
1 cup sifted flour
1½ teaspoons baking powder
½ teaspoon salt
1 egg, well beaten
⅓ cup milk
2 tablespoons melted shortening
Warm syrup, optional

Place sausages and apple slices in a pattern in the bottom of an 8 x 8 x 2-inch pan. Heat in 425° oven about 5 minutes. Combine chopped apple, cinnamon and sugar. Sift together flour, baking powder and salt. Add egg, milk, chopped apple mixture and melted shortening. Stir until the batter is blended. Spread batter over sausages and apple slices. Bake in 425° oven about 20 minutes. Turn upside down on warm platter. Serve with warm syrup, if desired.

*6 servings.*

# Cereal Flake Blueberry Kuchen

1 cup firmly packed brown sugar
4 teaspoons cinnamon
1 teaspoon salt
⅓ cup soft butter or margarine
1½ cups crushed corn flakes
½ cup chopped nuts
1 package white cake mix
1 12-ounce package frozen blueberries, thawed and drained OR
1¼ cups fresh or canned blueberries, drained

Combine sugar, cinnamon, salt and butter; mix well with pastry blender. Add corn flakes and nuts and blend thoroughly. Prepare white cake mix according to directions on package. Sprinkle 1½ cups of crumb mix evenly over bottom of greased and floured oblong baking pan, 13 x 9½ x 2-inches. Spread batter evenly over crumbs. Sprinkle berries and remaining crumbs evenly over cake batter. Fold berries and crumb mixture into cake batter, only until mixture resembles marble cake batter. Bake in 350° oven 35 to 40 minutes. Serve hot or cold.

*20 to 24 servings.*

# Peach Kuchen

**CAKE:**
2 cups sifted flour
¾ teaspoon salt
4 teaspoons baking powder
¼ teaspoon mace
½ cup sugar
1 cup milk
1 egg, well beaten
¼ cup butter, melted

**TOPPING:**
1½ cups thinly sliced canned peaches, drained
1 teaspoon cinnamon
2 tablespoons sugar
1 cup dairy sour cream

Sift together flour, salt, baking powder, mace and sugar. Combine milk, egg and melted butter; stir into dry ingredients just until blended. Pour batter into buttered 2-quart rectangular baking dish. Cover with peaches. Mix together cinnamon and sugar and sprinkle over peaches. Bake in 375° oven 35 minutes. Remove from oven and spread sour cream evenly over Kuchen. Return to oven for 5 minutes.

*8 to 10 servings.*

# Miniature Pan Rolls

1 package yeast, compressed or dry
¼ cup water (lukewarm for compressed yeast, warm for dry)

3 tablespoons sugar
2 teaspoons salt
¼ teaspoon baking soda
2 cups dairy sour cream
5 cups sifted flour (about)

Soften yeast in water. Let stand 10 minutes. Stir sugar, salt and baking soda into sour cream. Add flour to make a thick batter. Stir in softened yeast; mix well. Add enough more flour to make a soft dough. Turn out on lightly floured board or pastry cloth; knead until smooth and satiny. Shape dough into small balls about size of walnut. Place close together in 2 greased 8-inch square pans, allowing 6 or 7 balls for each row. Let rise until doubled, about 1½ hours. Bake in 375° oven 25 to 30 minutes.

*Makes about 8 dozen.*

# Hot Rolls
## (Standard Sweet Dough)

¾ cup milk
2 packages yeast (dry or
  compressed)
½ cup water (lukewarm for
  compressed yeast, warm for
  dry)
¼ cup sugar

5 cups flour
½ cup butter or margarine,
  softened
1 teaspoon salt
2 eggs
Roll Glaze OR
¼ cup butter, melted

Scald milk; cool to lukewarm. Put yeast and water in large mixing bowl; stir until dissolved. Add milk and sugar. Beat in 2 cups flour. Add butter, salt and eggs; beat until smooth. Add remaining flour placing ½ cup on board or pastry cloth for kneading. Turn out dough; knead until smooth and elastic. Twirl in greased bowl; cover well. Let rise until double in bulk, about 1½ hours. Punch down; let rise again until double in bulk, about ½ hour. Form in desired shapes. Cover; let rise until double in bulk, about ½ hour. Brush lightly with desired Roll Glaze or melted butter. Bake in 400° oven 10 to 12 minutes.

*Makes 3 to 3½ dozen.*

## HOW TO SHAPE ROLLS

**Fan Tans:** Roll ¼ of dough in a rectangle 10 x 15 inches. Cut lengthwise in five 2-inch strips. Brush each strip with melted butter; stack strips one on top of the other. Cut in 1½-inch pieces. Turn pieces so cut side is up showing 5 layers. Pinch pieces of dough together on each side of roll near bottom so cut side is showing 5 layers. Place in greased 2½-inch muffin cups.

**Double Snails:** Roll dough in finger size strips about 9 inches long. Hold one end of strip down on greased baking sheet with forefinger. Wind strip around and around until one-half of strip is used. Coil remaining half around and around in opposite direction. The curve is similar to a figure S.

**Figure 8's:** Roll dough in finger size strips about 8 inches long. Hold one end of strip firmly in one hand and twist the other end, stretching it slightly. Bring the two ends together; twist in a figure 8. Place on greased baking sheet.

**Bowknots:** Roll dough in strips about ½ x 6 inches. Twist and tie in knot. Place on greased baking sheet.

**Cloverleaf Rolls:** With a sharp knife or scissors cut off equal portions of dough the size of a large marble. Shape in small balls. Place 3 in each greased 2½-inch muffin cup.

**Muffins:** Shape dough in balls. Put one in each greased 2½-inch muffin cup.

**Snails:** Roll dough in finger size strips about 6 inches long. Hold one end of strip down on greased baking sheet with forefinger. Wind strip around and around. Tuck end underneath.

**Clothespin Rolls:** Roll dough in rectangle about 6 inches wide. Cut in strips about ½ x 6 inches. Wrap strips of dough around greased clothespins so edges barely touch. Put on greased baking sheet. When baked, twist clothespins and pull out.

# Roll Glazes

1 egg yolk, slightly beaten OR     1 egg white, slightly beaten
1 whole egg, slightly beaten OR

Brush glaze lightly on rolls just before baking.

# Corn Meal Rolls

| | |
|---|---|
| 1 package yeast, compressed or dry | ½ cup sugar |
| | 1 teaspoon salt |
| ½ cup water (lukewarm for compressed yeast, warm for dry) | 4½ to 5 cups sifted flour |
| | 2 eggs, slightly beaten |
| 2 cups scalded milk | 1 cup corn meal |
| ½ cup shortening | Melted shortening |

Soften yeast in water. Pour scalded milk over shortening, sugar and salt; stir occasionally until shortening melts. Cool to lukewarm. Stir in 1 cup flour and eggs. Add softened yeast and corn meal. Stir in enough more flour to make a soft dough. Turn out on lightly floured board or pastry cloth; knead until satiny, about 10 minutes. Round dough into ball, place in greased bowl, brush lightly with melted shortening. Cover and let rise in warm place until double in size, about 1 hour. Punch dough down; cover and let rest 10 minutes. Shape dough into small balls. Dip each ball into melted shortening; place three balls in each cup of greased muffin pans. Let rise until double in size, about 30 minutes. Bake in 400° oven 15 to 20 minutes.     *Makes 3 dozen.*

# Cottage Cheese Spirals

1 package compressed or dry
  yeast
¼ cup water (lukewarm for
  compressed yeast, warm for
  dry)
3 cups sifted flour
¼ cup granulated sugar
1 teaspoon salt
½ cup cold butter

1 cup creamed cottage cheese,
  sieved
1 egg, beaten
⅔ cup firmly packed brown
  sugar
3 tablespoons melted butter
½ teaspoon vanilla
⅔ cup chopped pecans
½ cup confectioners' sugar
1 tablespoon milk

Soften yeast in water. Sift together flour, sugar and salt. Cut butter into dry ingredients with a pastry blender until mixture resembles coarse crumbs. Stir in softened yeast, sieved cottage cheese and egg. Shape into ball. Place in lightly greased bowl, turning dough over once to coat top. Cover with damp cloth. Allow to rise in warm place until double in bulk. Punch down. Knead on lightly floured board until smooth and satiny, about 5 minutes. Roll into 12-inch square about ¼ inch thick. Combine brown sugar, melted butter, vanilla and pecans. Spread filling over dough and roll up as for jelly roll. Cut into 18 slices about ⅝ inch thick. Place slices cut side down in greased muffin cups. Allow to rise in warm place until double in bulk, about 45 minutes. Bake in 375° oven 12 minutes. Cool. Drizzle with frosting made by combining confectioners' sugar and milk.

*Makes* 18 *rolls.*

# Coffee Crescents

DOUGH:
4 cups sifted flour
1 tablespoon sugar
1 teaspoon salt
1 cup butter or margarine
1 cake compressed yeast
1 cup cold milk
3 egg yolks, well beaten
FILLING:
3 egg whites

1 cup sugar
3 teaspoons cinnamon
1½ cups finely chopped nuts
ICING:
1 tablespoon butter or
  margarine
1½ tablespoons boiling water
1 cup confectioners' sugar,
  sifted
½ teaspoon vanilla

Dough: Sift flour, sugar and salt together. Cut in butter with a pastry blender as for pie crust. Crumble yeast into cold milk; add egg yolks. Combine with first mixture; mix well. Cover. Chill several hours or overnight. Cut dough in 3 equal pieces. Roll each piece into a rectangle 12 x 16 inches.

**Filling:** Beat egg whites until stiff; add sugar gradually, beating continually. Spread ⅓ egg white mixture on each rectangle of dough. Sprinkle each with 1 teaspoon cinnamon and ½ cup nuts. Roll dough like a jelly roll beginning at wide side. Place on cooky sheet forming into crescent shape. Let rise one hour. Bake in 325° oven 35 to 40 minutes.

**Icing:** Combine butter and boiling water. Stir in confectioners' sugar and vanilla. Beat until smooth and creamy. Spread icing on warm crescents. *Makes 3 large crescents.*

# Italian Bread

| | |
|---|---|
| 2 packages yeast, compressed or dry | 2 tablespoons shortening |
| ½ cup water (lukewarm for compressed yeast, warm for dry) | 2 tablespoons sugar |
| | 1 teaspoon salt |
| | 6 cups sifted flour (about) |
| 2 cups boiling water | 1 egg white |
| | 1 tablespoon water |

Soften yeast in ½ cup water. To boiling water, add shortening, sugar and salt. Cool to lukewarm. Add 2 cups flour and beat until smooth. Add softened yeast and about 2 cups more flour. Beat well again. Cover and let rise in warm place until light and bubbly, about 45 minutes. Beat down and add enough more flour to make a moderately stiff dough. Turn out on lightly floured board or pastry cloth; knead until smooth and satiny. Place in greased bowl, cover and let rise until doubled, about 1½ hours. Punch down. Divide dough into 3 equal parts. Cover and let rest 10 minutes. Combine egg white and water. Roll each portion of dough to rectangle about ¼ inch thick and 13 inches long. Roll tightly like a jelly roll beginning at wide side and place on greased baking sheet. Tuck ends under slightly, sealing edges securely. Using scissors or sharp knife, make diagonal cuts across top of each loaf about ⅛ inch deep. Brush tops with egg white mixture. Let rise in warm place until almost doubled, about 45 minutes. Brush with egg white mixture again. Bake in 425° oven 35 to 40 minutes. *Makes 3 loaves.*

Note: Bread may be made a day ahead and heated before serving. Loaves freeze well.

For best results: Dissolve dry yeast in liquid at 105° and compressed yeast in liquid at 95°.

# Holiday Fruit Bread

2 packages yeast, compressed
    or dry
¼ cup water (lukewarm for
    compressed yeast, warm
    for dry)
1 cup milk
½ cup sugar
2 teaspoons salt

¼ cup shortening
5 cups sifted flour (about)
2 eggs
1 cup raisins
¾ cup chopped candied
    cherries
¼ cup chopped candied citron

Soften yeast in water. Scald milk. Add sugar, salt and shortening. Cool to lukewarm. Add flour to make a thick batter. Mix well. Add softened yeast, eggs and fruit. Beat well. Add enough more flour to make a soft dough. Turn out on lightly floured board or pastry cloth; knead until smooth and satiny. Place in greased bowl. Cover; let rise in warm place until doubled, about 1½ hours. When light, punch down and let rest 10 minutes. Divide dough in half and shape into two loaves. Place in greased loaf pans, 4½ x 8½ inches. Let rise until doubled, about 1 hour. Bake in 350° oven 35 to 40 minutes.          *Makes 2 loaves.*

# Cinnamon "Whizzes"

1 package yeast, compressed or
    dry
½ cup water (lukewarm for
    compressed yeast, warm
    for dry)
¼ cup lard OR part lard and
    part butter or margarine
1 tablespoon sugar
1 teaspoon salt

½ cup milk, scalded
2 eggs
3 cups sifted flour
¼ cup butter or margarine,
    melted
TOPPING:
2 tablespoons butter or
    margarine, melted
¼ cup sugar
¾ teaspoon cinnamon

Soften yeast in water. Add lard, sugar and salt to scalded milk, stirring to dissolve; cool to lukewarm. Add unbeaten eggs, softened yeast and flour; beat thoroughly for 2 minutes. Place in greased bowl, brush with a little of the ¼ cup melted butter. Cover and allow to rise until doubled in bulk, about 1 hour. Stir with four or five hard turns of the spoon; then dip spoon in melted butter before putting dough into each well greased muffin cup. Cover and let rise until double in bulk, about 30 minutes. Bake in 375° oven 15 to 20 minutes.     *Makes about 2 dozen.*

**Topping:** While muffins are still warm, dip top of each in melted butter and then in sugar-cinnamon mixture.

# Basic Coffee Cake Dough

1 package yeast, compressed
   or dry
1 tablespoon sugar
¼ cup water (lukewarm for
   compressed yeast, warm for
   dry)
2 cups milk, scalded

6¼ cups sifted flour
6 tablespoons soft butter or
   shortening
½ cup sugar
3 egg yolks
1½ teaspoons salt

Add yeast and sugar to water. Cool milk to lukewarm. Add milk and 3 cups flour to yeast mixture; beat until smooth. Beat in soft butter and sugar. Add egg yolks one at a time. Place ½ cup flour on pastry cloth for kneading. Add remaining flour sifted with salt into batter. Knead dough on cloth until smooth and elastic. Place in greased bowl; cover and let rise until double in bulk, about 1 to 1½ hours. Punch down; let rise until double in bulk. *Makes 1 Swedish Tea Ring and 2 dozen Pecan Rolls.*

# Swedish Tea Ring

½ Basic Coffee Cake Dough
2 tablespoons butter, melted
¼ cup sugar
¼ cup chopped blanched
   almonds

1 egg white, beaten slightly
1 tablespoon sugar
Thin Confectioners' Sugar Icing
Candied cherries
Pecan halves

Roll dough into rectangle about ½ inch thick. Brush with butter; sprinkle with sugar and almonds. Roll jelly roll fashion and shape into ring. Place on greased baking sheet; cut with scissors at 1-inch intervals almost through ring. Turn each slice slightly on its side. Brush with egg white; sprinkle with sugar. Cover; let rise until double in bulk, about 30 minutes. Bake in 375° oven 25 to 30 minutes. Top with Thin Confectioners' Sugar Icing (page 56), cherries and pecans.

# Pecan Rolls

½ Basic Coffee Cake Dough
½ cup melted butter
½ cup brown sugar

½ cup pecans, chopped
½ cup pecan halves

Roll dough in rectangle 9 x 24 inches. Brush dough with ¼ cup butter. Sprinkle with ¼ cup brown sugar and ½ cup chopped pecans. Roll jelly roll fashion to form 24-inch long roll. Pour remaining butter in 9 x 15 x 2 inch baking pan. Sprinkle ¼ cup brown sugar and ½ cup pecan halves over bottom of pan. Cut roll into 1-inch slices. Place in pan. Cover; let rise until double in bulk. Bake in 375° oven 25 to 30 minutes. *Makes 2 dozen.*

# Broiled Garlic Bread Slices

1 clove garlic, cut in half      12 slices French or Italian
¼ cup butter, melted          bread

Heat garlic in butter for 5 minutes. Discard garlic. Brush butter on both sides of sliced bread. Place on broiler pan or foil about 3 inches from source of heat. Broil both sides of bread until lightly browned.      6 *servings, 2 slices each.*

# Herb or Garlic French Bread

½ cup butter      1 1-pound loaf French bread
1 teaspoon garlic salt

Soften butter. Stir in garlic salt. Slice bread diagonally in 1½-inch pieces, without cutting through bottom crust. Spread seasoned butter between slices. Place in shallow pan or on foil. Heat in 425° oven 8 to 10 minutes.      8 *servings.*

**Variations:** Instead of garlic salt use 1 teaspoon celery salt, or 1 teaspoon celery seeds, or ½ teaspoon thyme, or ½ teaspoon curry powder or ¼ cup chopped chives.

# Mustard Bread

¼ cup butter      1 small loaf French, Vienna or
½ cup chopped green onions      Italian bread, 15 inches long
  with tops      2 tablespoons prepared mustard
2 tablespoons parsley flakes or      2 tablespoons sesame seeds or
  fresh chopped parsley      poppy seeds

Cream butter; blend in onion and parsley. Split loaf lengthwise. Spread cut surfaces with butter mixture. Spread with mustard, top with sesame seeds. Cut bread diagonally almost through in 1½-inch slices. Heat in a 350° oven 12 minutes or until browned lightly. Serve at once. Hard rolls may also be used. 10 *servings.*

# Wine French Toast

5 eggs, slightly beaten      ¾ cup sweet vermouth
¾ teaspoon salt      10 to 12 slices partially dry
1 teaspoon sugar      bread
¾ cup milk

Combine eggs, salt, sugar, milk and vermouth in shallow dish. Dip bread in mixture, turning to moisten. Place on well greased cooky sheet. Bake in 450° oven 10 to 12 minutes. Remove from oven; turn bread to brown the other side. Return to oven for an additional 10 to 12 minutes or until delicately browned.

*Makes 10 to 12 slices.*

Note: Milk may be used in place of vermouth.

# CAKES, COOKIES, PIES

FROSTY DATE CAKE
PINEAPPLE UPSIDE-DOWN CAKE
ORANGE LOAF CAKE
PARTY CAKE
APPLESAUCE CAKE
APPLE CIDER CAKE
APPLE UPSIDE-DOWN CAKE
STRAWBERRY POUND CAKE RING
CRUMB CAKE
WALNUT HONEY CAKE
SOUR CREAM SPICE CAKE
CHOCOLATE MARBLE CAKE
COCOA POUND CAKE
FUDGE SAUCE CAKE
MARIGOLD CAKE
SPRINGTIME CHIFFON CAKE
ELEGANT TORTE
OTHELLO TORTE
LEMON BUTTER FROSTING
VANILLA CREAM CHEESE
  FROSTING
ORANGE BUTTER CREAM
  FROSTING
THIN CONFECTIONERS' SUGAR
  ICING
FUDGE FROSTING
FLUFFY ICING
ROYALE FROSTING
DREAM BARS
PECAN BROWNIES
TWO-TONE BROWNIES
FUDGE-TOPPED BROWNIES
APRICOT SQUARES
TOFFEE NUT BARS
TOFFEE SQUARES
COCONUT KISSES
CHOCOLATE DROP COOKIES
CHOCOLATE NUT COOKIES
CHOCOLATE CHIP OATMEAL
  COOKIES
OLD FASHIONED OATMEAL
  COOKIES
GUMDROP OATMEAL COOKIES
LEMON COCONUT COOKIES
MOLASSES SNAPS
EARLY AMERICAN GINGER
  CUTOUTS

DIAMOND DAINTIES
CRISP MOLASSES COOKIES
PECAN OR ALMOND CRESCENTS
MINCEMEAT SQUARES
JUMBLES
ALMOND TEA CAKES (Cookies)
CHINESE ALMOND CAKES
FUDGE NUT COOKIES
EMPIRE BISCUITS (Cookies)
DUTCH ALMOND COOKIES
KRULLERS
PASTRY FOR 2-CRUST PIE
PASTRY FOR 8- OR 9-INCH
  PIE SHELL
PASTRY FOR 10-INCH PIE SHELL
9-INCH GRAHAM CRACKER CRUST
8-INCH GRAHAM CRACKER CRUST
GINGERSNAP CRUST
COCONUT TART SHELLS WITH
  STRAWBERRY PARFAIT FILLING
STRAWBERRY PIE GLACE
RICE AND PEACH GINGER PIE
SPARKLING RED CHERRY PIE
LATTICE CHERRY PIE
AUTUMN PEAR PIE
DUTCH APPLE PIE
CHOCOLATE CREAM MINT PIE
CHOCOLATE ALMOND DREAM PIE
CHOCOLATE FUDGE PIE
CONFETTI TOPPED CREAM PIE
MANDARIN ORANGE CREAM PIE
HONEYMOON LEMON MERINGUE
  PIE
LEMON-CRANBERRY MERINGUE
  PIE
FROZEN LEMON PIE
PEPPERMINT ICE CREAM PIE
  CHOCOLATE CRUST
BAKED ICE CREAM PIE
BAKED ALASKA RASPBERRY
  FLUFF PIE
FROZEN PUMPKIN "PEACE-PIPE"
  PIE WITH CARAMELIZED
  ALMONDS
LEMON FLUFF PIE
CARAMEL PECAN PIE
IRISH COFFEE PIE

*Illustrations:* Party Cake (page 48), Fluffy Icing (page 56).

# Cakes, Cookies, Pies

More good cooks have probably built their reputation by specializing in cakes, or cookies, or pies than in any other area of the culinary art. If you're a beginner in the cooking world these recipes will take you well past the first milestone on the road to fame. If you happen to be an undiscovered genius in the kitchen, the recipes will put you miles ahead. And if you've already established your reputation, you can keep it intact by serving these cakes, cookies and pies.

## Frosty Date Cake

**CAKE:**
2 tablespoons shortening
1 cup chopped dates
1 cup boiling water
½ teaspoon salt
1 cup sugar
1 egg, well beaten
1¼ cups sifted flour
1 teaspoon baking soda

1 teaspoon vanilla
½ cup chopped nuts
**TOPPING:**
2 tablespoons butter or
    margarine
¼ cup sifted flour
¼ cup sugar
½ cup chopped nuts

Mix shortening, dates and boiling water. Add salt, sugar and egg. Sift together flour and baking soda; add to date mixture; mix well. Add vanilla and nuts. Pour into greased 8-inch square pan. Mix together ingredients for topping; sprinkle over batter. Bake in 350° oven about 1 hour.

# Pineapple Upside-Down Cake

2 tablespoons salad oil
2 tablespoons pineapple syrup, drained from can
½ cup firmly packed brown sugar
4 canned pineapple slices
8 maraschino cherries
1½ cups sifted cake flour
2 teaspoons baking powder
½ teaspoon salt
⅓ cup salad oil
1 teaspoon vanilla
⅔ cup milk
1 egg
1 cup sugar

Combine 2 tablespoons oil and pineapple syrup in an 8-inch square pan; sprinkle with brown sugar. Halve the pineapple slices; arrange over brown sugar mixture, placing a maraschino cherry in center of each half. Sift together flour, baking powder and salt. Add ⅓ cup oil, vanilla and milk; beat until it forms a very smooth batter. In separate bowl beat egg until thick and foamy. Add sugar gradually; continue beating until well blended. Fold egg and sugar mixture thoroughly into batter. Pour over pineapple in pan. Bake in 350° oven 30 to 35 minutes. Let stand 5 minutes. Turn out on serving plate. Serve warm.    8 *servings*.

# Orange Loaf Cake

2¼ cups sifted flour
¼ teaspoon baking soda
2¼ teaspoons baking powder
¾ teaspoon salt
⅔ cup butter or margarine
¾ cup sugar
1 tablespoon grated orange peel
1 teaspoon orange extract
3 eggs, separated
¼ teaspoon salt
¼ cup sugar
½ cup buttermilk

Sift together flour, baking soda, baking powder and salt. Cream together butter, ¾ cup sugar, orange peel and orange extract thoroughly. Add egg yolks and beat until light. Beat egg whites and salt until foamy; beat in ¼ cup sugar, 1 tablespoonful at a time; beat until stiff peaks form, then set aside. Add dry ingredients to yolk mixture alternately with buttermilk, adding flour mixture first and last; beat until just blended after each addition. Fold in egg white mixture. Pour batter into greased and floured 9½ x 5¼ x 2¾-inch loaf pan. Bake in 350° oven about 1 hour.

# Party Cake

1 cup butter
1 pound confectioners' sugar, sifted
4 egg yolks, well beaten
1 teaspoon vanilla
3 cups sifted cake flour
2 teaspoons baking powder
¼ teaspoon salt
1 cup milk
2 cups shredded coconut
4 egg whites, beaten stiff
Fluffy Icing

Cream butter; add sugar and cream until light and fluffy. Add egg yolks and vanilla; beat well. Sift dry ingredients together 3 times. Add alternately with milk to first mixture. Fold in 1 cup coconut and egg whites. Grease and flour 4 square or 3 round 9-inch layer cake pans. Pour in cake batter. Bake round layers in 350° oven 25 to 30 minutes and square layers 20 to 25 minutes. When cold, put layers together with a thin coating of Fluffy Icing (page 56) between layers. Frost top and sides with remaining icing. Sprinkle with 1 cup coconut.

## Applesauce Cake

3 cups sifted flour
1¾ teaspoons baking soda
1 teaspoon cinnamon
1 teaspoon nutmeg
½ teaspoon salt
¼ cup cocoa
1 cup lard
1½ cups granulated sugar
½ cup firmly packed brown sugar, sieved
1 egg
2 cups applesauce
1 cup chopped nuts
1 cup raisins
2 teaspoons vanilla
Whipped cream, optional

Line a 9½ x 13-inch baking pan with waxed paper. Sift together flour, baking soda, cinnamon, nutmeg, salt and cocoa. Cream lard and sugars together until light and fluffy. Add egg and beat well. Add sifted dry ingredients alternately with applesauce, mixing thoroughly after each addition. Add nuts, raisins and vanilla. Pour batter into baking pan. Bake in 325° oven about 1 hour. Serve with whipped cream, if desired.

## Apple Cider Cake

2½ cups sifted cake flour
2 teaspoons baking powder
1 teaspoon salt
¼ teaspoon baking soda
1 teaspoon cinnamon
1½ cups sugar
¾ cup shortening
¾ cup sweet apple cider
3 eggs, unbeaten
Crab apple jelly
Royale Frosting, tinted yellow

Sift together flour, baking powder, salt, baking soda, cinnamon and sugar. Place shortening in mixing bowl; stir to soften. Sift in dry ingredients. Add cider and mix until all flour is dampened. Beat 2 minutes with mixer at low speed or 300 vigorous strokes by hand. Add eggs; beat 1 minute. Pour batter into 2 paper lined, greased round 8-inch pans. Bake in 350° oven 35 to 40 minutes. Cool. Split layers; spread jelly over 1 layer, cover with second layer; spread with Royale Frosting (page 57). Repeat, covering sides with remaining frosting.

# Apple Upside-Down Cake

3 tablespoons butter or
   margarine
1/4 cup firmly packed brown
   sugar
2 small red-skinned cooking
   apples, cored but not pared,
   finely sliced
1 1/4 cups sifted flour
1/2 teaspoon baking soda
1 teaspoon baking powder

1/4 teaspoon cinnamon
1/2 teaspoon ginger
1/8 teaspoon cloves
1/4 teaspoon salt
1/3 cup shortening
1/3 cup firmly packed brown
   sugar, sieved
1 egg
1/2 cup light molasses
1/2 cup hot water

Melt butter in an 8 x 8 x 1¾-inch baking pan; sprinkle with
¼ cup brown sugar. Slightly overlap apple slices in rows over
sugar. Set aside. Sift together flour, baking soda, baking powder,
spices and salt. Cream shortening and ⅓ cup brown sugar thoroughly. Beat in egg and molasses. Blend in dry ingredients alternately with hot water, adding flour mixture first and last; stir
until blended after each addition. Pour batter over apples in baking pan. Bake in 350° oven about 45 minutes. Remove from
oven; let stand 5 minutes. Invert onto plate. Serve warm.

8 *servings.*

# Strawberry Pound Cake Ring

3/4 cup butter
1 cup sugar
4 eggs
3/4 teaspoon vanilla
1/2 teaspoon finely grated lemon
   peel

2 1/4 cups sifted cake flour
1/2 teaspoon baking powder
1/4 cup milk
Lemon Butter Frosting
1 pint fresh strawberries

Butter and flour 1½-quart ring mold; set aside. Cream butter
and sugar until light and fluffy. Add eggs all at once and beat
until light and fluffy. Add vanilla and lemon peel. Sift flour and
baking powder together and add alternately with milk to creamed
mixture. Pour batter into ring mold. Bake in 325° oven 35 to 40
minutes. Cool 10 minutes. Remove from ring mold onto cooling
rack. After completely cooled, slice ring in 2 layers. Spread one
half of Lemon Butter Frosting (page 55) on cut surface of
both layers. Arrange 1 cup sliced strawberries over bottom layer.
Place frosted sides together. Swirl remaining frosting over top of
ring. Garnish with whole strawberries. Serve immediately.

For best baking results: Grease bottom and sides of pan. Dust
with flour until well coated. Shake out excess flour.

# Crumb Cake

1 cup butter
1 cup sugar
1 cup firmly packed brown
  sugar, sieved
3 cups sifted cake flour
2 eggs
⅔ cup sifted cake flour
¼ teaspoon salt

1 teaspoon baking soda
1 teaspoon baking powder
1 teaspoon cinnamon
½ teaspoon cloves
½ teaspoon nutmeg
½ teaspoon allspice
1 cup buttermilk or sour milk

Mix butter, sugars and 3 cups flour as for pie crust. Save 1 cup of this mixture for topping. To remainder add eggs; beat until light and fluffy. Sift remaining dry ingredients together; add alternately with buttermilk, beating until smooth after each addition. Turn into greased and floured 9 x 12-inch baking pan. Sprinkle with 1 cup crumb mixture. Bake in 350° oven 45 minutes.

Crumb cake can be frozen. *16 servings.*

# Walnut Honey Cake

SYRUP:
1 cup sugar
½ cup honey
¾ cup water
¾ teaspoon lemon juice
CAKE:
¾ cup butter
¾ cup sugar

3 eggs
1 cup sifted flour
1½ teaspoons baking powder
¼ teaspoon salt
½ teaspoon cinnamon
¼ cup milk
½ teaspoon grated orange peel
1 cup medium chopped walnuts
Confectioners' sugar, sifted

**Syrup:** Mix sugar, honey and water in small saucepan; boil gently 4 to 5 minutes. Add lemon juice; boil 2 minutes. Cool.
**Cake:** Cream butter. Add sugar; cream again. Add eggs, one at a time, beating well after each addition. Sift together flour, baking powder, salt and cinnamon; add to first mixture. Add milk and orange peel. Mix in walnuts. Pour into buttered 11 x 7¼ x 1½-inch pan. Bake in 350° oven 25 to 30 minutes. Cut in diamond shapes. While hot, pour Syrup over top. Cool 1 hour. Sprinkle with confectioners' sugar. *12 servings.*

It helps to know: ½ cup butter = 1 stick or ¼ pound or 8 tablespoons.

Pointers for brown sugar: To measure, pack firmly into cup. To remove lumps, press through sieve.

# Sour Cream Spice Cake

2¼ cups sifted cake flour
¾ teaspoon baking soda
1 teaspoon baking powder
¼ teaspoon salt
2 teaspoons cinnamon
1 teaspoon nutmeg
½ teaspoon cloves

1⅔ cups sugar
1 cup butter, melted
1 cup dairy sour cream
3 eggs
1 teaspoon vanilla
Orange Butter Cream Frosting
Walnuts

Butter and flour 2 round 9-inch cake pans or 1 pan, 9 x 13 x 2 inches. Set aside. Sift together flour, baking soda, baking powder, salt, cinnamon, nutmeg and cloves. Mix lightly with sugar in a large mixing bowl. Add butter, sour cream, eggs and vanilla all at once to dry ingredients. Mix together well with a spoon. Pour batter into pans. Bake in 350° oven 25 to 30 minutes for layers, or 40 minutes for loaf. Cool. Frost with Orange Butter Cream Frosting (page 56) and garnish with walnuts.

# Chocolate Marble Cake

3 cups sifted cake flour
3 teaspoons baking powder
½ teaspoon salt
½ cup shortening
1½ cups sugar
1 cup milk
1½ teaspoons vanilla
5 egg whites, beaten stiff

2 squares (2 ounces) unsweetened
    chocolate, melted
1½ tablespoons sugar
3 tablespoons hot water
½ teaspoon baking soda
Royale Frosting
Shaved unsweetened chocolate
    OR Pecan halves

Sift flour, baking powder and salt together three times. Cream shortening; add 1½ cups sugar gradually and cream together until light and fluffy. Add flour, alternately with milk, in small amounts, beating until smooth. Add vanilla. Fold in egg whites quickly and thoroughly. To melted chocolate, add 1½ tablespoons sugar and water, stirring until blended. Then add baking soda and stir until thickened; add to ⅓ of cake batter. Alternate light and dark batters by tablespoonfuls in 2 or 3 greased and floured 9-inch layer pans. Bake in 350° oven 30 to 35 minutes. When cool, spread Royale Frosting (page 57) between layers and over top and sides. Decorate with shaved chocolate or pecan halves.

# Cocoa Pound Cake

2 cups sifted flour
½ cup cocoa
1 cup soft butter or margarine

1¼ cups sugar
1 cup eggs well beaten
2 teaspoons vanilla

Sift together flour and cocoa. Cream butter thoroughly. Very gradually add sugar, beating until smooth and fluffy. (This requires 10 to 12 minutes.) Add eggs gradually, beating well after each addition. Blend in vanilla. Add flour mixture to creamed mixture and beat just until smooth. Turn batter into paper-lined greased 5¼ x 9½-inch loaf pan. Bake in 300° oven about 1 hour and 30 minutes. Cool in pan 10 minutes. Turn out on cooling rack. May be frosted with Butter Cream Frosting.

## Fudge Sauce Cake

1 cup sifted flour
¾ cup sugar
2 tablespoons cocoa
2 teaspoons baking powder
¼ teaspoon salt
¾ cup chopped pecans
½ cup milk

2 tablespoons melted butter
1 teaspoon vanilla
1 cup firmly packed brown
  sugar, sieved
¼ cup cocoa
1¾ cups hot water

Grease thoroughly an 8 x 8 x 2-inch square cake pan. Sift together into this pan flour, sugar, 2 tablespoons cocoa, baking powder and salt. Add pecans and toss lightly. Blend together milk, melted butter and vanilla. Add to flour mixture in baking pan and blend thoroughly into batter. Mix together brown sugar and ¼ cup cocoa. Spread on top of batter. Pour hot water over surface of batter. Bake in 375° oven about 1 hour. Remove from oven; turn cake upside down on cake plate.

## Marigold Cake

2 cups sifted flour
2 teaspoons baking powder
¼ teaspoon salt
1 cup (about 12) egg yolks
½ cup orange juice

¼ cup hot water
2 tablespoons grated orange peel
1 teaspoon orange extract
1¼ cups sugar
Orange Butter Cream Frosting

Sift together flour, baking powder and salt. Beat egg yolks until thick and lemon colored. Add orange juice and water gradually. Stir in orange peel and extract. Add sugar gradually, beating well after each addition. Gently fold in flour mixture in 4 additions, blending well after each. Carefully turn batter into ungreased 10-inch tube pan. Bake in 325° oven 60 to 65 minutes. Invert pan, cooling cake about 1 hour before removing from pan. Frost with Orange Butter Cream Frosting (page 56).

# Springtime Chiffon Cake

2¼ cups sifted flour
1 tablespoon baking powder
1 teaspoon salt
1½ cups sugar
½ cup salad oil
5 egg yolks

¾ cup unsweetened pineapple juice
1 cup egg whites (7 or 8)
½ teaspoon cream of tartar
⅓ cup flaked coconut
Royale Frosting
Pineapple pieces

Sift together flour, baking powder, salt and sugar. Make a "well" and add in order the salad oil, egg yolks and pineapple juice. Beat with spoon until smooth. Combine egg whites and cream of tartar. Beat until they form very stiff peaks. Pour egg yolk mixture over egg whites, a little at a time, folding after each addition. Fold in coconut. Turn into ungreased 10-inch tube pan. Cut through batter with knife to remove air bubbles. Bake in 325° oven about 65 minutes. Invert and cool 1 hour before removing from pan. Frost with Royale Frosting (page 57) and decorate with pineapple pieces.

# Elegant Torte

3 cups sifted cake flour
2 cups firmly packed brown sugar, sieved
½ teaspoon salt
1 cup shortening
1 egg, slightly beaten

1 cup buttermilk or sour milk
1 teaspoon baking soda
½ cup chopped nuts
Sweetened whipped cream OR
Peach Cream Filling

Combine flour, sugar and salt. Add shortening and blend with pastry blender until crumbly. Set aside 1 cup of this mixture. Combine egg, milk and soda. Add to dry ingredients; stir well. Pour into 2 paper-lined, greased round 9-inch pans. Sprinkle the 1 cup crumb mixture combined with nuts over top of each layer. Bake in 375° oven 25 to 30 minutes. Serve with sweetened whipped cream or Peach Cream Filling between the layers.

### PEACH CREAM FILLING

½ pint (1 cup) heavy cream, whipped
½ cup mashed peaches

1 tablespoon lemon juice
2 tablespoons sugar
Sliced peaches

Combine whipped cream, mashed peaches, lemon juice and sugar. Place between torte layers. Garnish with sliced peaches. Serve immediately.

# Othello Torte

**CAKE:**
6 eggs, separated
1 cup sugar
1 cup sifted cake flour
2 teaspoons baking powder
2 squares (2 ounces)
   unsweetened chocolate, grated
1 teaspoon vanilla

**FILLING:**
⅓ cup sugar
⅓ cup cornstarch
1 egg yolk
2 cups milk
1 cup butter
1 cup sifted confectioners'
   sugar
1 teaspoon vanilla
Semi-sweet chocolate, finely
   shaved

**Cake:** Beat egg yolks and sugar together. Sift flour with baking powder; fold into egg yolk and sugar mixture. Beat egg whites until stiff; fold into batter. Fold in chocolate and vanilla. Pour into ungreased 10-inch tube pan. Bake in 325° oven 30 minutes. When baked, turn cake upside down until cold.

**Filling:** Combine sugar and cornstarch. Blend in egg yolk. Add milk gradually. Cook until thickened, stirring constantly. Let stand until cold. (This custard will be very thick when cold.) Cream butter, sugar and vanilla together. Add custard and beat 20 minutes at medium speed. Cut cake into 3 layers; fill and frost with filling. Sprinkle sides and top of torte with finely shaved semi-sweet chocolate. Store in refrigerator several hours before serving.

Note: This cake improves if made 24 hours ahead of time. It freezes very satisfactorily. Freeze before packaging to firm the frosting.

# Lemon Butter Frosting

¾ cup butter
3½ cups sifted confectioners'
   sugar

1 tablespoon milk
2 tablespoons fresh lemon juice
2 tablespoons grated lemon peel

Cream butter and sugar together. Add milk, lemon juice and peel; beat until smooth.

# Vanilla Cream Cheese Frosting

1 3-ounce package cream cheese
1 tablespoon milk

3 cups sifted confectioners'
   sugar
½ teaspoon vanilla

Blend cream cheese and milk. Add sugar gradually, blending well. Add vanilla; mix again. Makes sufficient to frost 2 dozen Empire Biscuits or to fill and frost a 2-layer 8-inch cake.

## Orange Butter Cream Frosting

⅓ cup soft butter or margarine　　¼ cup orange juice
1 egg yolk　　1½ teaspoons lemon juice
1 pound (4½ cups) sifted
　confectioners' sugar

Cream butter and egg yolk until soft and fluffy. Add sugar gradually, beating well. Combine juices; blend in amount necessary to make a spreading consistency. Sufficient to frost and fill a 2-layer 9-inch round cake.

## Thin Confectioners' Sugar Icing

1 cup confectioners' sugar,　　2 tablespoons milk
　sifted　　¼ teaspoon vanilla

Mix together sugar, milk and vanilla. Beat until smooth. Spread or drizzle over coffee cake or rolls. Makes sufficient icing for 1 large coffee cake.

## Fudge Frosting

1 square (1 ounce) unsweetened　　1½ cups confectioners' sugar
　chocolate　　1 egg, well beaten
2 tablespoons butter or　　1 teaspoon vanilla
　margarine

Melt chocolate and butter in saucepan over low heat. Remove from heat; blend in sugar and egg. Add vanilla; beat until frosting is of spreading consistency. Frosting for brownies or an 8- or 9-inch square cake.

## Fluffy Icing

3 egg whites　　2 teaspoons light corn syrup
2¼ cups sugar　　1½ teaspoons vanilla
½ cup water

Mix egg whites, sugar, water and corn syrup together thoroughly in top of large double boiler. Place over gently boiling water, being careful that water in lower pan does not touch upper pan. Beat constantly with rotary beater until frosting stands in peaks, about 10 minutes. Remove from over boiling water. Add vanilla. Beat for 1 to 2 minutes stirring frosting up from bottom. Makes enough frosting for a large 3- or 4-layer cake.

# Royale Frosting

2 egg whites
1½ cups sugar
1 tablespoon light corn syrup

½ cup water
1½ teaspoons vanilla

Combine egg whites, sugar, corn syrup and water in top of double boiler. Mix until well blended. Cook over boiling water, beating constantly, until mixture forms stiff, glossy peaks (about 7 minutes). Beat in vanilla. Makes enough frosting for 10-inch cake or a 3-layer cake.

# Dream Bars

**PART 1:**
½ cup butter
½ cup firmly packed light
  brown sugar, sieved
1 cup sifted flour
**PART 2:**
2 eggs
1 cup firmly packed brown
  sugar, sieved

2 tablespoons flour
½ teaspoon baking powder
¼ teaspoon salt
1½ cups flaked coconut
1 cup chopped nuts
Sifted confectioners' sugar
Green grapes

**Part 1:** Cream together butter and brown sugar. Add flour; mix well. Pat into 8-inch square pan. Bake in 350° oven 10 minutes.

**Part 2:** Beat eggs until light; add brown sugar and beat until thoroughly mixed. Sift together flour, baking powder and salt. Fold into egg mixture; add coconut and nuts. Spread evenly over first part; return to oven and bake 15 to 20 minutes. Dust lightly with confectioners' sugar. Cool. Cut in 16 bars. Arrange on cake plate that is centered with a cluster of green grapes.

*Makes 16 bars.*

# Pecan Brownies

¼ cup butter or margarine
1 cup firmly packed brown
  sugar, sieved
1 egg, slightly beaten
1 teaspoon vanilla

½ cup sifted flour
1 teaspoon baking powder
½ teaspoon salt
¾ cup chopped pecans
Sifted confectioners' sugar

Melt butter; stir in brown sugar. Beat in egg and vanilla. Sift flour with baking powder and salt; stir into first mixture. Add pecans. Spread in greased 8-inch square pan. Bake in 350° oven 30 minutes. Sprinkle with confectioners' sugar. Cut in squares.

*Makes 16 brownies.*

# Two-Tone Brownies

**BUTTERSCOTCH LAYER:**
⅓ cup sifted flour
1 cup rolled oats, uncooked
⅓ cup firmly packed brown
   sugar, sieved
½ cup chopped nuts
⅓ cup melted butter
**CHOCOLATE LAYER:**
2 squares (2 ounces)
   unsweetened chocolate

⅓ cup shortening
1 cup sugar
2 eggs
¾ cup sifted flour
½ teaspoon baking powder
½ teaspoon salt
¼ cup milk
1 teaspoon vanilla

**Butterscotch Layer:** Mix flour with rolled oats, sugar and nuts. Pour butter over dry ingredients and blend well. Pack evenly in bottom of 9 x 12-inch baking dish. Bake in 400° oven 5 minutes. Let cool while preparing Chocolate Layer. (Reduce oven temperature to 350°.)

**Chocolate Layer:** Melt chocolate and shortening over very low heat. Beat in sugar and eggs. Sift flour, baking powder and salt together; stir into chocolate mixture alternately with milk. Add vanilla. Spread on top of cooled Butterscotch Layer. Bake in 350° oven 30 to 35 minutes. Cool; cut in squares.

*Makes 2½ dozen brownies.*

# Fudge-Topped Brownies

1 cup sifted flour
1 teaspoon baking powder
½ teaspoon salt
2 squares (2 ounces)
   unsweetened chocolate

½ cup butter or margarine
2 eggs, well beaten
1 cup sugar
1 cup chopped pecans
2 teaspoons vanilla
Fudge Frosting

Sift together flour, baking powder and salt. Melt chocolate and butter over low heat. Remove from heat. Add eggs, then sugar and beat well. Blend in flour mixture; mix thoroughly. Stir in pecans and vanilla. Spread batter in well greased 9-inch square pan. Bake in 350° oven about 35 minutes. When cool, frost with Fudge Frosting (page 56) and cut in squares.

*Makes 16 brownies.*

For best results: Store soft cookies in tightly covered container. Keep crisp cookies in loosely covered cooky jar.

# Apricot Squares

½ cup butter or margarine
1½ cups sifted flour
½ cup sugar
¼ teaspoon vanilla

2 egg yolks, well beaten
1 12-ounce can (1¼ cups)
  apricot filling
2 egg whites
¼ cup chopped nuts

Cut butter into flour with a pastry blender as for pie crust. Add ¼ cup sugar, vanilla and egg yolks. Mix well. Press like a crust into a shallow 8 x 12 x 1-inch pan. Spread apricot filling over dough. Beat egg whites stiff; beat in remaining ¼ cup sugar gradually. Spread meringue over filling. Sprinkle with chopped nuts. Bake in 350° oven 30 to 35 minutes. When cool, cut in 2-inch squares. *Makes 24 squares.*

# Toffee Nut Bars

1¼ cups granulated sugar
¾ cup firmly packed brown
  sugar, sieved
2 cups sifted flour
½ cup butter or margarine
1 cup chopped nuts

1 egg, well beaten
¾ teaspoon salt
¾ teaspoon nutmeg
¼ teaspoon allspice
1 teaspoon baking soda
1 cup buttermilk

Mix sugars, flour and butter together with fork or pastry blender. Sprinkle bottom of ungreased 13 x 9-inch pan with nuts; cover with 2 cups flour mixture. Beat together egg, salt, spices, baking soda and buttermilk. Stir in remaining flour mixture. Pour over mixture in pan, spreading evenly. Bake in 350° oven 45 minutes. Cool slightly; cut in bars. *Makes 24 bars.*

# Toffee Squares

1 cup margarine
1 cup firmly packed brown
  sugar, sieved
1 egg yolk
1 teaspoon vanilla

2 cups sifted flour
1 6-ounce package semi-sweet
  chocolate pieces, melted
½ cup chopped nuts

Cream margarine and sugar. Blend in egg yolk and vanilla. Add flour; mix well. Spread in greased 15½ x 10½-inch jelly roll pan. Bake in 350° oven 15 to 20 minutes. Remove from oven; spread immediately with chocolate. Sprinkle with nuts. Cool; cut in squares. *Makes 24 squares.*

# Coconut Kisses

4 egg whites
¼ teaspoon salt
1⅓ cups sugar

1 teaspoon vanilla
2½ cups moist, shredded
coconut

Beat egg whites and salt until frothy. Add sugar gradually, beating until mixture forms stiff peaks. Beat in vanilla. Fold in coconut. Drop from teaspoon onto well greased baking sheet. Bake in 325° oven 18 to 20 minutes. *Makes 4 dozen.*

# Chocolate Drop Cookies

**COOKY DOUGH:**
⅓ cup butter
1 cup firmly packed brown
sugar, sieved
1 egg
2 squares (2 ounces)
unsweetened chocolate,
melted
½ teaspoon vanilla
½ teaspoon baking soda
¼ teaspoon salt

2 cups sifted flour
¾ cup buttermilk or sour milk
½ cup chopped nuts
**FROSTING:**
1 square (1 ounce)
unsweetened chocolate
2 tablespoons butter
1½ cups sifted confectioners'
sugar
1 tablespoon warm water
½ teaspoon vanilla

**Cooky Dough:** Cream butter and sugar until light. Beat in egg. Add melted chocolate and vanilla; mix well. Sift baking soda, salt and flour together. Add to first mixture alternately with buttermilk. Stir in nuts. Drop from teaspoon onto ungreased baking sheet. Bake in 375° oven 10 to 12 minutes.

**Frosting:** Melt chocolate over very low heat. Add butter, sugar, water and vanilla. Beat until smooth. Spread on cool cookies.
*Makes 4 dozen.*

# Chocolate Nut Cookies

2 cups sifted flour
½ teaspoon baking soda
½ teaspoon salt
¾ cup shortening
1¼ cups firmly packed brown
sugar, sieved
2 teaspoons vanilla

1 egg
3 squares (3 ounces)
unsweetened chocolate,
melted and cooled
¼ cup buttermilk
½ cup chopped nuts

Sift together flour, baking soda and salt. Cream shortening, sugar and vanilla thoroughly. Beat in egg and chocolate. Add dry ingredients alternately with buttermilk, adding flour mixture first and last; beat until smooth after each addition. Blend in nuts. Drop from teaspoon onto ungreased baking sheet. Bake in 375° oven about 12 minutes. *Makes 5 dozen 2-inch cookies.*

# Chocolate Chip Oatmeal Cookies

½ cup shortening
½ cup firmly packed brown
  sugar, sieved
½ cup granulated sugar
1 egg
1 tablespoon water
½ teaspoon vanilla

¾ cup sifted flour
½ teaspoon baking soda
½ teaspoon salt
1½ cups rolled oats, uncooked
1 6-ounce package semi-sweet
  chocolate pieces
¼ cup chopped nuts

Beat shortening until creamy; add sugars gradually; beat thoroughly. Beat in egg until fluffy. Add water and vanilla. Sift together flour, baking soda and salt; add to creamed mixture. Add rolled oats, chocolate pieces and nuts. Drop from teaspoon onto greased baking sheet. Bake in 375° oven about 12 minutes.

*Makes 3½ dozen.*

# Old Fashioned Oatmeal Cookies

¾ cup butter
½ cup granulated sugar
1 cup firmly packed brown
  sugar, sieved
2 eggs
1½ cups sifted flour
1 teaspoon baking soda

1 teaspoon salt
1½ teaspoons cinnamon
½ teaspoon nutmeg
¼ cup milk
3 cups rolled oats, uncooked
1 cup raisins

Cream butter; add sugars; cream thoroughly. Beat in eggs, one at a time, beating well after each addition. Sift dry ingredients together and add alternately with milk. Stir in oats and raisins; mix well. Drop rounded tablespoonfuls of dough onto ungreased baking sheet; flatten slightly. Bake in 375° oven 10 to 12 minutes.

*Makes about 3½ dozen cookies, 3 inches in diameter.*

# Gumdrop Oatmeal Cookies

1 cup sifted flour
½ teaspoon baking soda
½ teaspoon salt
½ cup shortening (room
  temperature)
½ cup firmly packed brown
  sugar, sieved

½ cup granulated sugar
1 egg
1 teaspoon vanilla
2 tablespoons milk
1½ cups rolled oats, uncooked
¾ cup finely cut mixed spiced
  gumdrops

Sift together flour, baking soda and salt into bowl. Add shortening, sugars, egg, vanilla and milk. Beat until smooth, about 2 minutes. Fold in rolled oats and gumdrops. Drop from teaspoon onto greased baking sheet. Bake in 375° oven 12 to 15 minutes.

*Makes 3½ dozen.*

# Lemon Coconut Cookies

| | |
|---|---|
| 1 cup butter or margarine | 2 cups sifted flour |
| ½ cup sugar | ¼ teaspoon salt |
| 1 egg | 1 cup flaked coconut |
| ½ teaspoon grated lemon peel | |

Cream butter. Add sugar and continue creaming until light and fluffy. Add egg and lemon peel. Beat well. Sift together flour and salt. Stir into creamed mixture. Blend in coconut. Drop by teaspoonfuls on ungreased baking sheet. Bake in 325° oven until lightly browned around the edges, 15 to 20 minutes.

*Makes about 6 dozen 2-inch cookies.*

# Molasses Snaps

| | |
|---|---|
| 1⅓ cups sifted flour | ⅓ cup shortening |
| 1 teaspoon baking soda | ⅔ cup sugar |
| ¾ teaspoon ginger | ⅓ cup light molasses |
| ½ teaspoon salt | 1 egg |

Sift together flour, baking soda, ginger and salt. Cream shortening, sugar and molasses thoroughly. Add egg and beat until fluffy. Blend in dry ingredients. Drop by teaspoonfuls onto greased baking sheet, allowing 2 inches between cookies. Bake in 350° oven about 15 minutes or until delicately browned.

*Makes 4½ dozen.*

# Early American Ginger Cutouts

| | |
|---|---|
| 2¾ cups sifted flour | ¼ cup firmly packed dark |
| ½ teaspoon baking soda | brown sugar, sieved |
| 1 teaspoon ginger | ¾ cup dark molasses |
| ½ teaspoon cinnamon | 1 egg, beaten |
| ½ teaspoon cloves | 1 teaspoon hot water |
| ½ teaspoon salt | 1 teaspoon vinegar |
| ½ cup butter | |

Sift dry ingredients together. Cream butter and sugar. Add molasses and egg, beating until smooth. Mix in sifted dry ingredients; then add water and vinegar and blend well. Chill dough 2 hours. Roll out on lightly floured board to ¼ inch thickness and cut with gingerbread man and animal cooky cutters. Place on buttered baking sheet and bake in 350° oven 15 minutes. When cooled, decorate with various colored butter frostings, if desired.

# Diamond Dainties

¾ cup butter or margarine
1¼ cups sugar
2 eggs
1 teaspoon vanilla
1 teaspoon grated lemon peel

2½ cups sifted flour
½ cup corn meal
Gumdrops OR
Flaked coconut

Cream butter. Gradually add sugar and beat until light and fluffy. Add eggs, vanilla and lemon peel. Sift together flour and corn meal; add to creamed mixture, blending well. Chill dough several hours. Roll out on lightly floured board or pastry cloth to ⅛ inch thickness. Cut dough into small diamond-shaped cookies. Place gumdrop or a little coconut in center of each. Place on greased baking sheets. Bake in 375° oven 6 to 8 minutes.

*Makes 10 dozen small cookies.*

# Crisp Molasses Cookies

1 cup shortening
1 cup molasses
2 eggs, slightly beaten
1 cup sugar
3½ cups sifted flour

½ teaspoon salt
1 teaspoon baking soda
¼ teaspoon cinnamon
¼ teaspoon ginger
½ teaspoon cloves

Heat shortening and molasses in saucepan until shortening is melted; stir constantly. Slowly pour this mixture over eggs. Add sifted dry ingredients; mix thoroughly. Chill overnight. Roll 1/16 inch thick on floured board or pastry cloth; cut with 2-inch cooky cutter. Place on baking sheet. Bake in 350° oven 10 minutes.

*Makes 10 dozen 2-inch cookies.*

# Pecan or Almond Crescents

1 cup butter
1 teaspoon vanilla
½ teaspoon salt
6 tablespoons confectioners'
  sugar

2 cups sifted flour
1 cup finely chopped nuts
Confectioners' sugar

Cream butter; add vanilla, salt and 6 tablespoons confectioners' sugar. Cream well. Add flour gradually. Add nuts; mix well. Wrap in waxed paper. Chill. Pinch off small pieces of dough; shape by rolling in rolls 2½ to 3 inches long, ½ inch thick. Form in crescents. Place on ungreased baking sheet. Bake in 400° oven 10 to 15 minutes. While warm, dust with confectioners' sugar.

*Makes 45 to 50 crescents.*

# Mincemeat Squares

2 cups sifted flour
2 teaspoons baking powder
½ teaspoon salt
¾ cup sugar
½ cup melted shortening

2 eggs
½ teaspoon orange extract
1 tablespoon grated orange peel
¾ cup prepared mincemeat

Sift together flour, baking powder and salt. Add sugar to shortening and mix well. Beat in eggs until mixture is smooth. Stir in extract and orange peel. Gradually add flour mixture, stirring until well blended. Place half of dough in well greased 9-inch square pan. Spread dough with mincemeat; cover with remaining dough. Bake in 375° oven about 30 minutes. When cool, cut in 1½-inch squares. *Makes about 2 dozen squares.*

# Jumbles

½ cup shortening
1 cup sugar
1 egg
1 teaspoon vanilla
2 cups sifted flour
½ teaspoon baking soda

½ teaspoon salt
½ cup buttermilk
TOPPING:
½ cup chopped nuts
¼ cup sugar
1 teaspoon cinnamon

Cream shortening; add sugar gradually, creaming thoroughly. Add egg and vanilla; beat well. Sift dry ingredients together; add alternately with buttermilk to creamed mixture. Turn into greased and floured 10 x 15-inch baking pan. Sprinkle with Topping made by mixing nuts, sugar and cinnamon. Bake in 400° oven 15 minutes. Cut in squares while still warm.

Jumbles can be frozen. *Makes 20 to 24 squares.*

# Almond Tea Cakes (Cookies)

½ cup butter or margarine
1¼ cups sugar
3 eggs, separated
1 cup sifted flour
1 teaspoon baking powder

3 tablespoons milk
1 cup chopped almonds
1 tablespoon sugar
½ teaspoon cinnamon

Cream butter and half of the sugar. Add well beaten egg yolks, flour, baking powder and milk. Mix well; spread in 11 x 7 x 1½-inch greased baking pan. Beat egg whites until stiff; beat in remaining sugar gradually. Fold in almonds; spread on top of dough. Mix together sugar and cinnamon. Sprinkle over egg whites. Bake in 350° oven about 30 minutes. Cool and cut in strips. *9 servings.*

# Chinese Almond Cakes

| | |
|---|---|
| 1 cup butter or margarine | 1 tablespoon cream |
| 2¼ cups sifted flour | 1 teaspoon almond extract |
| ¾ cup sugar | ½ cup blanched almonds, |
| ½ teaspoon salt | halved |

Cut butter into flour with pastry blender. Add sugar, salt, cream and extract; knead into a dough. Shape into 2 rolls about 1 inch in diameter. Wrap in waxed paper. Chill. Cut roll in ½-inch slices. Place 1 inch apart on ungreased baking sheet. Press half an almond into each cake. Bake in 375° oven 10 to 12 minutes.

*Makes 5 to 6 dozen cakes.*

# Fudge Nut Cookies

| | |
|---|---|
| ⅔ cup butter | 1 teaspoon baking powder |
| 1⅔ cups sugar | ½ teaspoon baking soda |
| 8 ounces (1 cup) creamed | ½ teaspoon salt |
| cottage cheese, sieved | ½ cup chopped nuts |
| 2 eggs | Sifted confectioners' sugar OR |
| 2 teaspoons vanilla | Chopped nuts OR |
| 2¾ cups sifted flour | Granulated sugar |
| ½ cup cocoa | |

Cream butter and sugar until light and fluffy. Beat in cottage cheese. Beat in eggs and vanilla. Gradually add sifted dry ingredients. Stir in nuts. Chill dough several hours. Form into balls about 1 inch in diameter. Roll in sifted confectioners' sugar, chopped nuts or granulated sugar. Place on lightly greased baking sheet. Bake in 350° oven 15 minutes or until done.
Cookies can be frozen.

*Makes 5 dozen.*

# Empire Biscuits
## (Cookies)

| | |
|---|---|
| ½ cup margarine | 1 teaspoon baking powder |
| ½ cup sugar | Red raspberry preserves |
| 1 egg, slightly beaten | Chopped nuts |
| 2 cups sifted flour | Vanilla Cream Cheese Frosting |
| 2 teaspoons cinnamon | |

Cream margarine and sugar. Blend in egg. Add flour sifted with cinnamon and baking powder; mix well. Roll thin; cut with 2-inch round cutter. Place on ungreased baking sheet. Bake in 350° oven 12 to 15 minutes. Cool. For each biscuit, spread preserves between 2 rounds. Frost top with Vanilla Cream Cheese Frosting (page 55). Decorate with chopped nuts and preserves.

*Makes 2 dozen.*

# Dutch Almond Cookies

½ cup plus 1 tablespoon butter
  or margarine
⅔ cup firmly packed brown
  sugar, sieved
1⅓ cups sifted flour
¼ teaspoon baking powder
1 teaspoon cinnamon
¼ teaspoon nutmeg
¼ teaspoon cloves

¼ teaspoon ginger
⅛ teaspoon salt
Dash pepper
½ cup almond filling (canned)
¼ cup sifted flour
1 teaspoon slightly beaten egg
18 blanched almonds, split
  in halves

Cream butter and brown sugar. Sift together 1⅓ cups flour, baking powder, cinnamon, nutmeg, cloves, ginger, salt and pepper. Add to creamed mixture; stir well. Divide dough in half. Place each half on waxed paper; pat out to a 7-inch square. Combine almond filling and ¼ cup flour. Spread evenly over one layer of cooky dough. Top with second layer of dough. Brush with egg. Cut in 36 squares. Place almond half on each square. Bake on lightly greased baking sheet in 350° oven 20 to 25 minutes. Store in airtight container. *Makes 3 dozen.*

# Krullers

5 egg yolks
½ teaspoon salt
¼ cup sugar
5 tablespoons dairy sour cream
1 tablespoon brandy or rum

1 teaspoon vanilla
2 cups sifted flour
Fat for deep frying
Confectioners' sugar

Combine egg yolks and salt; beat until thick and lemon colored. Beat in sugar. Add sour cream, brandy and vanilla. Stir in 1¾ cups flour reserving ¼ cup for flouring pastry cloth. Turn dough out on floured cloth and knead lightly, about 2 minutes. Cover and let rest 10 minutes. Work with half of dough at a time. Keep unused portion covered. Roll out dough paper thin. Cut into 1-inch wide strips. Cut each strip diagonally in 3-inch pieces. Slit each piece in center and pull one end through to other side. Fry in deep fat, preheated to 350°, until edges begin to turn light brown. Turn, fry other side to golden brown. Avoid overcrowding pan. Drain on absorbent paper. Sprinkle with confectioners' sugar. *Makes 7 to 7½ dozen.*

Baking hint: Remove cookies from baking sheet as soon as taken from the oven. Cool on wire rack.

# Pastry for 2-Crust Pie

1½ cups sifted flour  
½ teaspoon salt  

½ cup shortening  
5 tablespoons cold water  

Sift together flour and salt; cut in shortening with pastry blender. Add water all at once and mix with blender. Turn out on lightly floured pastry cloth; mixture will be crumbly. Bring ends of cloth together and hit cloth on table so as to form pastry into a ball. Divide dough in half. Form one half into a flat circle on cloth. Roll out to fit a 9-inch pie pan. Roll remaining dough for top crust two inches larger than pie pan. Perforate top crust with fork. After placing top crust on pie, fold the extra crust under edge of bottom crust; press together. Crimp edge. Bake according to pie recipe.

Note: Pastry is sufficient for 1 2-crust pie or 2 8- or 9-inch pie shells. Bake pie shells in 450° oven 10 to 12 minutes.

# Pastry for 8- or 9-Inch Pie Shell

1 cup sifted flour  
½ teaspoon salt  

⅓ cup shortening  
1 to 2 tablespoons cold water  

Sift flour with salt into bowl. Cut in shortening, using a pastry blender or fork, until mixture is consistency of corn meal and small peas. Sprinkle water, a little at a time, over different parts of flour mixture. Toss together lightly with fork. Use as little water as possible, just enough to moisten dough. Place dough on waxed paper. Knead 3 times. Press gently with paper into ball. Let stand at room temperature 15 to 20 minutes. Lightly flour pastry cloth or board and stockinette covered rolling pin. Roll dough into circle ⅛ inch thick. Use light strokes, working out from center. Lift rolling pin as it nears edge. To measure, invert pie pan on dough to be sure circle extends 1½ inches beyond edge of pan. Fold rolled out dough over rolling pin and lift onto pan. Fit pastry into pan. Do not stretch pastry. Press with fingertips from center out to remove air bubbles. Fold edge of pastry under to fit rim of pie pan. Flute edge with fingertips.

**For baked pie shell:** Prick pastry dough with fork. Bake in 450° oven 10 to 12 minutes.

# Pastry for 10-Inch Pie Shell

1⅓ cups sifted flour      ½ cup shortening
½ teaspoon salt      3 to 4 tablespoons cold water

Sift together flour and salt; cut in shortening with pastry blender. Add water all at once and mix with blender. Turn out on lightly floured pastry cloth; mixture will be crumbly. Bring ends of cloth together and hit cloth on table to form pastry into ball. Form into flat circle on cloth. Roll out to fit 10-inch pie pan. Trim crust around edge of pan, leaving about 1 inch. Fold extra crust under and press together. Flute edge. Perforate crust with fork. Bake in 425° oven 15 to 18 minutes.

# 9-Inch Graham Cracker Crust

1 cup graham cracker crumbs      ⅓ cup butter or margarine,
¾ teaspoon flour      melted
¼ cup sugar

Crush graham crackers; measure 1 cup. Add remaining ingredients; mix well. Pat mixture into bottom and sides of 9-inch pie pan. Bake in 375° oven 8 minutes. Chill well before adding filling.

# 8-Inch Graham Cracker Crust

1 cup graham cracker crumbs      ¼ cup softened butter
¼ cup sugar

Crush graham crackers; measure 1 cup. Thoroughly mix together all ingredients. Press evenly on bottom and sides of 8-inch pie pan to make a layer ⅛ inch thick. Bake in 375° oven about 8 minutes. Chill before adding filling.

# Gingersnap Crust

1¼ cups finely crushed      ¼ cup melted butter
  gingersnaps (about 20)

Save a few crumbs for topping pie. Mix remaining crumbs and butter. Press into 9-inch pie pan. Bake in 325° oven 10 minutes. Cool before filling.        *Makes 1 baked 9-inch crust.*

# Coconut Tart Shells with Strawberry Parfait Filling

**TART SHELLS:**
¼ cup soft butter
2 4-ounce packages moist
  shredded coconut
**STRAWBERRY PARFAIT
FILLING:**
1 12-ounce package frozen
  strawberries

**Water**
1 (3-ounce) package strawberry
  flavored gelatin
¼ cup cold water
1 pint vanilla ice cream
**WHIPPED CREAM SWIRLS:**
½ cup whipping cream
1½ teaspoons sugar
⅛ teaspoon vanilla

**Tart Shells:** Divide butter into 8 equal pieces. Spread each piece evenly in a 3-inch muffin cup. Divide each package of coconut into 4 equal portions. Pat each portion into buttered muffin cup as evenly as possible. Bake in 350° oven 8 to 10 minutes or until crisp and golden brown. Cool 1 hour. Remove from muffin cups to shallow pan.

**Filling:** Thaw and drain frozen berries. Measure drained berry juice; add enough water to it to make 1 cup. Bring to boiling point. Pour over gelatin; stir until dissolved. Add cold water. Cut ice cream into chunks and dissolve by stirring into hot gelatin mixture. Cool. When partially thickened, fold in well drained berries. Pour into cold coconut shells. Place in refrigerator to chill.

**Whipped Cream Swirls:** Whip cream; when stiff, add sugar and vanilla. Mix thoroughly. Drop by teaspoons or put through pastry tube into bottom of shallow pan. Put in freezing compartment of refrigerator until ready to use. Just before serving, place swirls in center of each tart. *8 servings.*

# Strawberry Pie Glacé

1 cup sugar
3 tablespoons cornstarch
½ teaspoon salt
1 cup water

2 teaspoons lemon juice
Few drops red food coloring
3 cups sliced strawberries
1 baked 9-inch pie shell

Combine sugar, cornstarch and salt. Stir in water, lemon juice and red coloring. Cook, stirring constantly, until thick and clear. Remove from heat; cool slightly. Arrange strawberries in cooled pie shell. Pour cornstarch mixture over strawberries. Refrigerate until set. *Makes 1 9-inch pie.*

Note: Frozen strawberries that have been well drained may be substituted for fresh berries.

# Rice and Peach Ginger Pie

½ cup uncooked rice
⅔ cup water
¾ teaspoon salt
2½ cups milk
½ cup heavy cream
2 sticks cinnamon
½ cup sugar
1½ tablespoons cornstarch
¾ teaspoon nutmeg
2 eggs

1 cup diced peaches
2 tablespoons butter or margarine
½ teaspoon vanilla
1 baked 9-inch gingersnap crumb crust
Sweetened whipped cream, optional
Gingersnap crumbs, optional

Bring rice, water and salt to a boil in top part of double boiler. Lower heat to simmer; cover and cook until water is absorbed, about 5 minutes. Add milk, cream and cinnamon sticks and bring to boil. Place over boiling water; cover and cook until rice is tender, about 40 minutes. Remove cinnamon sticks. Combine sugar, cornstarch and nutmeg. Beat eggs. Gradually add sugar mixture and beat thoroughly. Add to rice and milk mixture; cook until thickened, stirring constantly. Add diced peaches, butter and vanilla. Cool before pouring into crust. If desired, decorate with a ruff of sweetened whipped cream sprinkled with gingersnap crumbs. *Makes 1 9-inch pie.*

# Sparkling Red Cherry Pie

FILLING:
2 1-pound cans (4 cups) unsweetened pie cherries
1 cup sugar
¼ cup cornstarch
⅛ teaspoon salt
1 tablespoon butter or margarine
⅛ teaspoon cinnamon

⅛ teaspoon almond extract
Few drops red food coloring
1 baked 9-inch pie shell
ALMOND CREAM TOPPING:
⅔ cup whipping cream
2 teaspoons sugar
¼ teaspoon vanilla
2 drops almond extract

Filling: Drain cherries well. Save ⅔ cup juice. Combine sugar, cornstarch and salt in saucepan. Slowly add cherry juice, stirring to prevent lumping. Bring mixture to boiling point. Cook over low heat, stirring constantly, until clear and thick, about 10 minutes. Add butter, cinnamon, extract, food coloring and cherries. Continue cooking over low heat, stirring gently, until mixture is very thick, about 8 minutes. Cool. Pour into cooled pie shell. Chill well. Serve with Almond Cream Topping.

Topping: Beat cream until it begins to stiffen. Add sugar, vanilla and extract. Continue beating until cream is of desired stiffness. *Makes 1 9-inch pie.*

# Lattice Cherry Pie

3 tablespoons cornstarch
1 cup sugar
¼ teaspoon salt
1 cup cherry juice, drained
   from can
¼ teaspoon red food coloring

3 cups canned waterpack, red
   tart pitted cherries, drained
⅛ teaspoon almond extract
2 tablespoons butter or
   margarine
Pastry for 2-crust pie

Sift cornstarch, sugar and salt into saucepan. Add juice and coloring. Stir until smooth. Cook and stir until thickened and clear. Add cherries, almond extract and butter. Mix well; cool. Roll out and line pie pan with half of pastry. Roll out remaining pastry and cut in ½-inch strips for lattice crust. Pour cherry mixture into prepared pan. Weave pie crust strips over cherries. Flute edges. Bake in 425° oven 40 minutes or until browned.

*Makes* 1 9-*inch pie.*

# Autumn Pear Pie

2 tablespoons lemon juice
4 cups sliced fresh pears
⅓ cup granulated sugar
⅓ cup firmly packed brown
   sugar, sieved

2 tablespoons cornstarch
¼ teaspoon salt
¼ teaspoon nutmeg
Pastry for 2-crust pie
Butter or margarine

Add lemon juice to sliced pears. Combine sugars, cornstarch, salt and nutmeg. Divide dough in half. Roll one half to circle ⅛ inch thick and fit into 9-inch pie pan. Roll remaining half of dough for top crust. Arrange half of sliced pears in bottom crust. Sprinkle half of sugar mixture over pears. Add remaining pears; sprinkle with remaining sugar mixture. Dot with butter. Arrange top crust over filling. Trim and flute edge. Prick or slash pastry to allow steam to escape. Bake in 425° oven 35 to 40 minutes.

*Makes* 1 9-*inch pie.*

# Dutch Apple Pie

Pastry for 1-crust 9-inch pie
5 to 6 cooking apples
1 tablespoon lemon juice
1 cup sugar

3 tablespoons flour
1 cup dairy sour cream
Cinnamon

Roll out and line pie pan with pastry; flute edges. Pare and slice apples; sprinkle with lemon juice and place in lined pie pan. Combine sugar, flour and sour cream; pour over apples. Sprinkle with cinnamon. Bake in 425° oven 10 minutes; reduce heat to 375° and bake 35 minutes or until apples are tender. Serve slightly warm.

*Makes* 1 9-*inch pie.*

# Chocolate Cream Mint Pie

½ cup soft butter
1 cup sifted confectioners'
   sugar
2 squares (2 ounces)
   unsweetened chocolate,
   melted and cooled

2 unbeaten eggs
⅛ teaspoon peppermint extract
1 teaspoon vanilla extract
1 baked 8-inch graham cracker
   crust, chilled
½ pint (1 cup) whipping cream

Cream butter. Add sugar; cream until light and fluffy. Gradually add chocolate. Add eggs, one at a time, stirring well after each addition. Stir in extracts. Pour into crust. Refrigerate 4 to 6 hours. Just before serving, whip cream and spread over top of pie. *Makes 1 8-inch pie.*

# Chocolate Almond Dream Pie

1 4½-ounce chocolate almond
   candy bar
24 marshmallows
⅓ cup milk

½ pint (1 cup) whipping cream
1 teaspoon vanilla
1 baked 9-inch pie shell
Yellow food coloring

Combine chocolate bar, 20 marshmallows and milk in top of double boiler. Melt and stir until mixture is smooth and creamy. Remove from heat; cool. To cool quickly place in pan of ice water. Whip cream; add vanilla. When chocolate mixture is cool, fold into whipped cream and blend well until smooth. Pour into cooled pie shell. Chill several hours. Before serving decorate with easy marshmallow daisies. With scissors, cut each of the 4 remaining marshmallows into petal shaped pieces. Arrange the marshmallow petals to resemble daisies on the surface of the pie. Center each daisy with a small piece of marshmallow tinted yellow with food coloring. *Makes 1 9-inch pie.*

# Chocolate Fudge Pie

4 eggs
2 cups sugar
3 squares (3 ounces)
   unsweetened chocolate,
   melted
⅓ cup butter or margarine,
   melted

1 cup chopped nuts
1 teaspoon vanilla
1 9-inch pie pan lined with
   unbaked pastry
Whipped cream OR
Ice cream

Beat eggs until thick and lemon colored. Gradually add sugar, beating continually. Combine melted chocolate and butter; cool slightly. Pour into egg mixture. Stir to combine thoroughly. Stir in nuts and vanilla. Pour mixture into pastry lined pie pan. Bake in 350° oven 40 minutes. Serve with whipped cream or ice cream.

*Makes 1 9-inch pie.*

# Confetti Topped Cream Pie

**FILLING:**
⅓ cup cornstarch
⅔ cup sugar
½ teaspoon salt
2½ cups milk, heated
3 egg yolks, slightly beaten
2 tablespoons butter or
  margarine

1 teaspoon vanilla
1 baked 9-inch pie shell
**TOPPING:**
½ cup whipping cream
½ teaspoon vanilla
½ cup gumdrops, cut in small
  pieces

**Filling:** Mix cornstarch, sugar and salt in saucepan. Gradually add milk. Cook slowly until very thick. Gradually add small amount of hot mixture into egg yolks. Add this slowly to the rest of the hot mixture; blend well. Place saucepan over low heat. Stir and cook until mixture just comes to a boil, about 4 to 5 minutes. Add butter and vanilla. Cool. Pour into cooled pie shell. Chill.

**Topping:** Whip cream; beat in vanilla. Spread over pie. Top with gumdrops. Serve cold. *Makes 1 9-inch pie.*

# Mandarin Orange Cream Pie

⅔ cup sugar
½ cup sifted flour
½ teaspoon salt
1½ cups scalded milk
3 eggs, separated
2 tablespoons butter or
  margarine

½ teaspoon orange extract
⅓ cup sugar
1 11-ounce can (1 cup) mandarin
  orange sections, drained
1 baked 9-inch pie shell
2 teaspoons grated orange peel

In top of double boiler, combine ⅔ cup sugar, flour and salt. Add milk gradually, stirring constantly. Cook over direct heat until thickened, stirring constantly. Remove from heat. Beat egg yolks slightly. Blend a small amount of hot sauce into egg yolks. Then blend egg mixture back into sauce. Cook over boiling water about 5 minutes, stirring frequently. Stir in butter and orange extract. Cool slightly. For meringue, beat egg whites until frothy. Add ⅓ cup sugar gradually, beating until stiff, glossy peaks are formed. Arrange orange sections over bottom of cooled pie shell. Turn filling over oranges. Top with meringue. Sprinkle orange peel around edge of meringue. Bake in 350° oven 10 to 15 minutes to brown meringue. *Makes 1 9-inch pie.*

# Honeymoon Lemon Meringue Pie

**FILLING:**
¼ cup cornstarch
1½ cups milk
¾ cup sugar
½ teaspoon salt
2 egg yolks, beaten well
1 tablespoon butter or
    margarine

1 teaspoon shredded lemon peel
5 tablespoons lemon juice
1 baked 8-inch pie shell
**MERINGUE:**
¼ teaspoon salt
2 egg whites
¼ cup sugar
1 teaspoon shredded lemon peel

Filling: Dissolve cornstarch in a little of the milk. Add remaining milk, sugar and salt. Cook over low heat until thick, stirring constantly. Gradually stir a little of the hot mixture into egg yolks. Add egg mixture to the rest of hot mixture. Stir constantly and cook 2 minutes longer. Add butter, lemon peel and juice. Cool while making meringue. Pour into cooled pie shell.

Meringue: Sprinkle salt over egg whites. Beat until soft peaks form when the beater is lifted. Sprinkle sugar, a little at a time, over whites beating until meringue forms definite peaks. Fold in shredded peel. Spoon over pie, making sure meringue touches crust all the way around. Bake in 300° oven 15 to 20 minutes.

*Makes* 1 8-*inch pie.*

# Lemon-Cranberry Meringue Pie

1 baked 9-inch pie shell
**FILLING:**
⅓ cup cornstarch
¼ cup sifted flour
1½ cups sugar
½ teaspoon salt
1½ cups boiling water
3 egg yolks, slightly beaten
1½ tablespoons butter or
    margarine

1 teaspoon grated lemon peel
7 tablespoons lemon juice
    (½ cup minus 1 tablespoon)
1 1-pound can (2 cups) jellied
    cranberry sauce
**MERINGUE:**
3 egg whites
⅛ teaspoon salt
6 tablespoons sugar

Filling: Mix cornstarch, flour, sugar and salt. Add boiling water gradually, stirring constantly to prevent lumping. Place over direct heat. Cook slowly until thickened throughout, stirring constantly. Cook, uncovered, over simmering water, about 10 minutes, until clear and thick. Stir 2 or 3 times. Stir a small amount of hot mixture into egg yolks. Combine with remaining hot mixture. Continue cooking over simmering water, about 5 minutes, stirring constantly. Remove from heat. Add butter, lemon peel and juice. Blend thoroughly. Cool about 5 minutes.

Pour ⅔ of filling into cooled pie shell; spread filling up side to fluted edge to prevent cranberry sauce from touching pastry. Spread with ¾ of the cranberry sauce (1½ cups) that has been finely broken with a fork. Top with remaining filling.

Meringue: Beat egg whites and salt until frothy. Add sugar gradually, beating constantly until peaks form when beater is withdrawn. Cover filling with meringue. Bake in 350° oven 12 to 15 minutes or until tops of the irregular surface are golden brown. Best served the same day pie is made.     *Makes 1 9-inch pie.*

Note: Use remaining cranberry sauce (½ cup) as an accompaniment to meat or poultry meal.

## Frozen Lemon Pie

| | |
|---|---|
| 1 6-ounce can (⅔ cup) evaporated milk | ¼ cup lemon juice |
| | 2 egg whites |
| ⅓ cup sugar | 2 tablespoons sugar |
| 2 egg yolks, well beaten | ½ cup sifted graham cracker |
| ½ teaspoon grated lemon peel | OR vanilla wafer crumbs |

Pour milk into ice cube tray of refrigerator. Chill until milk begins to freeze around edges. Add ⅓ cup sugar to egg yolks; mix well. Stir in peel and juice. Cook over low heat, stirring constantly, until mixture thickens slightly, about 3 minutes. Remove from heat; cool. Chill in bowl of ice. Beat egg whites stiff; gradually beat in 2 tablespoons sugar. Fold into cold lemon mixture. Line loaf pan, 9 x 5 x 2¾ inches, with waxed paper; sprinkle half of crumbs over bottom. Whip chilled milk until stiff; fold into lemon mixture. Pour into prepared pan. Sprinkle with remaining crumbs. Freeze until firm.     *6 servings.*

## Peppermint Ice Cream Pie
## Chocolate Crust

| | |
|---|---|
| CRUST: | ¼ cup finely chopped pecans |
| 14 crisp chocolate cookies, crushed | FILLING: |
| | 1 quart peppermint ice cream, |
| 5 tablespoons butter or margarine, melted | softened |

Crust: Mix crushed cookies, butter and pecans. Press mixture on bottom and sides of 9-inch pie pan. Bake in 300° oven 8 minutes. Cool.

Filling: Spoon softened ice cream into cold crust. Place in freezing compartment of refrigerator until serving time.

*Makes 1 9-inch pie.*

# Baked Ice Cream Pie

1 baked 8-inch pie shell
2 pints vanilla ice cream
2 egg whites
¼ teaspoon cream of tartar
¼ cup sugar
1½ cups crushed and sweetened
   fresh berries

Fill the cooled pie shell with slightly softened ice cream. Cover with freezer wrapping. Keep in freezer until ready to use. At serving time make meringue topping. Beat egg whites with cream of tartar until frothy. Gradually add sugar, beating until glossy and very stiff. Cover ice cream in pie shell with berries, then cover with meringue. Spread meringue to rim of shell to completely cover berries and ice cream. Bake in 450° oven 3 to 5 minutes or until delicately browned. Serve immediately.

*Makes 1 8-inch pie.*

# Baked Alaska Raspberry Fluff Pie

3 egg whites
3 tablespoons sugar
½ teaspoon lemon juice
½ cup red raspberry preserves
1 pint vanilla ice cream
1 pint chocolate ice cream
1 baked 9-inch pie shell, pastry
   or crumb, chilled

Beat egg whites until foamy. Add sugar gradually, continuing to beat until very stiff. Gradually beat in lemon juice and preserves. Spoon ice cream into pie shell. Cover with meringue. Bake in 450° oven for a few minutes until lightly browned.

*Makes 1 9-inch pie.*

# Frozen Pumpkin "Peace-Pipe" Pie
# with Caramelized Almonds

1 pint vanilla ice cream,
   softened
1 baked 10-inch pie shell
1 1-pound can (2 cups) pumpkin
1½ cups sugar
½ teaspoon salt
1 teaspoon cinnamon
½ teaspoon ginger
¼ teaspoon cloves
1 teaspoon vanilla
1½ cups whipping cream
1 cup slivered almonds
¼ cup sugar

Spread softened ice cream in cooled pie shell; place in freezer. Mix pumpkin with 1½ cups sugar, salt, spices and vanilla. Whip 1 cup cream until stiff; fold into pumpkin mixture. Pour mixture over ice cream in shell. Cover with foil; freeze about 4 hours. Meanwhile, caramelize almonds: Combine almonds and ¼ cup sugar in small skillet. Place over low heat, stirring constantly and rapidly, as the sugar begins to turn color. Remove from heat when almonds are caramel-colored; spread on greased cooky sheet. Break apart when cool. Before serving pie, whip remaining ½ cup cream, spread over top of pie; garnish with almonds. Makes 1 10-inch pie.

Note: If a 9-inch pie pan is used, freeze the extra cup of pumpkin filling in paper cupcake pan liners and serve topped with maple nut or vanilla ice cream.

# Caramel Pecan Pie

½ pound (28) caramels
½ cup water
¼ cup margarine
¾ cup sugar
¼ teaspoon salt

½ teaspoon vanilla
2 eggs, slightly beaten
1 cup pecan halves
1 9-inch pie pan lined with
   unbaked pastry

Place caramels, water and margarine in top of double boiler. Heat, stirring frequently, until caramels are melted and sauce is smooth. Combine sugar, salt, vanilla and eggs. Gradually add caramel sauce, mixing well. Add pecan halves. Pour into pastry lined pie pan. Bake in 400° oven 10 minutes; reduce heat to 350°, continue baking 20 minutes.       *Makes 1 9-inch pie.*

Note: The pie filling will appear to be very soft while it is hot, but it becomes firm as it cools.

# Irish Coffee Pie

1 tablespoon (1 envelope)
   unflavored gelatin
¾ cup sugar
¼ teaspoon salt
1 tablespoon powdered instant
   coffee
1 egg yolk
¾ cup milk
¼ cup Irish whiskey

1 egg white, beaten stiff
1½ cups whipping cream,
   whipped
½ cup slivered almonds,
   blanched and toasted
1 10-inch baked pie shell
TOPPING:
1½ cups sweetened whipped
   cream

Combine gelatin, sugar, salt and coffee in top of double boiler. Beat egg yolk and milk slightly; add to double boiler. Cook, stirring occasionally, until gelatin is melted and sugar is dissolved. Chill until thick and syrupy. Add Irish whiskey; beat until light and frothy. Fold in egg white, whipped cream and almonds. Heap into cooled pie shell; chill until set. Spread Topping over pie.       *Makes 1 10-inch pie.*

# Lemon Fluff Pie

4 eggs, separated
1 cup sugar
¼ cup lemon juice
3 tablespoons water

Grated peel of 1 lemon
1 baked 9-inch pie shell OR
6 individual pie shells

As eggs are separated, put whites into mixing bowl and yolks into top of double boiler. Beat yolks until thick, adding ½ cup of sugar gradually while beating. When thick and lemon colored, stir in lemon juice, water and peel. Cook over hot water, stirring until quite thick. Remove from hot water. Rinse egg beater thoroughly to free it of egg yolk before whipping egg whites. Beat whites until fluffy but not stiff, then add remaining ½ cup sugar gradually while beating, until smooth, stiff peaks are formed. Fold approximately half the egg white mixture into the cooked egg and lemon filling; when evenly blended place in cooled pie shell. Heap remaining meringue (egg white mixture) around edges of pie like a wreath. Place in 425° oven long enough to brown peaks of meringue. Cool before serving.

*Makes 1 9-inch pie or 6 individual pies.*

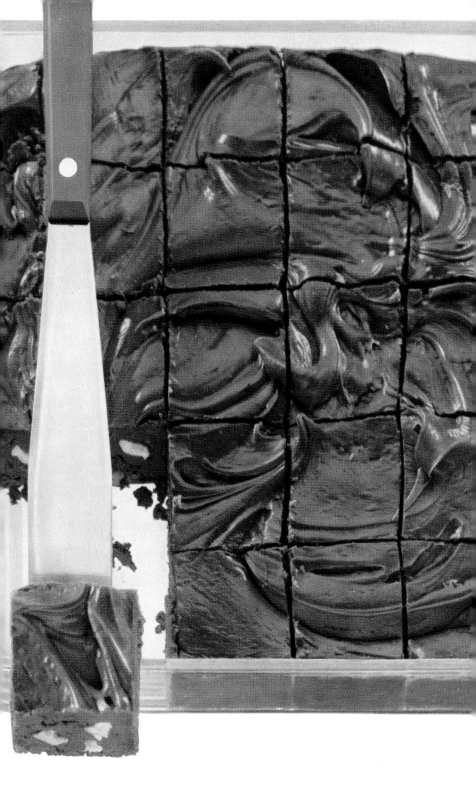

# DESSERTS, CANDIES, CONFECTIONS

CREME DE CACAO
  BAVARIAN
FROZEN HAWAIIAN CREAM
PINA SCHOONER
DOUGHNUT CARTWHEELS
CHIFFON DESSERT WAFFLES
  WITH FROZEN STRAWBER-
  RIES AND WHIPPED CREAM
CREAM PUFFS WITH CHOCO-
  LATE CHIP CREAM FILLING
SHERBET RING WITH STRAW-
  BERRIES
LIME OR LEMON SHERBET
ICE CREAM PARTY LOAF
ICE CREAM AND FRUIT
  COMPOTE
CRACKER TORTE CONFETTI
INDIVIDUAL ALASKAS
PINEAPPLE CHEESE CAKE
COTTAGE BLINTZES
CREAMY CHEESE CAKE

CHERRIES JUBILEE
RUM TORTE
RASPBERRY CREAM TORTE
CHOCOLATE RUM
  REFRIGERATOR CAKE
APPLE CARAMEL
APPLE SLICES
PEACHES DELIGHTFUL
CURRIED FRUIT
CHEESE AND FRUIT
MILLION DOLLAR FUDGE
DIVINITY FUDGE
CHOCO-MINT BALLS
CHOCOLATE NO-BAKE
  CLUSTERS
BUTTER TOFFEE
LOUISIANA CREAM PRALINES
ORANGE COCONUT CREAMS
LEMON COCONUT CREAMS
ORANGE SUGARED WALNUTS
SPICED PECANS OR WALNUTS

*Illustration:* Million Dollar Fudge (page 89).

# Desserts, Candies, Confections

In the days before sugar was known, figs, dates and nuts were mixed with honey to satisfy the longing for sweets. The recipes given here are for modern-day enjoyment and include handsome puddings and favored frozen desserts . . . providing an excellent source for the homemaker searching for something special in the line of sweets.

## DESSERTS

### Creme de Cacao Bavarian

| | |
|---|---|
| 1 tablespoon (1 envelope) unflavored gelatin | ¼ pound marshmallows |
| ¼ cup cold water | ½ pint (1 cup) whipping cream |
| 2 cups creme de cacao | Shaved sweet chocolate |

Soften gelatin in cold water. Heat creme de cacao over low heat. DO NOT BOIL. Add marshmallows to hot creme de cacao. Remove from heat when marshmallows are melted. Add softened gelatin; stir until gelatin is dissolved. Pour into 2-quart mixing bowl; set bowl in pan of ice. Whip cream. Fold into gelatin mixture when mixture starts to congeal. Keep refrigerated until serving time. Garnish with shaved chocolate.      *8 servings.*

# Frozen Hawaiian Cream

1 cup fine graham cracker
  crumbs
1 egg, beaten
½ cup dairy sour cream
¾ cup sugar
½ teaspoon salt

1 teaspoon grated orange peel
½ teaspoon vanilla
¼ teaspoon almond extract
1 cup well drained crushed
  pineapple
1 cup whipping cream, whipped

Cover bottom of an 8 x 8 x 2-inch pan with ½ cup graham cracker crumbs. Mix together egg, sour cream, sugar, salt and orange peel in top of double boiler. Cook over simmering water until mixture coats a spoon. Remove from heat; stir in vanilla and almond extracts. Cool thoroughly. Stir in pineapple. Fold whipped cream into mixture, blending well. Pour gently on top of crumbs in square pan. Spread remaining crumbs on top. Freeze several hours or overnight. Cut in six oblong pieces.

*6 servings.*

# Pina Schooner

1 quart vanilla ice cream
2 4-ounce cans shredded
  coconut

1 teaspoon almond extract
1 fresh pineapple
3 tablespoons sugar, optional

Soften ice cream slightly. Save ¾ cup coconut for garnish. Cut remaining coconut into small pieces with scissors. Fold coconut and almond extract into ice cream. Refreeze ice cream. Leave green top on pineapple; wash leaves and outside shell. Cut pineapple in half lengthwise. Cut around each pineapple half ¼ inch from shell, scooping out entire center of pineapple and leaving only the ¼-inch thick shell. Remove and discard core. Cut remaining pineapple meat in cubes. Sprinkle with sugar, if desired. Place four scoops of the prepared coconut ice cream into each half pineapple shell. Spoon pineapple cubes over ice cream. Sprinkle reserved ¾ cup coconut over top. Place in bed of crushed ice. Serve from pineapple shell.

*8 servings.*

# Doughnut Cartwheels

1 cup Fluffy Icing
4 to 6 fresh doughnuts (plain)

Chopped nuts, toasted
Ice cream

Spread Fluffy Icing (page 56) around outer edge of doughnuts. Roll in chopped nuts. Top with scoop of ice cream.

*4 to 6 servings.*

# Chiffon Dessert Waffles with Frozen Strawberries and Whipped Cream

1 cup sifted flour
1½ teaspoons baking powder
¾ cup sugar
½ teaspoon salt
2 egg yolks
¼ cup salad oil

⅓ cup cold water
½ teaspoon vanilla
¾ teaspoon grated lemon peel
2 egg whites
Frozen strawberries, thawed
Whipped cream

Sift together flour, baking powder, sugar and salt. Add egg yolks, salad oil, water, vanilla and lemon peel. Beat until smooth and well blended. Beat egg whites until very stiff and dull in appearance. Pour egg yolk mixture into the beaten whites, folding gently until well blended. Bake in waffle baker. Serve warm with strawberries and cream. *8 servings.*

# Cream Puffs with Chocolate Chip Cream Filling

**CREAM PUFFS:**
½ cup butter
¼ teaspoon salt
1 cup boiling water
1 cup sifted flour
4 eggs
**CHOCOLATE CHIP CREAM FILLING:**
3 tablespoons flour
3 tablespoons cornstarch

¾ cup sugar
¾ teaspoon salt
3 cups milk, scalded
3 eggs, beaten
1½ teaspoons vanilla
1 6-ounce package semi-sweet chocolate pieces

**Cream Puffs:** Add butter and salt to water; stir until butter melts and mixture comes to a boil. Add flour all at once; stir vigorously until mixture is smooth and forms soft ball. Remove from heat. Beat in eggs, one at a time. Beat well. Drop by tablespoonfuls, 2 inches apart, on lightly greased cooky sheet. Bake in 375° oven 50 minutes. Remove from oven; cut a small slit in side of each puff. Cool. Fill with Chocolate Chip Cream Filling.
*Makes 10 to 12 cream puffs.*

**Chocolate Chip Cream Filling:** Combine flour, cornstarch, sugar and salt in saucepan. Gradually stir in milk. Cook over low heat, stirring constantly, until slightly thickened. Add small amount of hot mixture to eggs. Stir into remaining hot mixture. Cook over low heat for about 5 minutes. Remove from heat; cool. Add vanilla and chocolate pieces. *Makes about 4 cups filling.*

# Sherbet Ring with Strawberries

1 quart lemon sherbet
⅓ cup green creme de menthe
1 quart strawberries, hulled
½ cup shredded coconut
Galax leaves

Let sherbet stand at room temperature until slightly softened. Add creme de menthe and blend well. Cut 6 strips of wax paper 1 inch wide by 12 inches long. Lay them crosswise in a 5-cup ring mold with the ends of the strips hanging over the edge. Pack in sherbet. Freeze until firm in freezer. Remove from freezer and dip mold quickly in warm water. Run knife around edge; invert on serving platter. Peel off paper and return to freezer. At serving time fill center with strawberries. Sprinkle top with shredded coconut and garnish with galax leaves.     8 *servings.*

# Lime or Lemon Sherbet

1 cup boiling water
1 3-ounce package lime- or
   lemon-flavored gelatin
1 cup sugar
¼ cup lemon juice
1 teaspoon grated lemon peel
1 quart light cream

Pour boiling water over gelatin and stir until dissolved. Add sugar, lemon juice and peel. Stir until sugar is dissolved. Chill. Pour slowly into cream. Turn into refrigerator trays. Freeze to a mush. Beat with rotary beater. Freeze firm.     *Makes 1½ quarts.*

# Ice Cream Party Loaf

½ gallon ice cream, packed
   in rectangular carton
1 cup heavy cream, whipped
1 teaspoon vanilla
3 tablespoons sugar
Food coloring, optional
Thin chocolate wafers

Remove ice cream from carton and place whole "loaf" of ice cream on metal serving tray or small cooky sheet. Flavor whipped cream with vanilla and sugar; tint with food coloring, if desired. Frost sides and ends of your favorite flavored ice cream loaf with whipped cream. Decorate top with thin chocolate wafers, forming flowers or other designs. Use additional whipped cream as "glue," if necessary. Make additional flower decorations on ends, if desired. Place decorated ice cream loaf in freezer and store until ready to serve. (If stored more than an hour or two, wrap carefully with freezer wrap after whipped cream has hardened.) To serve, slice in 1-inch slices.

10 *servings.*

# Ice Cream and Fruit Compote

1 quart pistachio ice cream
2 10-ounce packages frozen
   sliced peaches, thawed
   slightly and drained
1 quart strawberry ice cream
2 15-ounce cans (3½ cups)
   blueberries, drained

1 quart vanilla ice cream
2 10-ounce packages frozen
   red raspberries, thawed
   slightly and drained

Chill your favorite big, deep, impressive glass dish (4 quart size).
Put pistachio ice cream in bottom of dish. Arrange peaches
over ice cream. Add strawberry ice cream, then blueberries. Over
the blueberries put vanilla ice cream. Top with raspberries. Serve
immediately.                               *12 servings.*

# Cracker Torte Confetti

3 egg whites
1 teaspoon baking powder
¾ cup sugar
14 rich, crisp, round crackers,
   crushed
1 cup finely chopped walnuts
WHIPPED CREAM TOPPING:
1 cup whipping cream

¼ cup confectioners' sugar
3 tablespoons chocolate shot
ICE CREAM CONFETTI BALLS:
Chocolate ice cream
Strawberry ice cream
Peppermint stick ice cream
Mint ice cream (green)

Beat egg whites until stiff; add baking powder and sugar, beating
in thoroughly. Fold in crushed crackers and chopped walnuts.
Spread on bottom and sides of 12 small buttered tart pans or
buttered 9-inch pie pan. Bake in 300° oven 30 to 35 minutes.
Turn out on cooling rack; refrigerate until ready to serve.

**Whipped Cream Topping:** Whip cream until smooth but not
dry. Fold in confectioners' sugar and chocolate shot.

**Ice Cream Confetti Balls:** Use a melon ball cutter or measuring
spoon to scoop out small balls of each variety of ice cream.
Spoon whipped cream topping into tortes. Spoon 1 to 2 balls of
each cream into tortes, giving a "confetti" effect. *Makes 12 tortes.*

# Individual Alaskas

4 egg whites
¼ teaspoon vanilla
¼ cup sifted confectioners'
  sugar

1 pint ice cream
6 individual sponge cake shells

Beat egg whites until stiff, not dry. Add vanilla. Add sugar gradually; continue beating until meringue stands in peaks. Divide ice cream into 6 portions; place a portion in center of each cake shell. Spread meringue over cake and ice cream so they are completely covered. Place on cooky sheet. Brown in 450° oven about 5 minutes. Serve immediately.                        6 *servings.*

Note: Individual Alaskas may be frozen before baking.

# Pineapple Cheese Cake

**CRUST:**
2⅔ cups malted cereal nuts,
  crushed to make 2 cups
½ cup sugar
½ teaspoon cinnamon
½ cup melted butter or
  margarine
**FILLING:**
2 envelopes (2 tablespoons)
  unflavored gelatin
¼ cup cold water
2 eggs, slightly beaten
1¼ cups sugar
1 teaspoon salt

½ cup milk
2 teaspoons vanilla
¼ cup pineapple syrup, drained
  from can
1 8-ounce package cream cheese
2 teaspoons grated lemon peel,
  optional
1 cup well drained crushed
  canned pineapple
1 pint (2 cups) small curd dry
  cottage cheese
1 cup heavy cream
Whipped cream, optional
Pineapple slices, optional
Maraschino cherries, optional

**Crust:** Combine crushed malted cereal nuts, sugar, cinnamon and butter. Mix thoroughly. Press ⅔ of mixture into bottom of 9-inch spring form pan. Save remaining crumbs for decorating top of cheese cake.

**Filling:** Soften gelatin in cold water. Combine eggs, sugar, salt and milk in top of double boiler. Cook over hot water, stirring constantly, until mixture coats a metal spoon. Remove from heat. Add gelatin, stir until dissolved. Cool. Add gelatin mixture, vanilla and pineapple syrup to cream cheese; stir until smooth. Blend in lemon peel, pineapple and cottage cheese. Whip cream and fold into mixture. Pour into crumb-lined pan. Sprinkle top with reserved crumbs. Chill overnight. If desired, garnish with additional whipped cream, pineapple slices and maraschino cherries.                        12 *servings.*

# Cottage Blintzes

1 egg, beaten
1 cup milk
1 cup sifted flour
½ teaspoon salt
3 tablespoons butter
1 cup creamed cottage cheese,
  drained
2 tablespoons butter, softened
1 egg
Confectioners' sugar
Dairy sour cream

TOPPINGS:
Blueberry or blackberry jam OR
Currant jelly OR
Cinnamon flavored orange
  sections OR
Golden raisins OR
Butter 'n' brown sugar baked
  banana slices

Beat egg, milk, flour and salt together thoroughly. Melt 3 table-spoons butter in 6-inch skillet. Make one blintz at a time. Pour ¼ cup batter to cover bottom of pan. Cook over low heat until the one side is set. Slide off onto a clean cloth, cooked side down; cool. Make filling by beating together cottage cheese, butter and egg; spread each blintz thickly with this mixture and roll. Place sealed side down on baking sheet. Bake in 350° oven 20 minutes or until golden. Just before serving, sprinkle with confectioners' sugar. Serve with sour cream and one or several of the toppings.

*8 servings.*

# Creamy Cheese Cake

1½ cups fine graham cracker
  crumbs
⅓ cup firmly packed brown
  sugar, sieved
½ teaspoon cinnamon
⅓ cup melted butter
1 8-ounce package cream cheese

1 12-ounce carton (1½ cups)
  creamed cottage cheese
2 eggs, well beaten
½ cup sugar
½ teaspoon vanilla
1 cup dairy sour cream

Mix crumbs, brown sugar, cinnamon and butter until crumbly. Press in an even layer over bottom and sides of a round, spring form pan or an 8-inch square pan. Soften cream cheese to room temperature. Press cottage cheese through sieve; mix with cream cheese. Beat in eggs, sugar and vanilla. Pour into crumb-lined pan. Bake in 350° oven about 35 minutes. Spread with sour cream while still hot. Cool; chill thoroughly before serving.

*8 to 10 servings.*

# Cherries Jubilee

| | |
|---|---|
| 1 1-pound can (2 cups) dark sweet pitted cherries, drained | ¼ cup cherry brandy |
| ½ cup cherry syrup, drained from can | ½ cup orange curacao |
| | ½ cup cognac |
| | 1 quart vanilla ice cream |

Heat cherries and cherry syrup in chafing dish over boiling water until hot. Add cherry brandy, orange curacao and cognac. Continue heating until warm. Ignite, stirring constantly. Serve over ice cream.                    6 *servings.*

Note: Ice cream may be spooned into dessert dishes and placed in the freezer until serving time.

# Rum Torte

**SPONGE CAKE:**
6 egg yolks
1 cup sugar
1 teaspoon lemon extract
½ cup boiling water
1½ cups sifted cake flour
½ teaspoon salt
2 teaspoons baking powder
3 tablespoons rum

**FILLING:**
3 egg yolks
½ cup sugar
¼ cup sifted flour
2 cups milk
3 egg whites
¼ cup confectioners' sugar
1 cup whipping cream, whipped
¼ cup toasted slivered almonds

Sponge Cake: Beat egg yolks until thick and lemon colored. Add sugar gradually, beating continually. Add extract and water. Sift together flour, salt and baking powder. Fold into first mixture. Pour into 2 greased and floured 9-inch layer cake pans. Bake in 350° oven 25 minutes. Put on cooling racks. Remove from pans; split cake crosswise forming 4 round thin layers. Sprinkle 3 halves with 1 tablespoon rum each. Set aside until ready to fill torte.

Filling: Beat yolks until thick and lemon colored. Add sugar gradually, beating continually. Fold in flour. Pour in milk, stirring constantly. Cook over medium heat until mixture bubbles, stirring constantly. Cool. Beat egg whites until stiff. Beat in confectioners' sugar. Fold in cooled egg yolk mixture. Spread between layers of cake. Place in spring form pan. Refrigerate several hours or overnight. Remove from pan. Decorate with whipped cream forced through pastry bag; sprinkle with almonds.                    12 *servings.*

# Raspberry Cream Torte

⅔ cup margarine
1¾ cups sugar
2 eggs
1½ teaspoons vanilla
3 cups sifted cake flour
2½ teaspoons baking powder

1 teaspoon salt
1¼ cups milk
RASPBERRY CREAM
FILLING:
½ cup red raspberry preserves
1 cup heavy cream, whipped

Cream margarine and sugar. Add eggs and vanilla; beat well. Sift together flour, baking powder and salt; add alternately with milk, mixing well after each addition. Pour into 3 waxed paper lined 9-inch layer pans. Bake in 350° oven 25 minutes. Turn out on cooling racks.

**Raspberry Cream Filling:** Fold preserves into whipped cream. Spread between torte layers and on top. *12 servings.*

# Chocolate Rum Refrigerator Cake

1½ cups butter
3 cups confectioners' sugar
3 squares (3 ounces)
  unsweetened chocolate,
  melted and cooled

⅓ cup rum
3 eggs
1 10-inch angel food or sponge
  cake, uniced
Whipped cream

Cream butter until smooth and fluffy. Gradually work in 1½ cups sugar, blending well. Beat in chocolate, rum and remaining sugar. Add eggs, which have been beaten until thick and lemon colored. Cut strips from cake to line sides of 9-inch spring form pan. Cut remaining cake in small pieces and cover bottom of pan. Pour in half the chocolate filling. Cover with a layer of remaining cake pieces and pour on rest of filling, spreading evenly. Chill overnight. When ready to serve, coat sides of cake with whipped cream and decorate top with cream. *8 to 12 servings.*

# Apple Caramel

6 Roman Beauty apples
¾ cup sugar
¾ cup butter

1 teaspoon vanilla
Cream

Pare, core and cut each apple in 8 wedges. Spread sugar evenly in very large skillet. Heat until sugar melts and turns a light brown color. Stir occasionally. Add butter; mix well. Add apples in 1 single layer. Cover; cook over medium heat 10 minutes. Turn; cook 10 more minutes. Add vanilla. Serve warm with cream. *8 servings.*

# Apple Slices

**DOUGH:**
2 cups sifted flour
1 teaspoon salt
¾ cup shortening
2 egg yolks
1 tablespoon lemon juice
7 tablespoons cold water
**FILLING:**
5 to 7 apples
1 cup sugar
¼ teaspoon salt
1 tablespoon flour
½ teaspoon cinnamon
½ teaspoon nutmeg
¼ cup butter
**ICING:**
1 cup confectioners' sugar,
  sifted
1 tablespoon milk
½ teaspoon vanilla

**Dough:** Sift flour and salt into mixing bowl; cut in shortening. Mix egg yolks, lemon juice and water; stir into first mixture to make soft dough. Toss on lightly floured board or pastry cloth. Divide dough in two portions, having a little larger piece for the bottom. Roll larger piece to fit an oblong pan, 9 x 13 inches, having dough extend up around sides.

**Filling:** Pare, core and slice apples as for pie. Combine sugar, salt, flour and spices; sift over apples, tossing lightly to mix. Turn into prepared crust; dot with butter. Wet top edge of dough. Roll other portion of dough to fit top. Perforate with fork; place over filling; press edges firmly together to seal. Bake in 350° oven 55 to 60 minutes.

**Icing:** Mix confectioners' sugar, milk and vanilla until smooth. Spread on partially cooled apple slices. Cut in slices. 12 *servings*.

# Peaches Delightful

⅔ cup sugar
1 cup water
3 slices lemon
6 fresh peaches, peeled, halved
  and pitted
½ teaspoon vanilla
Dash salt
1 pint fresh raspberries,
  washed and drained OR
1 1-pound package frozen
  raspberries, thawed
Shredded coconut
Toasted slivered almonds

Cook sugar, water and lemon slices until sugar is completely dissolved. Add peaches; simmer until just tender. Stir in vanilla and salt. Chill. Lift two peach halves onto individual dessert plates. Spoon raspberries into peach cavities. Sprinkle with coconut and almonds. 6 *servings*.

# Curried Fruit

1 1-pound can (2 cups) pears
1 1-pound can (2 cups) peaches
1 1-pound can (2 cups) apricot
halves
1 1-pound can (2 cups)
pineapple chunks

1 1-pound can (2 cups) black
sweet cherries
1/3 cup butter or margarine
3/4 cup firmly packed brown
sugar
2 teaspoons curry powder
1 cup dairy sour cream

Drain fruit; place in 2½-quart casserole. Melt butter; blend in sugar and curry powder; spread over fruit. Bake in 325° oven 1 hour. Serve warm topped with sour cream.     8 to 10 *servings.*

# Cheese and Fruit

| | |
|---|---|
| **Cheddar** | Best with tart Jonathan apples. |
| **Swiss** | Best with tangy Greening apples and slender green Finger grapes. |
| **Blue** | Best with sweet, juicy Anjou pears or spicy, cinnamon colored Bosc pears. |
| **Brick** | Best with sweet-sour Tokay grapes. |
| **Gouda** | Best with Golden Delicious apples. |
| **Soft-Ripened Variety** | Best with deep purple Ribier grapes. |
| **Provolone** | Best with sweet Bartlett pears. |

# Million Dollar Fudge

4½ cups sugar
Dash salt
2 tablespoons butter
1 14½-ounce can (1⅔ cups)
evaporated milk
2 cups chopped nuts

2 6-ounce packages semi-sweet
chocolate pieces
4 squares (4 ounces)
unsweetened chocolate, cut
in small pieces
1 pint marshmallow cream

Mix sugar, salt, butter and evaporated milk in large saucepan. Bring to a boil; boil 6 minutes. Meanwhile place remaining ingredients in a large mixing bowl. Pour boiling syrup over ingredients in bowl; beat until chocolate is all melted. Pour into buttered pan, 9 x 14 x 2 inches. Let stand a few hours before cutting. Store in tin box.     *Makes 8 dozen pieces.*

Note: Twelve ounces German sweet chocolate (broken in pieces) may be used in place of the 4 squares unsweetened chocolate.

# Divinity Fudge

2½ cups sugar
½ cup water
½ cup light corn syrup
2 egg whites
¼ teaspoon salt

1 teaspoon vanilla
½ cup chopped nuts
¼ cup chopped candied cherries
¼ cup chopped candied
   pineapple

Put sugar, water and syrup in saucepan; bring to boil. Beat egg whites with salt until foamy. Pour 2 tablespoons boiling syrup on egg whites; continue beating. Cook syrup to soft ball stage (234°). Pour ½ of syrup slowly on beaten egg whites; continue beating. Cook remaining syrup to soft crack stage (272°). Pour slowly on egg white and syrup mixture. Continue beating until beater leaves its impression. Quicky add remaining ingredients. Drop from teaspoon onto buttered tray or marble slab.

*Makes* 40 *pieces.*

Note: Nuts and fruits may be omitted.

# Choco-Mint Balls

1½ cups evaporated milk
4 cups sugar
Dash salt
2 6-ounce packages semi-sweet
   chocolate pieces

1 7½-ounce jar marshmallow
   cream
½ teaspoon peppermint extract
Finely chopped nuts

Place evaporated milk, sugar and salt in a large saucepan. Cook and stir over low heat until sugar is dissolved. Bring to a rolling boil and cook 5 minutes, stirring constantly. Remove from heat; add semi-sweet chocolate pieces, marshmallow cream and flavoring. Beat until smooth. Cool. Scoop out a teaspoon of candy at a time and roll into a ball between palms of hands. Roll in chopped nuts to coat. *Makes about* 80 *balls.*

# Chocolate No-Bake Clusters

¾ cup butter or margarine,
   softened
1 cup firmly packed brown
   sugar, sieved
2 cups rolled oats, uncooked

¼ cup shaved semi-sweet
   chocolate
Confectioners' sugar
Pecan halves

Beat butter and sugar together until creamy. Stir in oats and chocolate. Shape into balls. Sprinkle with confectioners' sugar. Press pecan half on top of each. Refrigerate. *Makes* 2½ *dozen.*

# Butter Toffee

2¼ cups sugar
1 teaspoon salt
½ cup water
1¼ cups butter
1½ cups (½ pound) chopped
 blanched almonds

1 cup finely chopped walnut
 meats
¼ pound milk chocolate,
 melted

Combine sugar, salt, water and butter; heat to boiling. Add half the almonds and cook, stirring constantly, to the hard crack stage (290°). Stir in the rest of the almonds and half of the walnut meats. Pour into buttered 9 x 13-inch pan and cool. Brush with melted chocolate; sprinkle with remaining walnut meats. When cool break into pieces. *Makes 3 dozen pieces.*

# Louisiana Cream Pralines

1 pound light brown sugar
Dash salt
¾ cup evaporated milk

1 tablespoon butter
2 cups (½ pound) pecan
 halves

Cover a large baking sheet with aluminum foil, or butter baking sheet lightly. Mix sugar, salt, evaporated milk and butter in medium size saucepan. Stir over low heat until sugar is dissolved. Add pecans; cook over medium heat to soft ball stage (234°), stirring constantly. Remove from heat and let cool 5 minutes. Stir rapidly until mixture begins to thicken and coat pecans lightly. Drop rapidly from a teaspoon onto baking sheet to form patties. (If candy becomes too stiff at the last to handle easily, stir in a few drops of hot water.) Let pralines stand until cool and set. *Makes about 44 small pralines.*

Note: To make large pralines, drop from a tablespoon. Recipe makes about 20 large pralines.

**To make Orange Cream Pralines:** Add 1 teaspoon grated orange peel to sugar mixture before cooking, then proceed as above.

**To make Coffee Cream Pralines:** Add 1½ teaspoons instant coffee to sugar mixture before cooking, then proceed as above.

**To make Ginger Cream Pralines:** Add 2 to 3 tablespoons finely cut crystallized ginger root or ¾ to 1 teaspoon ginger during last few minutes of cooking to soft ball stage, then proceed as above.

# Orange Coconut Creams

| | |
|---|---|
| 3 cups sugar | 1 teaspoon orange juice |
| 1 cup evaporated milk | ¾ cup flaked coconut |
| 1½ tablespoons butter | ¼ teaspoon yellow food |
| 1 teaspoon grated orange peel | coloring, if desired |

Butter an 8 x 8 x 2-inch baking pan. Mix sugar, evaporated milk and butter in a medium size saucepan. Stir over low heat until sugar is dissolved. Then cook over medium heat to soft ball stage (236°), stirring constantly. Remove from heat and cool to lukewarm (110°). Stir in orange peel, juice and coconut, and food coloring, if desired. Beat until mixture loses its glossy finish. Turn at once into buttered pan and quickly smooth top with spatula or knife. Let stand until cold, then mark into squares and cut. *Makes 4 to 5 dozen.*

# Lemon Coconut Creams

Follow recipe for Orange Coconut Creams. Use grated lemon peel and lemon juice in place of grated orange peel and orange juice. Omit food coloring. After cutting creams in squares, press red dots cut from maraschino cherries on top of each square, if desired. *Makes 4 to 5 dozen.*

# Orange Sugared Walnuts

| | |
|---|---|
| 3 cups sugar | 1 teaspoon grated orange peel |
| ½ cup water | 1 pound walnut halves |
| ½ cup orange juice | |

Cook sugar, water and orange juice together to soft ball stage (238°). Remove from heat, add orange peel and walnuts; stir until syrup begins to look cloudy. Before mixture hardens drop from spoon onto waxed paper or buttered surface. Separate into smaller pieces. *Makes about 3½ dozen.*

# Spiced Pecans or Walnuts

| | |
|---|---|
| 1 cup pecans or walnuts | ⅛ teaspoon cinnamon |
| 2 tablespoons butter or | ⅛ teaspoon allspice |
| margarine | Salt |

Melt butter. Add nuts; heat slowly 5 minutes or until nuts are thoroughly heated, stirring occasionally. Drain on absorbent paper. Shake in bowl with spices; return to absorbent paper to drain. Sprinkle with salt.

# MAIN DISHES

## BEEF

Standing Rib Roast of Beef
Pot Roast with Vegetables
Sweet Sour Pot Roast
Savory Swiss Steak
Sauerbraten
Italian Style Beef Stew
City Chicken-Beef Style
Grecian Beef with Cheese Noodles
Sukiyaki
Beef Stroganoff
Chopped Round Steak and Fresh Mush-
  rooms in Sour Cream
Sausage-Stuffed Beef Birds in Barbecue
  Sauce
Beef-Zucchini Casserole
Beef and Broccoli Skillet Dinner
Frozen Meat Sauce
Lemon Barbecued Beef Loaves
Hamburger-Cream Cheese Casserole
Kick-Off Burgers
Meat Balls in Onion Soup
Egg and Beef Scramble
Beef Helene
Corned Beef Hash with Shirred Eggs
Cereal Flake Corned Beef Casserole

## PORK

Pork Chops with Caper Sauce
Chinese Pork Chops
Pork Chop—Rhubarb Casserole
Gourmet Pork Chops
Chicken Lickin' Good Pork Chops
Pork 'n' Potatoes
Chicken-Pork Divinity
South Sea Island Treat
Creamy Planked Pork
Spareribs-Tangy Plum Glaze
Maikai Spareribs

## HAM

Baked Ham with Cumberland Sauce
Golden Glazed Ham
Glazed Ham Balls in Noodle Ring
Baked Ham Slice with Apricot Glaze
Ham and Asparagus Rolls with Cheese
  Sauce
Indonesian Sausage

## LAMB

Shish Kabob with Pilaff
Sweet 'n' Sour Lamb Chops
Lamb and Bean Whirls
Barbecued Lamb Shanks
Rotisserie Rolled Leg of Lamb

## VEAL

Veal Paprika with Buttered Noodles
Veal Divine
Veal En Casserole

## CHICKEN

Chicken Loaf
Oven-Fried Chicken
Sauce Variations
Ginger Glazed Chicken
Orange Kissed Chicken
Chicken and Rice Casserole
Chicken Cashew Casserole
Celestial Chicken
Chicken a La Romano
Chicken Tropicale
One-Bowl Chicken and Curried Rice

## TURKEY

Pretzel-Fried Turkey
Smothered Turkey with Potatoes
Creamed Turkey with Lemon-Buttered
  Noodles
Poultry Chart
Delectable Turkey Hash

## STUFFINGS

Cranberry-Orange Stuffing for Roast
  Chicken
Almond-Herb Stuffing

## FISH, SEAFOOD

Savory Tuna Roll
Shrimp a La Ming
Tuna Suey
Lobster and Crab Meat Casserole
Individual Crab Meat Souffles
Jiffy Crab Meat Eleanor
Lobster Thermidor
Savory Baked Fish
Dolmades American Style

## MEATLESS MAIN DISHES

Poached Eggs on Wild Rice—Western
  Sauce
Savory Scrambled Eggs
Baked Eggs Au Gratin with Nippy
  Cheese Sauce
Egg Fondue
Creamy Poached Eggs
Danish Egg Casserole
Swiss Cheese Fondue
Rice and Cheese Timbales
Green Rice Casserole
Rice and Vegetables
Wild Rice and Mushroom Casserole
Tomato-Corn Scramble
Gourmet Macaroni
Spaghetti Marinara
Pancake Hawaiian

*Illustration:* Savory Tuna Roll (page 121).

# Main Dishes

Meat . . . poultry . . . fish . . . eggs . . . cheese . . . hearty make-ahead casseroles. What's your preference for the protein-rich dish to provide the mainstay for the meal? Here are dozens of delicious suggestions which run the gamut . . . some planned for "thrift" days . . . some for "splurge" days. All are geared for commendations from those who partake of them.

## Standing Rib Roast of Beef

**Standing rib roast of beef,**        **Parsley**
   **(3 ribs) 6 to 8 pounds**

Place beef in open roasting pan with fat side up. Roast in 325° oven 22 to 26 minutes per pound for rare, 26 to 30 minutes per pound for medium and 33 to 35 minutes per pound for well done. Allow the larger number of minutes per pound for smaller roasts. If using a meat thermometer it should read 140° for rare, 160° for medium and 170° for well done. Remove to platter. Garnish with parsley.

*Amount of meat to buy per serving:*

Boneless meat        — ¼ pound
Bone in meat         — ½ pound
Bony meat (such as
sparefibs, short ribs)   ¾ to 1 pound

# Pot Roast with Vegetables

| | |
|---|---|
| 3 pounds beef pot roast | 6 potatoes, pared, cut in half |
| Flour | 6 medium carrots, pared |
| ¼ cup fat | 6 medium onions, peeled |
| 2 teaspoons salt | 6 small turnips, pared |
| ¼ teaspoon pepper | ¼ cup flour |
| 1 cup water | ½ cup cold water |

Dip beef into flour so it is coated on all sides. Brown meat well on each side in hot fat in Dutch oven or heavy kettle. Add salt, pepper and 1 cup water. Slip a low rack under the meat. Cover; cook slowly 2 hours; add more water, if necessary. Add vegetables. Cook ½ hour more or until meat and vegetables are fork tender. Arrange meat and vegetables on hot platter. Measure juices in kettle and add water to make 2 cups broth. Mix ¼ cup flour with ½ cup cold water. Add slowly to broth; cook, stirring constantly, until thickened. Cook 5 minutes. Taste; season more if necessary.                                    6 *to* 8 *servings.*

# Sweet Sour Pot Roast

| | |
|---|---|
| 2 tablespoons fat | ¾ cup firmly packed brown |
| 5 pounds round bone pot roast |   sugar |
| ½ cup sliced onion | ¼ teaspoon nutmeg |
| 1 cup vinegar | |

Melt fat in heavy kettle. Brown meat in melted fat. Remove meat. Add onion and cook until transparent. Return meat to kettle. Add remaining ingredients. Cover tightly; simmer 3 hours or until meat is tender. If gravy is desired, thicken broth. Use 1½ tablespoons flour for every cup of broth.    8 *to* 10 *servings.*

# Savory Swiss Steak

| | |
|---|---|
| 2 pounds round steak, 1 inch | 1 teaspoon pepper |
|   thick | 1 8-ounce bottle (1 cup) |
| ½ cup flour |   French dressing |
| 2 teaspoons salt | 2 medium onions, sliced |

Cut steak in serving size pieces. Combine flour, salt and pepper; pound into steak. Heat ¾ cup dressing in skillet. Add meat; brown slowly on both sides. Add onions and remaining dressing. Cover tightly. Cook slowly 2 to 2½ hours, until meat is tender.

6 *servings.*

# Sauerbraten

4 to 5 pounds beef rump,
  rolled and tied
2 large cloves garlic, slivered
2¼ cups water
¾ cup cider vinegar
½ cup sliced onion
2 bay leaves
2 tablespoons sugar
1 teaspoon whole peppercorns
3 slices lemon
3 whole allspice
2 cups chopped onion

4 tablespoons sugar
3 tablespoons fat
¼ cup flour
1 teaspoon paprika
1 large tomato OR
¾ cup canned tomatoes
1 carrot, sliced
6 gingersnaps, crushed
1¼ cups (about) beef consommé
Salt
¼ cup water
1¼ tablespoons arrowroot

Make deep slits in beef; insert slivers of garlic. Combine 2¼ cups water, vinegar, onion slices, bay leaves, 2 tablespoons sugar, peppercorns, lemon slices and allspice. Bring to boil, reduce heat and simmer 2 minutes. Cool. Marinate beef in this mixture 12 hours or overnight in refrigerator. Turn meat occasionally during marinating.

In Dutch oven, brown chopped onion and 1 tablespoon sugar in 1 tablespoon fat. Remove onion. Remove beef from marinade; dry meat thoroughly. Dredge meat with flour; brown well in remaining fat. Pour off excess fat. Strain marinade; add to meat. Add browned onion, paprika, tomato, carrot and remaining 3 tablespoons sugar. Cover; cook on top of range 15 to 20 minutes, skimming surface frequently. Place meat, covered, in 350° oven; braise 3½ to 4 hours. Turn meat twice during braising time. When tender, remove from oven. Slice meat; place on serving platter. Skim fat from juices in pan; add gingersnaps. Cook on top of range 5 minutes. Strain cooking liquid; add consommé to make 1 quart liquid. Season with salt. Mix ¼ cup water and arrowroot until smooth; stir into cooking liquid. Cook and stir until thickened and smooth. To serve, pour sauce over sliced beef.                                                    6 *servings.*

## Italian Style Beef Stew

2 pounds beef stew meat
2 tablespoons fat or drippings
1 small onion, chopped
1 16-ounce can (2 cups)
  tomatoes

1½ teaspoons salt
½ teaspoon oregano
¼ teaspoon rosemary
1 3-ounce can grated
  Parmesan cheese

Brown meat in hot fat. Add onion, tomato, salt, oregano and rosemary. Cover pan; simmer over low heat 2 hours or until meat is tender. Stir in cheese.                                 6 *servings.*

# City Chicken-Beef Style

1 blade bone chuck roast, cut
1½ inches thick
3 tablespoons salad oil
¼ cup water
1 cup catsup
½ cup vinegar
1 tablespoon Worcestershire
sauce
2 tablespoons chopped onion

2 tablespoons chopped green
pepper
½ teaspoon salt
½ teaspoon thyme
1 tablespoon cornstarch
½ cup water
3 cups cooked rice (1 cup
uncooked)

Cut beef in 1½-inch cubes. Thread 3 or 4 pieces of beef on each wooden skewer. Add oil to skillet. Brown beef cubes. Add barbecue sauce made by combining ¼ cup water, catsup, vinegar, Worcestershire sauce, onion, green pepper, salt and thyme. Cover tightly; cook over low heat about 1½ hours. Remove meat. Make a paste of 1 tablespoon cornstarch and about 2 tablespoons of the water; then add remainder of ½ cup water. Stir cornstarch mixture into drippings in pan. Bring to boiling and stir 1 or 2 minutes. Arrange hot beef on rice. Pour barbecue gravy over all. Meat and barbecue sauce may be prepared day before serving and refrigerated.                    6 *or* 8 *servings.*

# Grecian Beef with Cheese Noodles

2 pounds sirloin steak, 1 inch
thick
Juice of ½ lemon
½ teaspoon salt
Dash pepper
¼ cup salad oil
2 tablespoons flour
¼ cup tomato paste
¾ cup hot water
1 small onion
6 whole cloves

1 stick cinnamon
⅛ orange
1 clove garlic

CHEESE NOODLES:

1 8-ounce package broad
noodles
4 teaspoons salt
6 cups boiling water
2 tablespoons butter, melted
2 tablespoons Parmesan cheese

Cut meat in strips, ¼ inch thick and 3 inches long. Sprinkle with lemon juice, salt and pepper. Brown on both sides in oil; remove meat. Brown flour in oil; add tomato paste diluted with water. Add meat. Stud onion with cloves. Tie onion, cinnamon, orange and garlic in cheesecloth bag; add to mixture. Cover and simmer 25 to 30 minutes or until tender. Remove bag. Serve with Cheese Noodles.                    6 *servings.*

Cheese Noodles: Stir noodles and salt into boiling water. Cook, stirring constantly, 2 minutes. Cover. Let stand 10 minutes. Drain; rinse in hot water. Add butter and cheese. Toss lightly.

# Sukiyaki

1 beef bouillon cube
½ cup boiling water
¼ cup sugar
1 teaspoon monosodium
  glutamate
1½ cups soy sauce
1½ pounds sirloin steak
2 tablespoons salad oil
1 cup sliced fresh mushrooms
1 green pepper, thinly sliced
1 cup diagonally sliced celery
1 cup diagonally sliced green
  onions

1 8-ounce can (1 cup) water
  chestnuts, drained and sliced
1 1-pound can (2 cups) bean
  sprouts, drained
1 4⅔-ounce can (½ cup)
  bamboo shoots, drained

WHITE RICE:

1 cup rice
2¼ cups water
1 teaspoon salt

Dissolve bouillon cube in water. Add sugar, monosodium glutamate and soy sauce. Mix well. Cut meat in slices, ¼ inch thick and 3 inches long. Heat oil in skillet. Brown meat slightly on both sides. Add half of sauce to meat. Push meat to one side of skillet. In separate wedges in skillet add mushrooms, green pepper, celery and onions. Cook 1 minute; toss-stir each vegetable with a spoon and fork during cooking. In separate wedges add water chestnuts, bean sprouts and bamboo shoots. Pour remaining sauce over vegetables. Heat 3 to 4 minutes. Serve with White Rice.                                                           *4 servings.*

**White Rice:** Wash and drain rice. Put rice, water and salt in heavy saucepan. Cover. Heat to boiling point over medium heat. Boil hard 3 minutes. Reduce heat to very low; cook 30 minutes.
                                                          *3 to 4 cups.*

# Beef Stroganoff

1½ pounds top round steak,
  ½ inch thick
5 tablespoons flour
3 tablespoons fat
1 large onion, thinly sliced
1½ cups sliced fresh
  mushrooms

1 cup consommé or bouillon
1 teaspoon lemon juice
½ teaspoon salt
¼ teaspoon pepper
⅛ teaspoon dry mustard
1 cup dairy sour cream
Hot rice or noodles

Cut meat in strips 2 inches wide; dredge in 3 tablespoons flour and brown in fat. Push meat to one side of pan. Add onion; cook until soft. Add mushrooms, ½ cup consommé, lemon juice, salt, pepper and mustard. Cover pan; cook over low heat 45 to 60 minutes or until meat is tender. Blend remaining 2 tablespoons flour with remaining consommé, add to hot mixture; cook over low heat until sauce is smooth and thickened, stirring constantly. Blend in sour cream and heat; do not boil. Serve over hot rice or noodles.                                                      *6 servings.*

# Chopped Round Steak and Fresh Mushrooms in Sour Cream

4 slices onion
½ cup butter
2 pounds fresh mushrooms, sliced
2 pounds ground lean round steak

¼ teaspoon powdered ginger
2 teaspoons salt
¼ teaspoon black pepper
2 cups dairy sour cream

Cook onion in butter until soft. Add mushrooms; cook over medium heat 15 minutes. Add meat; cook 2 minutes. Stir in ginger, salt and pepper. Add sour cream; cook only until cream is heated. *8 servings.*

# Sausage-Stuffed Beef Birds in Barbecue Sauce

**BEEF BIRDS:**

2 pounds round steak, ½ inch thick
½ cup flour
Salt
Pepper
½ cup shortening

**SAUSAGE STUFFING:**

½ pound pure pork sausage meat
¼ cup finely chopped onion
¼ cup finely chopped celery
½ cup finely chopped apple
3 cups toasted small bread cubes

1 teaspoon salt
⅛ teaspoon pepper
¼ cup water

**BARBECUE SAUCE:**

1 cup catsup
1½ cups water
1 tablespoon flour
3 tablespoons tarragon vinegar
1 tablespoon Worcestershire sauce
¼ teaspoon oregano
¼ teaspoon marjoram
⅛ teaspoon thyme

**Beef Birds:** Cut steak in 6 pieces. Pound to flatten in flour seasoned with salt and pepper. Put small mound of Sausage Stuffing on each piece of steak. Roll tightly; fasten with wooden picks. Brown in hot shortening. Place in Dutch oven. Pour Barbecue Sauce over all. Cover. Bake in 350° oven 2 hours.   *6 servings.*

**Sausage Stuffing:** Cook sausage in skillet until pink color disappears. Drain off fat. Add onion, celery and apple to sausage; cook until onion is soft. Add bread cubes and seasonings. Sprinkle with water; toss lightly to mix.

**Barbecue Sauce:** Combine ingredients. Heat to boiling point before pouring over Sausage-Stuffed Beef Birds.

## Beef-Zucchini Casserole

6 small zucchini
½ cup chopped onion
2 tablespoons lard or drippings
1 pound ground beef
½ cup cracker crumbs
1 teaspoon salt
⅛ teaspoon pepper

⅛ teaspoon oregano
¼ cup butter or margarine
¼ cup flour
1 teaspoon salt
¼ teaspoon pepper
2 cups milk
1 cup shredded Cheddar cheese

Wash zucchini and cut off ends. Cook whole zucchini in boiling salted water about 8 minutes. Drain; cut in ½-inch slices. Cook onion in lard about 3 minutes. Add ground beef and cook until very lightly browned. Pour off drippings. Stir in crumbs, 1 teaspoon salt, ⅛ teaspoon pepper and oregano. Remove from heat. Melt butter in saucepan. Stir in flour, 1 teaspoon salt and ¼ teaspoon pepper. Add milk and cook, stirring constantly, until mixture is thickened. Add cheese and stir until melted. Place half of zucchini slices in greased 2-quart baking dish. Add half of beef mixture, then half of cheese sauce. Repeat layers. Bake in 350° oven 25 minutes. *6 to 8 servings.*

## Beef and Broccoli Skillet Dinner

2 pounds fresh broccoli
¼ cup olive oil
2 cloves garlic, crushed
2 pounds boneless beef (round or chuck) sliced very thin and cut diagonally into 4 x ½-inch strips

3 cups chicken bouillon or stock
¼ cup water
1½ tablespoons cornstarch
3 tablespoons soy sauce
1 teaspoon salt
1 16-ounce can (2 cups) bean sprouts, drained
Cooked rice

Wash broccoli, discard outer leaves and tough ends; soak in salted water 30 minutes. Cut in 2½ x ½-inch pieces. Add 2 tablespoons oil and garlic to hot skillet. Brown beef quickly on all sides in oil; remove from skillet; set aside. Pour remaining oil into skillet. Add broccoli; cook over high heat ½ minute. Add bouillon, cover, cook 2 minutes. Stir in mixture of water, cornstarch, soy sauce and salt; bring to boil, stirring gently; cook until mixture thickens. Add bean sprouts and beef. Cook several minutes longer. Serve immediately with rice. *6 to 8 servings.*

# Frozen Meat Sauce

½ cup salad oil
2 cloves garlic, crushed
1½ cups chopped onion
⅔ cup chopped green pepper
5 pounds ground beef
2 8-ounce cans (3 cups)
   mushrooms, sliced
4 6-ounce cans (3 cups) tomato
   paste

2 quarts tomato juice
2 teaspoons salt
1½ teaspoons celery salt
1 teaspoon sugar
1½ teaspoons Worcestershire
   sauce
¼ teaspoon pepper
1 cup red wine, optional

Heat salad oil in large kettle, add garlic, onion and green pepper. Cook slowly 5 minutes. Add meat; stir well and brown over high heat. Add mushrooms and mushroom liquid, tomato paste, juice and seasonings. Simmer 2 hours until thick. If wine is used, add 1 hour before cooking is completed. *Makes 8 pints.*

**To freeze:** Cool quickly and package in pint containers. Freeze.

**To thaw for use:** Place in food compartment of refrigerator overnight or let it stand at room temperature several hours. Heat in covered saucepan over medium heat; stir occasionally.

**SPAGHETTI AND MEAT SAUCE**
2 pints meat sauce
1½ quarts boiling water

2 teaspoons salt
12 ounces spaghetti
1 cup grated Parmesan cheese

Thaw and heat meat sauce according to directions. Boil water and salt in large kettle. Add spaghetti and cook until tender, about 15 minutes. Drain spaghetti, rinse, drain again. Serve with meat sauce and Parmesan cheese. *5 to 6 servings.*

**CHILI CON CARNE**
2 pints meat sauce
1 6-ounce can (¾ cup) tomato
   sauce

1 pound 4-ounce can (2½ cups)
   kidney beans
½ teaspoon chili powder

Thaw meat sauce according to directions; add remaining ingredients. Heat until bubbling. *6 servings.*

**EGGPLANT WITH MEAT SAUCE**
1 eggplant

1 pint meat sauce, thawed
6 tablespoons grated Parmesan
   cheese

Peel and slice eggplant in ½-inch slices. Alternate slices of eggplant with meat sauce and cheese in a 1½-quart casserole. Bake in 350° oven 1 hour. *4 servings.*

**BARBECUED BEEF ON BUNS**　　**12 hamburger buns**
**2 pints meat sauce**

Thaw and heat meat sauce according to directions. Split buns into halves. Heat in 400° oven 5 minutes. Use ⅓ cup meat sauce to each bun.　　　　　　　　　　　　　　　　12 *servings.*

# Lemon Barbecued Beef Loaves

**MEAT LOAVES:**

1½ pounds ground beef
¼ cup lemon juice
½ cup water
1 egg, slightly beaten
4 slices dry bread, crumbled
¼ cup finely chopped onion
2 teaspoons seasoned salt

**TOPPING:**

½ cup catsup
⅓ cup firmly packed brown
　sugar
1 teaspoon dry mustard
¼ teaspoon ground cloves
¼ teaspoon ground allspice
6 thin lemon slices

Combine all ingredients for meat loaves. Mix well; shape into 6 individual loaves; place in greased oblong baking pan. Combine ingredients for topping, with the exception of the lemon slices. Bake loaves in 350° oven 15 minutes, then cover with topping and place a lemon slice on each loaf. Continue baking 30 minutes, basting occasionally. Serve with sauce in pan spooned over loaves.　　　　　　　　　　　　　　　　　　6 *servings.*

# Hamburger-Cream Cheese Casserole

1 pound hamburger
1 onion, chopped
1 tablespoon butter or
　margarine
1 teaspoon salt
½ teaspoon pepper
2 8-ounce cans (2 cups) tomato
　sauce

1 8-ounce package noodles
1 cup creamed cottage cheese
1 8-ounce package cream cheese
¼ cup dairy sour cream
⅓ cup sliced green onion
¼ cup chopped green pepper

Brown hamburger and onion in butter in skillet. Stir in salt, pepper and tomato sauce. Remove from heat. Cook noodles according to directions on package. Drain. Combine cottage cheese, cream cheese, sour cream, green onion and green pepper. In 3-quart casserole spread half the noodles; cover with cheese mixture; top with remaining noodles. Pour hamburger mixture over top. Bake in 350° oven about 30 minutes. 8 *to* 10 *servings.*
Note: Casserole can be frozen.

# Kick-Off Burgers

1 pound ground beef
¼ cup chopped onion
2 tablespoons butter, melted
1 10½-ounce can condensed
   vegetable soup
½ teaspoon salt
2 tablespoons flour

1 cup dairy sour cream

CHEESE FOOTBALL BUNS:

Butter, softened
6 to 8 wiener buns, halved
8 to 10 slices Cheddar cheese

Brown ground beef and onion in butter. Stir in soup; simmer 10 minutes. Blend in salt, flour and sour cream; cook an additional minute. Spoon onto Cheese Football Buns.  *6 to 8 servings.*

**Cheese Football Buns:** Butter both sides of buns; place on cooky sheet. Put a slice of cheese on bottom halves of buns; cut strips of cheese ⅛ inch wide by 1¼ inches long and place on tops of buns to look like football laces. Heat in oven or under broiler just until cheese begins to melt. Bring buns to table with meat mixture in chafing dish and let guests make own burgers.

# Meat Balls in Onion Soup

1 pound ground beef
¾ cup rolled oats, uncooked
1 egg
½ cup milk
1 teaspoon salt
⅛ teaspoon pepper
½ teaspoon tarragon

⅓ cup flour
2 tablespoons fat
1 envelope dry onion soup mix
2¼ cups water
½ cup dry wine, optional
Grated Parmesan cheese

Combine beef, rolled oats, egg, milk and seasonings. Blend thoroughly. Shape into 18 medium size balls; roll lightly in flour (save excess flour). Melt fat in skillet; brown meat balls over moderate heat. Dissolve onion soup mix in 2 cups water; add to meat balls. Cover; cook over low heat until done, 20 to 25 minutes. Mix remaining flour and ¼ cup water to a smooth paste; stir into onion soup. Cook until smooth and thickened. If desired, five minutes before serving stir in dry wine and blend. Just before serving sprinkle with cheese.  *6 servings.*

# Egg and Beef Scramble

2 tablespoons butter
1 3½-ounce package dried beef
6 eggs, slightly beaten

⅛ teaspoon pepper
½ cup dairy sour cream

Melt butter in large skillet. Cut or tear beef in bite size pieces. Cook in butter 3 to 4 minutes until lightly browned. Add eggs and pepper; cook and stir until eggs are set. Remove from heat. Fold in sour cream. Serve immediately.  *4 servings.*

# Beef Helene

1 4-ounce package sliced dried
   beef
3 tablespoons butter or
   margarine
2 tablespoons flour
½ teaspoon paprika
⅛ teaspoon nutmeg

½ teaspoon Worcestershire
   sauce
1½ cups milk
1 cup cooked sliced mushrooms
¼ cup sliced ripe olives
Corn Bread

Put beef in bowl. Rinse with hot water. Drain. Melt butter in skillet. Stir in flour, paprika, nutmeg, Worcestershire sauce and milk. Cook and stir until thickened. Stir in dried beef and mushrooms. Cook and stir until mushrooms and shredded beef are heated through. Add olives. Serve on hot Corn Bread (page 33).

*4 servings.*

# Corned Beef Hash with Shirred Eggs

2 16-ounce cans (4 cups)
   corned beef hash
6 large eggs
Dash salt

Dash pepper
¼ to ⅓ cup milk
1 10½-ounce can cream of
   mushroom soup

Butter six individual casseroles. Fill each with corned beef hash, making a depression in top of each. Bake in 350° oven 15 minutes or until heated. Break an egg into center of each. Continue to bake until egg is set to desired degree, 4 to 5 minutes. Season egg with salt and pepper. Meantime, add milk to soup and heat to bubbling. To serve, spoon mushroom sauce on top of contents of each casserole. Serve at once.

*6 servings.*

# Cereal Flake Corned Beef Casserole

⅓ cup melted butter or
   margarine
3 cups whole wheat or corn
   flakes
1¼ cups cooked cut green beans
½ cup finely chopped onion
1 1-pound can (2 cups) corned
   beef hash

½ cup milk
1 10½-ounce can condensed
   cream of chicken or celery
   soup
1 cup chopped process American
   cheese (¼ pound)
½ teaspoon salt
Dash pepper

Drizzle butter over cereal and toss lightly with spoon to evenly coat flakes. Combine remaining ingredients and blend carefully. Spread ⅓ of the cereal flakes over bottom of 2-quart casserole. Cover flakes with ½ of hash mixture. Repeat, ending with cereal flakes on top. Bake in 375° oven until heated through, about 40 minutes.

*6 to 8 servings.*

# Pork Chops with Caper Sauce

4 rib or loin pork chops, 1
  inch thick
2 tablespoons flour
2 tablespoons lard or drippings
½ teaspoon salt
⅛ teaspoon pepper
1 bouillon cube

⅓ cup hot water
¼ cup chopped onion
1 teaspoon prepared mustard
1 tablespoon capers
1 tablespoon flour
¼ cup water
½ cup dairy sour cream

Dredge chops in 2 tablespoons flour. Brown in lard. Pour off drippings. Season chops with salt and pepper. Dissolve bouillon cube in hot water. Add bouillon, onion, prepared mustard and capers to chops. Cover tightly; simmer 45 minutes to 1 hour or until done. Remove chops to warm platter. Add 1 tablespoon flour to drippings; mix well. Add water and cook, stirring constantly, until thickened. Fold in sour cream; cook just until heated through. Serve sauce over chops. *4 servings.*

# Chinese Pork Chops

8 pork chops, ½ inch thick
¼ cup soy sauce
¼ cup chili sauce

1 tablespoon honey
Salt
Pepper

Trim fat from pork chops. Place in baking dish. Combine soy sauce, chili sauce and honey. Spoon over chops. Sprinkle with salt and pepper. Bake in 350° oven about 45 minutes, basting occasionally with soy-chili mixture. *4 servings.*

# Pork Chop—Rhubarb Casserole

6 loin or rib pork chops, ¾ to
  1 inch thick
1 teaspoon salt
⅛ teaspoon pepper
2 cups soft bread crumbs,
  toasted
¼ teaspoon salt

½ cup firmly packed brown
  sugar
½ cup granulated sugar
3 tablespoons flour
½ teaspoon cinnamon
6 cups sliced rhubarb (1½
  pounds)

Brown chops in skillet. Pour off drippings and save ¼ cup. Season chops with salt and pepper. Combine crumbs, ¼ cup drippings and ¼ teaspoon salt. Mix together sugars, flour and cinnamon and add to rhubarb. Place half of crumbs in bottom of 2-quart casserole or baking dish. Spoon half of rhubarb over crumbs and arrange chops on rhubarb. Place remaining rhubarb on chops. Cover tightly and bake in 350° oven 40 minutes. Remove cover and top with remaining crumbs. Bake 10 minutes longer. *6 servings.*

# Gourmet Pork Chops

6 rib pork chops, ¾ inch thick
2 tablespoons lard or drippings
1 teaspoon salt
⅛ teaspoon pepper
⅓ cup chopped onion
¾ cup chopped celery
6 ounces fresh mushrooms,
  quartered
3 tablespoons butter or
  margarine
2 bouillon cubes
¼ teaspoon salt
2 cups cooked wild rice (about
  ¾ cup uncooked)
⅓ cup light cream

Brown chops in lard or drippings. Pour off drippings. Season chops with 1 teaspoon salt and pepper. Cook onion, celery and mushrooms in butter until onions and celery are tender and mushrooms are lightly browned. Add bouillion cubes to hot mushroom mixture. Crush cubes and stir until dissolved. Add ¼ teaspoon salt, rice and cream. Put rice mixture in greased 8 x 12-inch baking dish. Place chops on top. Cover. Bake in 350° oven 30 minutes. Uncover and continue baking 15 minutes or until chops are done. *6 servings.*

# Chicken Lickin' Good Pork Chops

6 loin pork chops, 1 inch thick
½ cup flour
1 tablespoon salt
1 teaspoon dry mustard
½ teaspoon garlic powder
1 tablespoon fat
1 10½-ounce can chicken rice
  soup

Dredge pork chops with blended flour, salt, dry mustard and garlic powder. Brown chops slowly in fat about 15 minutes in skillet. Reduce heat and add soup. Cover. Cook over low heat about 1 hour or until chops are thoroughly done. *6 servings.*

# Pork 'n' Potatoes

4 pork shoulder steaks, ½ inch
  thick
1 10½-ounce can condensed
  tomato soup
⅓ cup chopped onion
1 teaspoon salt
¼ teaspoon pepper
2 tablespoons chopped parsley
3 cups thinly sliced potatoes

Brown pork steaks. Pour off drippings. Mix together soup, onion, salt, pepper and parsley. Combine half of soup mixture with potatoes; place in bottom of 9 x 12-inch baking dish. Place meat on top of potatoes and spread remaining soup mixture over top. Cover and bake in 350° oven 1 hour. Remove cover; continue baking 15 minutes or until meat is done. *4 servings.*

# Chicken-Pork Divinity

1 pound boneless, lean pork, cut in 2-inch strips (about 2 cups)
2 5½-ounce jars (2 cups) white chicken meat, cut in 2-inch strips
¼ cup butter, melted
1 12-ounce can (1½ cups) apple juice
1 teaspoon salt
¼ teaspoon rosemary
¼ teaspoon mace
½ cup shredded Swiss cheese
½ cup sliced Macadamia nuts
2 cups dairy sour cream
Cream, if necessary
Cheddar Noodle Cups

Brown pork and chicken in butter in large skillet. Add apple juice, salt, rosemary and mace; simmer about 45 minutes or until meat is tender. Stir in Swiss cheese and nuts, cooking until cheese melts. Add sour cream and heat over low temperature; do not allow to boil. Thin with a little cream if too thick. Serve from a chafing dish in Cheddar Noodle Cups.    *4 to 6 servings.*

**CHEDDAR NOODLE CUPS:**

1 5-ounce can (2½ cups) chow mein noodles
1 cup shredded Cheddar cheese
1 egg white

Stir ingredients together to uniform consistency. Press mixture firmly into bottom and sides of medium size muffin cups. Bake in 300° oven 12 to 15 minutes.    *Makes 8 cups.*

# South Sea Island Treat

1 12-ounce can pork and ham luncheon meat
1 tablespoon cornstarch
1 cup water
⅓ cup pineapple syrup, drained from can
1 tablespoon vinegar
½ teaspoon Worcestershire sauce
1 teaspoon soy sauce
¼ teaspoon prepared mustard
1 9-ounce can pineapple slices (4 slices), drained and cubed
1 tomato, cut in sixths
½ green pepper, sliced lengthwise
½ cup chopped celery
3 cups cooked rice (or half rice and half chow mein noodles)

Cut luncheon meat in cubes, approximately ¾ inch; brown lightly in skillet. Combine cornstarch, liquids and seasonings. Add to the meat; cook until mixture is thickened and clear, stirring constantly. Add remaining ingredients, except rice; simmer 5 minutes. (Vegetables should remain crisp.) Serve over cooked rice.    *4 servings.*

## Creamy Planked Pork

2 pounds lean pork shoulder,
cut in 1-inch cubes
1/4 cup butter
2 cups whipping cream
1 teaspoon salt
1/8 teaspoon pepper
Dash ground cloves
3 whole cloves
1/2 pound fresh mushrooms
1/4 cup butter

1 10-ounce package frozen peas,
thawed
1 tablespoon flour
1 package instant potato
mix OR
2 cups mashed potatoes
1 egg
1 egg yolk
1/2 cup shredded Cheddar cheese

In large skillet, brown pork cubes in 1/4 cup butter. Add cream, salt, pepper, ground and whole cloves. Cover; simmer until pork is tender, about 30 minutes. Meanwhile, wash and slice mushrooms; then brown lightly in 1/4 cup butter. Mix the mushrooms and peas into pork-cream mixture, sprinkle on flour and heat an additional 10 minutes. Prepare instant potatoes according to package directions, using milk for the liquid. Beat in whole egg, egg yolk and cheese to make "Duchess" potatoes. Using a pastry tube, make a border of potatoes around edge of plank (or spoon around if pastry tube is unavailable). Place under broiler a few minutes to brown; then fill center with pork-cream-vegetable mixture. Serve immediately. *6 servings.*

*Planks—their care and use:* Planks are well seasoned hardwood platters about 1 inch thick used for heating and serving fish, meat or vegetables. Before using, planks should always be oiled and heated in the oven. To clean planks after use, wipe off and scrub with soft paper.

## Spareribs—Tangy Plum Glaze

3 pounds spareribs
2 1/2 teaspoons salt
1 1-pound 13-ounce can (3 1/2
cups) plums

1/4 cup frozen concentrated
orange juice
1/2 teaspoon Worcestershire
sauce

Cut spareribs in individual servings; place on rack in roasting pan. Season with salt. Cover tightly; cook in 350° oven 45 minutes. Drain plums, reserving 1/2 cup syrup. Force plums through sieve. Add the 1/2 cup plum syrup, orange juice and Worcestershire sauce to sieved plums. Pour off drippings from ribs and remove rack. Spread half the plum sauce over ribs. Bake uncovered 1/2 hour. Turn ribs. Spread with remaining sauce and continue baking 1/2 hour. *6 to 8 servings.*

# Maikai Spareribs

4 pounds spareribs
Salt
Pepper
⅓ cup coarsely chopped celery
⅓ cup coarsely chopped green
    pepper
2 tablespoons butter or
    margarine
2 tablespoons cornstarch
2 cups liquid (juice drained
    from pineapple tidbits and
    water)

2 13½-ounce cans (3 cups)
    pineapple tidbits
1 small clove garlic, finely
    chopped
⅓ cup vinegar
2 tablespoons soy sauce
1 tablespoon sugar
½ teaspoon salt
½ teaspoon ginger

Cut spareribs in 2- or 3-rib portions. Place ribs, meaty side up, in a large shallow roasting pan. Season with salt and pepper. Bake uncovered in 450° oven about 45 minutes or until well browned. Pour off all fat. Reduce oven temperature to 350°. While ribs are browning, cook celery and green pepper in melted butter until tender, about 5 minutes. Blend in cornstarch. Add liquid and cook, stirring constantly, until clear and thickened. Stir in pineapple tidbits, garlic, vinegar, soy sauce, sugar, salt and ginger. Pour hot pineapple mixture over browned spareribs. Cover and bake in 350° oven about 1½ hours or until fork-tender. Uncover and bake 15 minutes longer to brown.

*4 to 6 servings.*

# Baked Ham with Cumberland Sauce

1 ham
Thin slices orange
Thin slices lemon
CUMBERLAND SAUCE:
1 10-ounce glass red currant
    jelly
Juice and grated peel of
    1 orange

Juice and grated peel of
    1 lemon
¼ teaspoon ground ginger
1 teaspoon prepared mustard
1 tablespoon cornstarch
1 tablespoon cold water

Prepare ham according to directions on the wrapper.

Cumberland Sauce: Combine jelly, orange and lemon peels and juices, ginger and mustard in a saucepan. Bring to a boil; simmer 10 minutes. Strain. Blend cornstarch with water; add to jelly mixture. Bring to a boil. Cook until slightly thickened, stirring constantly. One-half hour before time indicated on the schedule, remove ham from oven. Pour off drippings. Remove shank skin if present. Coat with Cumberland Sauce and return ham to oven to brown and complete baking. Garnish with slices of orange and lemon. Serve with remaining Cumberland Sauce.

# Golden Glazed Ham

| | |
|---|---|
| 1 fully-cooked ham | 1 cup strained honey |
| 1 cup apricot jam, preserves or marmalade | ½ teaspoon salt |
| | Green grapes |

Place ham in uncovered baking dish. Heat in 325° oven, allowing 15 minutes per pound. Combine apricot jam, honey and salt in saucepan. Warm mixture, stirring constantly. Take ham from oven ½ hour before end of heating time. Spread with glaze and return to oven to finish heating. Baste at 10 minute intervals with additional glaze. Garnish serving platter with small bunches of green grapes.

# Glazed Ham Balls in Noodle Ring

**HAM BALLS:**

½ pound ground lean ham
¾ pound ground pork
⅔ cup rolled oats, uncooked
1 egg, slightly beaten
½ cup milk

**SAUCE:**

⅓ cup firmly packed brown sugar
2 tablespoons flour
1 teaspoon dry mustard

⅔ cup fruit juice (pineapple, apricot or peach) OR water
2 tablespoons vinegar
6 whole cloves
⅓ cup dark corn syrup

**NOODLE RING:**

1 8-ounce package medium noodles
2 eggs, slightly beaten
2 cups milk
1½ teaspoons salt
Buttered crumbs

**Ham Balls:** Combine ham, pork, rolled oats, egg and milk. Mix until thoroughly blended. Chill. Shape into small balls and place in shallow baking pan. Bake in 325° oven 1 hour. Drain.

**Sauce:** Combine ingredients for sauce in saucepan; cook over direct heat until slightly thickened, stirring frequently. Pour over ham balls in pan; continue baking 15 minutes.

**Noodle Ring:** While ham balls are baking, prepare noodle ring. Cook noodles according to package directions; drain. Place in greased 1½-quart ring mold; pour combined eggs, milk and salt over noodles. Sprinkle with crumbs; bake in oven with ham balls 45 minutes. Let stand about 8 minutes before unmolding. Loosen edges of noodle ring carefully; unmold onto platter. Fill center with hot ham balls and sauce.                    6 *servings.*

*Amount of ham to buy per serving:*

| | |
|---|---|
| Uncooked bone in | – ½ to ¾ pound |
| Uncooked boneless | – ⅓ pound |
| Cooked bone in | – ⅓ pound |
| Cooked boneless | – ⅛ to ¼ pound |

# Baked Ham Slice with Apricot Glaze

| | |
|---|---|
| 1 center cut slice fully cooked ham, 1 inch thick | 1 cup firmly packed brown sugar |
| ½ cup apricot syrup, drained from canned apricots OR apricot nectar | 1 teaspoon dry mustard |
| | Firm bananas, all-yellow or slightly green-tipped |
| 1 tablespoon lemon juice | Drained canned apricot halves |
| | Water cress |

Slash fat edge of ham slice at 1-inch intervals; place in shallow pan or casserole. Bake in 325° oven 20 minutes. Blend apricot syrup and lemon juice into brown sugar and mustard; heat until bubbly, stirring occasionally. Remove ham from oven, spoon ⅓ of glaze over ham and return to oven. Apply remaining glaze at two 10-minute intervals, adding peeled and halved bananas to baking dish with last application of glaze. (Total baking time, 50 minutes.) Serve ham slice garnished with baked banana halves, apricot halves and water cress.                    5 *to* 6 *servings.*

# Ham and Asparagus Rolls with Cheese Sauce

| | |
|---|---|
| 2 1-pound 3-ounce cans asparagus spears (40 to 60 spears) | 1 teaspoon Worcestershire sauce |
| | 2 cups milk |
| 8 slices cooked ham, ¼ inch thick | 1 cup shredded Cheddar cheese |
| **CHEESE SAUCE:** | **BROWNED PINEAPPLE SLICES:** |
| ¼ cup butter | 8 slices canned pineapple |
| ¼ cup flour | ¼ cup flour |
| ¼ teaspoon paprika | 2 tablespoons butter or margarine |
| ¼ teaspoon salt | |

Drain asparagus; divide into 8 equal portions. Roll each portion in a slice of ham; fasten with wooden picks. Place in shallow pan. Bake in 350° oven 25 to 30 minutes. Remove to serving dish; remove wooden picks. Garnish with Browned Pineapple Slices.                    8 *servings.*

**Cheese Sauce:** Melt butter in saucepan. Stir in flour and seasonings. Cook until bubbly; add milk. Cook, stirring constantly, until thickened; reduce heat very low and cook 10 minutes. Add cheese; stir until cheese is melted. Pour sauce over ham rolls.

**Browned Pineapple Slices:** Drain pineapple slices thoroughly on absorbent paper. Cut in halves; dip in flour. Melt butter in skillet. Add pineapple; brown to a golden color on both sides.

# Indonesian Sausage

1 8-ounce package brown'n
  serve sausage
1 10½-ounce can condensed
  cream of chicken soup

½ teaspoon curry powder
1 cup fresh or canned apple
  slices
2 cups hot cooked rice

Lightly brown sausage in a skillet. Add soup, curry powder and apple slices. Heat until apples are tender. Serve over hot cooked rice.
    *4 servings.*

# Shish Kabob with Pilaff

2 pounds boned sirloin end
  leg of lamb
2 tablespoons olive oil
Juice of 1 lemon
½ teaspoon salt
Dash pepper
1 medium onion, sliced in rings
2 bay leaves
1 large green pepper
½ cup boiling water
9 small, equal size, onions
½ cup boiling water

9 mushroom caps, 1½ inches
  in diameter
3 medium tomatoes, sliced
Parsley

PILAFF:

1 tablespoon butter
¼ teaspoon rosemary
3 cups water
1 chicken bouillon cube
1 teaspoon salt
1½ cups long grain rice
⅓ cup butter

Cut meat in 9 cubes about 2 inches square. Mix oil and lemon juice to make marinade. Dip meat cubes in marinade. Place in casserole. Sprinkle with seasonings, onion rings, bay leaves and 1 tablespoon marinade. Cover. Chill 4 to 5 hours. Cut green pepper lengthwise in thirds; remove seeds. Cook in ½ cup water 1 minute. Cook onions in ½ cup water 5 minutes. Cut each green pepper third in thirds crosswise. Alternate meat, green pepper, onions and mushroom caps on rotisserie spits placing spits lengthwise through onions and stem section of mushroom caps. Brush with marinade. Place in rotisserie compartment of range. Cook 20 minutes with medium heat, then 10 minutes with high heat or until meat is browned. Serve on large platter with Pilaff. Garnish with tomatoes and parsley.    *4 to 6 servings.*

Pilaff: Melt 1 tablespoon butter. Add rosemary; brown very lightly 3 to 4 minutes. Bring water to boil; add bouillon cube and salt. Stir until dissolved. Wash rice; drain. Melt ⅓ cup butter in saucepan. Add rice; heat 6 minutes or until butter is absorbed. Gradually add chicken stock. Cover; simmer 15 minutes. Add rosemary butter. Stir 5 minutes over low heat. Cover. Let stand 25 minutes.

# Sweet 'n' Sour Lamb Chops

| | |
|---|---|
| 4 shoulder lamb chops, about 1 inch thick | 1 teaspoon salt |
| ¼ cup vinegar | ⅛ teaspoon pepper |
| ¼ cup firmly packed brown sugar | ¼ teaspoon ginger |
| | 1 medium orange, sliced |
| | 1 medium lemon, cut in wedges |

Brown shoulder lamb chops on both sides over low heat. Combine vinegar, brown sugar, salt, pepper and ginger; mix well. Pour sugar mixture over chops. Add orange slices and lemon wedges. Cover; continue cooking about 30 minutes or until chops are tender. *4 servings.*

# Lamb and Bean Whirls

| | |
|---|---|
| 1½ pounds ground lamb | ½ cup tomato juice |
| 1½ teaspoons salt | 1 10½-ounce package frozen green beans, French style, cooked |
| ⅛ teaspoon pepper | |
| ¼ teaspoon basil | |
| ¼ teaspoon thyme | |

Mix together lamb, salt, pepper, basil, thyme and tomato juice. Place on waxed paper; shape into 10 x 12-inch rectangle. Spread green beans over meat. Beginning with a 10-inch side, roll as for a jelly roll. Cut into 10 slices, each 1 inch thick. Place on broiler rack. Place broiler pan so top surface of lamb whirls is 2 to 3 inches from heat. Broil until brown on first side, 8 to 10 minutes. Turn and brown on second side, 2 to 3 minutes. *5 servings.*

# Barbecued Lamb Shanks

| | |
|---|---|
| 4 lamb shanks | 2 tablespoons Worcestershire sauce |
| 2 tablespoons shortening | ½ cup vinegar |
| 1 cup sliced onion | ¼ cup firmly packed brown sugar |
| 1 cup catsup | 2 teaspoons dry mustard |
| 1 cup water | |
| 2 teaspoons salt | |

Brown lamb shanks in shortening in heavy skillet. Combine remaining ingredients; pour over lamb shanks; cover. Bake in 350° oven, or simmer on top of range 1¾ hours or until tender. Baste sauce over shanks 2 or 3 times during cooking period. Uncover; continue cooking 15 minutes. *4 servings.*

Note: This recipe may be made the day before it is served. The meat and sauce should be refrigerated. Barbecued Lamb Shanks can be reheated in a moderate oven or over low heat on top of range.

# Rotisserie Rolled Leg of Lamb

1 6- to 8-pound leg of lamb
1 1-pound 4-ounce can (2½ cups) minted pineapple chunks, drained
Water cress
Radish roses

BASTING SAUCE:
¼ teaspoon garlic juice

⅓ cup salad oil
¼ cup water
¼ cup lemon juice
¼ cup soy sauce
½ teaspoon Worcestershire sauce
1 teaspoon sugar
½ teaspoon salt
Dash Tabasco

Have butcher bone, roll lengthwise and tie leg of lamb. Insert spit lengthwise through center of meat. Fasten securely. Insert metal meat thermometer in front end as close to center as possible without touching spit. Place spit in rotisserie compartment of range. Turn on medium heat. Cook 30 to 35 minutes per pound or until thermometer reaches 175° to 180°. After the first half hour of cooking, brush every 15 minutes with Basting Sauce. Remove to serving platter. Garnish with minted pineapple, water cress and radishes. *8 servings.*

**Basting Sauce:** Combine all ingredients. Mix well.

# Veal Paprika with Buttered Noodles

2 pounds veal, cut in ½-inch slices
⅓ cup flour
1¼ teaspoons salt
⅛ teaspoon pepper
5 tablespoons shortening
2 onions, minced
1¼ teaspoons paprika

1 14½-ounce can (1¾ cups) chicken broth
1 cup dairy sour cream
Paprika for garnish

BUTTERED NOODLES:
1 8-ounce package broad noodles
2 tablespoons butter

Cut sliced veal in 2-inch squares. Mix flour, salt and pepper; dredge meat in mixture. Place 3 tablespoons shortening in skillet. Heat until shortening melts. Add onions and cook 5 minutes or until very lightly browned. Remove onions from skillet. Add remaining 2 tablespoons shortening, then veal. Brown veal 8 minutes on each side. Place onions over meat; sprinkle with 1¼ teaspoons paprika and add chicken broth. Bring to boil. Cover skillet; simmer 45 minutes or until meat is tender. Stir in sour cream gradually. Heat, stirring constantly, until mixture bubbles. Serve over Buttered Noodles. Sprinkle with paprika.

*4 to 5 servings.*

**Buttered Noodles:** Cook noodles according to package directions. Add butter.

# Veal Divine

2 veal round steaks, cut in
  6 pieces (6 cutlets)
1 egg, slightly beaten
¼ teaspoon salt
⅛ teaspoon pepper
⅔ cup dry bread crumbs
3 tablespoons lard or drippings

3 slices boiled ham
¾ cup water
1 10½-ounce can condensed
  mushroom soup
½ cup shredded sharp Cheddar
  cheese
Paprika

Pound steak pieces on both sides. Mix together egg, salt and pepper. Dip veal in egg mixture and then in crumbs. Brown in lard. Cut ham slices in half. Place ½ slice ham over each veal cutlet. Add water to mushroom soup; mix well. Pour soup over ham and veal. Cover tightly; simmer on top of range or bake in 300° oven 45 minutes. Remove cover. Sprinkle cheese over ham. Cover and continue cooking until cheese is melted, about 10 minutes. Sprinkle with paprika. *6 servings.*

# Veal en Casserole

2 eggs
1 tablespoon water
3 pounds veal, cut in 2-inch
  cubes
1¼ cups cracker crumbs
3 tablespoons shortening

SAUCE:
3 tablespoons butter

3 tablespoons flour
3 cups strained tomatoes
2 teaspoons salt
2 teaspoons sugar
¼ teaspoon marjoram
¼ teaspoon garlic salt
2 small bay leaves
Dash Tabasco

Beat eggs slightly; add water. Roll veal cubes in cracker crumbs; dip in egg mixture, then roll again in cracker crumbs. Brown meat in shortening.

**Sauce:** Melt butter, stir in flour until smooth. Add tomatoes slowly, blending well. Stir in remaining ingredients; cook until thick. Place meat in 2-quart casserole; pour sauce over top; cover. Bake in 375° oven 1 hour. *6 servings.*

# Chicken Loaf

1 4-pound stewing chicken,
  cooked and diced
2 cups fresh bread crumbs
3 cups chicken broth
1 cup cooked rice

1½ teaspoons salt
⅛ cup chopped pimiento
4 eggs, well beaten
Parsley sprigs

Mix all ingredients for loaf; add eggs last. Pour into 1-pound bread pan. Bake in 325° oven 1 hour. Serve garnished with parsley. *8 to 10 servings.*

# Oven-Fried Chicken

| | |
|---|---|
| 1 2- to 3-pound broiler-fryer chicken, cut up | ¼ teaspoon pepper |
| 1 cup flour | 2 teaspoons paprika |
| 2 teaspoons salt | ½ cup butter |

Dip chicken pieces in mixture of flour, salt, pepper and paprika. Melt butter in shallow baking pan in 400° oven. Remove baking pan from oven. As pieces of floured chicken are placed in pan, turn to coat with butter, then arrange skin side down in a single layer. Bake in 400° oven 30 minutes. Turn chicken. Bake another 30 minutes or until tender. If chicken cannot be served at once, reduce oven heat and brush chicken with more melted butter. *4 servings.*

## Sauce Variations

Follow directions for Oven-Fried Chicken but when chicken is turned after it has baked 30 minutes, pour one of the three following sauces over the pieces. Continue baking as directed.

**Lemon Barbecue Sauce:** Mash 1 small clove garlic with ½ teaspoon salt in bowl. Add ¼ cup salad oil, ½ cup lemon juice, 2 tablespoons finely chopped onion, ½ teaspoon freshly ground black pepper and ½ teaspoon thyme.

**Spicy Barbecue Sauce:** Combine the following ingredients in saucepan: ½ cup sliced onion, 1 teaspoon salt, 1 tablespoon vinegar, 1 tablespoon sugar, 1 tablespoon Worcestershire sauce, ½ teaspoon chili powder, ¼ teaspoon black pepper, ½ cup catsup and ¼ cup water. Simmer 15 minutes.

**Butter-Honey Sauce:** Melt ¼ cup butter in saucepan. Add ¼ cup honey and ¼ cup lemon juice.

# Ginger Glazed Chicken

| | |
|---|---|
| 2 1½- to 2-pound broiler-fryer chickens | ¾ cup apricot OR pineapple preserves |
| 1 8-ounce bottle Italian-style salad dressing | 2 teaspoons ginger |
| | Dash white pepper |

Cut chickens in half. Place in shallow pan and coat all sides with dressing. Let stand at room temperature 2 to 3 hours or overnight in refrigerator. Remove chicken from pan and place skin side up on broiler rack. Combine marinade liquid with preserves, ginger and pepper. Brush mixture over chicken. Broil 20 to 30 minutes, basting frequently with remaining mixture. Turn, coat again and broil until chicken is done and golden brown in color. *4 servings.*

# Orange Kissed Chicken

| | |
|---|---|
| 1 2½-pound broiler-fryer chicken, cut up | 2 teaspoons salt |
| 1 egg, slightly beaten | 2 teaspoons paprika |
| ¼ cup orange juice | 1 tablespoon grated orange peel |
| 1 cup flour | ½ cup butter |

Dip chicken pieces into mixture of egg and orange juice, then into mixture of flour, salt, paprika and grated orange peel. Melt butter in shallow baking pan in 400° oven. Remove baking pan from oven. As pieces of floured chicken are placed in pan, turn to coat with butter, then arrange skin side down in a single layer. Bake in 400° oven 30 minutes. Turn chicken. Bake another 30 minutes. *4 servings.*

# Chicken and Rice Casserole

| | |
|---|---|
| ½ cup butter | 1¼ cups uncooked rice |
| 1 10½-ounce can cream of chicken soup | 3 chicken breasts, split to make 6 halves |
| 1 10½-ounce can cream of mushroom soup | 2 tablespoons melted butter |
| 1 10½-ounce can cream of celery soup | Paprika |

Melt butter, add soups. Heat and stir until smooth; add rice. Spread in shallow 9 x 13-inch baking dish. Lay chicken breasts on top, skin side up. Brush with melted butter; sprinkle lightly with paprika. Bake in 275° oven 2½ hours. *6 servings.*

# Chicken Cashew Casserole

| | |
|---|---|
| 1 tablespoon butter | 1 tablespoon soy sauce |
| ¼ cup chopped onion | 3 drops Tabasco |
| 1 cup finely diced celery | Dash pepper |
| 1 3-pound can whole chicken | 1 cup canned chow mein noodles |
| 1 10½-ounce can condensed cream of mushroom soup | ⅓ cup cashew nuts |

Melt butter in saucepan. Add onion and celery; brown lightly. Drain chicken stock from canned chicken, measure ⅔ cup stock; add to browned vegetables. Stir in mushroom soup, soy sauce, Tabasco and pepper. Bring to the boiling point. Remove chicken meat from bones; dice in medium size pieces. Add to mushroom soup mixture; simmer a few minutes. Pour into 1-quart casserole. Sprinkle chow mein noodles and cashew nuts on top. Bake in 350° oven 20 minutes or until bubbly. *4 servings.*

# Celestial Chicken

8 6- to 8-ounce chicken breasts,
   split
2 eggs, slightly beaten
2 tablespoons water
1 teaspoon soy sauce
½ teaspoon monosodium
   glutamate
¼ teaspoon salt
¼ teaspoon pepper
Flour
1 cup salad oil

MUSHROOM CREAM SAUCE:
¼ cup butter or margarine
¼ cup flour
2 cups light cream
2 4-ounce cans (1⅓ cups)
   button mushrooms, drained

BROWNED SESAME SEEDS:
½ cup sesame seeds

Remove skin and bone from chicken or have butcher bone them. Mix together eggs, water, soy sauce, monosodium glutamate, salt and pepper in a shallow dish. Dip boned chicken into this mixture coating thoroughly; then dip into flour until thoroughly coated. Heat oil in skillet. Add chicken; fry until golden brown and tender, 6 to 10 minutes on each side. Serve hot with Mushroom Cream Sauce and sprinkle with Browned Sesame Seeds.

*8 servings.*

Mushroom Cream Sauce: Melt butter over low heat. Add flour; blend well. Stir in cream. Continue cooking about 5 minutes longer until thickened; stir occasionally. Add mushrooms; cover and cook about 5 minutes longer until mushrooms are heated.

*Makes about 3 cups sauce.*

Browned Sesame Seeds: Spread sesame seeds over bottom of an 8-inch round or square shallow baking pan. Bake in 350° oven 12 to 15 minutes or until golden brown.

# Chicken a La Romano

1 3-pound broiler-fryer chicken,
   split lengthwise
1 teaspoon salt
½ teaspoon ground pepper
Dash red pepper
¼ teaspoon crushed oregano

⅓ cup minced parsley
1 clove garlic, minced
1 1-pound can (2 cups)
   tomatoes
¼ cup grated Romano cheese
¼ cup olive oil

Bring wing tips onto back to expose thick breast meat to heat. Place chicken, skin side down, in shallow baking pan. Bake in 350° oven 20 minutes. Meanwhile combine salt, pepper, red pepper, oregano, parsley and garlic; sprinkle over chicken. Pour tomatoes over all. Sprinkle with cheese. Drizzle with olive oil. Continue baking, uncovered, 1½ hours or until drumstick twists easily out of thigh joint.

*2 to 4 servings.*

# Chicken Tropicale

| | |
|---|---|
| ½ cup pineapple juice | 6 chicken breasts |
| ¼ cup sherry | ½ cup salad oil |
| 3 tablespoons lemon juice | 2 cups crushed potato chips |
| 2 tablespoons light corn syrup | ½ cup slivered almonds |
| ½ teaspoon salt | 1 tablespoon melted butter |
| ¼ teaspoon rosemary seasoning salt | Parsley |
| | Pineapple chunks |
| ¼ teaspoon nutmeg | Flaked coconut |

Mix first 7 ingredients for marinade. Marinate chicken several hours or overnight. Drain well. Dip in salad oil, roll in crushed chips. Bake in shallow greased pan in 375° oven 1 hour or until tender. Combine almonds and butter. Sprinkle over chicken. Continue baking 10 minutes or until almonds are lightly toasted. Garnish with parsley and pineapple chunks rolled in coconut.

*6 servings.*

# One-Bowl Chicken and Curried Rice

| | |
|---|---|
| 1 3-pound can cooked chicken, cut up | 1½ teaspoons curry powder |
| 1½ cups uncooked rice | Paprika |
| 1 medium onion, finely chopped | Dairy sour cream |

Pour broth from canned chicken (about 4 cups) into large kettle. Stir in rice, onion and curry powder. Bring to boiling point, reduce heat, cover pan; simmer 15 minutes. Stir once gently. Place whole pieces of chicken on top of rice. Cover and simmer 10 minutes longer. Sprinkle chicken with paprika. Serve hot chicken and curried rice with sour cream. *4 to 6 servings.*

# Pretzel-Fried Turkey

| | |
|---|---|
| 2 eggs, slightly beaten | 1 4-pound fryer-roaster turkey, cut up |
| 2 tablespoons water | |
| 1 teaspoon salt | 1⅓ cups fine pretzel crumbs |
| Pepper | Fat for frying |

Combine eggs, water, salt and pepper. Dip turkey pieces in egg mixture and coat with pretzel crumbs. Brown slowly in medium hot fat in skillet, turning as necessary. When turkey is lightly browned, about 20 minutes, reduce heat and cover tightly. If skillet cannot be covered tightly, add 1 to 2 tablespoons water. Cook slowly until fork-tender, 50 to 60 minutes. Uncover skillet the last 5 to 10 minutes to re-crisp coating. *5 to 6 servings.*

# Smothered Turkey with Potatoes

| | |
|---|---|
| 1 4- to 5-pound fryer-roaster turkey, cut up | ½ cup cooking fat |
| ½ cup flour | ½ cup turkey broth or water |
| 4 teaspoons salt | 4 to 5 medium potatoes, cut in ½-inch slices |
| 2 teaspoons paprika | 1 teaspoon salt |
| 1 teaspoon ground pepper | ⅓ cup chopped parsley |

Coat turkey for frying by shaking 2 or 3 pieces at a time, in a paper bag containing flour, 4 teaspoons salt, paprika and pepper. Heat fat in skillet. Brown meaty pieces first, slipping less meaty pieces in between as the turkey browns, turning as necessary. When all pieces are browned, reduce heat. Add broth. Cover tightly; simmer 30 minutes. Spread potatoes over turkey, season with 1 teaspoon salt and continue cooking, covered, about 1 hour or until turkey and potatoes are fork-tender. Sprinkle with parsley.          *6 servings.*

# Creamed Turkey with Lemon-Buttered Noodles

| | |
|---|---|
| 1 tablespoon salt | Dash pepper |
| 6 ounces broad or medium noodles | 2 cups milk |
| 4½ cups boiling water | 1 cup chopped cooked turkey |
| ⅓ cup butter or margarine | ½ cup sliced pitted ripe olives |
| 2 tablespoons minced onion | 1 tablespoon capers |
| ⅓ cup flour | 1 teaspoon grated lemon peel |
| 1 teaspoon salt | ¼ cup butter or margarine, melted |
| ¼ teaspoon basil | 2 tablespoons lemon juice |

Add 1 tablespoon salt and noodles to boiling water. Boil rapidly, stirring constantly, for 2 minutes. Cover, remove from heat and let stand 10 minutes. Meanwhile, melt ⅓ cup butter; add onion; cook 3 minutes without browning. Stir in flour, salt, basil and pepper. Add milk gradually; cook until thickened, stirring constantly. Stir in turkey, olives, capers and lemon peel. Heat thoroughly. Rinse noodles with hot water; drain well. Turn into large bowl. Combine ¼ cup butter and lemon juice. Pour over noodles; mix lightly. Turn noodles onto heated serving platter; spoon creamed turkey over top.          *6 servings.*

*Keep in Mind:* 2 ounces uncooked macaroni, spaghetti or noodles, yields 1 generous serving. Interchange different shapes by weight.

# Delectable Turkey Hash

4 cups cubed cooked turkey
1 cup butter or margarine
2 cups chopped green onions
1 cup diced celery
2 green peppers, chopped
¼ cup slivered, salted almonds
1 4-ounce can (⅔ cup) button
   mushrooms, drained

⅓ cup flour
1 tablespoon curry powder
2 teaspoons basil
2 teaspoons salt
½ teaspoon ground pepper
2 cups turkey broth
½ cup sweet vermouth
Wine French Toast

Cook turkey in butter until lightly browned. Add onion, celery
and green pepper; continue cooking until vegetables are soft but
not browned. Add almonds, mushrooms, and flour blended with
seasonings. Stir together until flour has been absorbed. Add
broth all at once; simmer until thickened, stirring constantly.
Add vermouth; simmer for several minutes. Serve on Wine
French Toast (page 46).                                   8 *servings.*

Note: If vermouth is not used, substitute an equal amount of broth.

# Cranberry-Orange Stuffing
# for Roast Chicken

1 8-ounce package seasoned
   bread stuffing
1 cup cranberry-orange relish
⅓ cup melted butter

½ teaspoon salt
¼ teaspoon nutmeg
1 tablespoon sugar

Combine ingredients. Toss. Makes enough stuffing for one roasting chicken or small turkey.

# Almond-Herb Stuffing

2 quarts soft bread cubes
1 cup slivered blanched almonds
1½ teaspoons salt
1 teaspoon thyme
½ teaspoon tarragon

¼ teaspoon savory
¼ teaspoon pepper
⅓ cup butter or margarine
¾ cup minced onion
2 cups warm chicken broth

Empty bread cubes into large bowl. Add almonds, salt, thyme,
tarragon, savory and pepper. Melt butter in saucepan. Add
onion and cook about 5 minutes, stirring frequently. Pour onion
mixture and broth over bread cubes. Toss lightly, mixing thoroughly, until bread is well moistened. Turn into buttered 1½-
quart casserole; cover. Bake in 350° oven 35 minutes. Uncover
and bake 15 minutes longer. If desired, stuff a large chicken or
small turkey with the stuffing.                           6 *servings.*

Note: For chicken broth you may use two chicken bouillon cubes dissolved in 2 cups boiling water.

# Savory Tuna Roll

**CHEESE PASTRY:**
1 cup sifted flour
½ teaspoon salt

⅓ cup shortening
¼ cup shredded Cheddar cheese
3 to 4 tablespoons cold water

**SAVORY TUNA FILLING:**
2 tablespoons chopped onion
2 tablespoons butter, melted
1 tablespoon flour
¼ teaspoon salt
⅛ teaspoon salt
⅛ teaspoon marjoram

⅛ teaspoon thyme
Dash pepper
¼ cup light cream
1 9¼-ounce can tuna
⅓ cup chopped parsley
1 egg, slightly beaten

**CHEESE SAUCE:**
2½ tablespoons butter
2½ tablespoons flour
1 14½-ounce can (1⅔ cups)
   evaporated milk
⅔ cup water

1 cup shredded Cheddar cheese
2 egg yolks, beaten
Salt
Pepper
1 10-ounce package frozen
   mixed vegetables, cooked

**Cheese Pastry:** Sift flour and salt into bowl. Cut in shortening. Stir in cheese. Sprinkle water over mixture. Stir with fork until dough is moist enough to hold together. Form into ball. Refrigerate while making Savory Tuna Filling. Roll out dough on floured pastry cloth to 7 x 12-inch rectangle. Spread filling lengthwise down center. Moisten edges. Fold sides around filling to meet; seal sides and ends. Place seam side down on baking sheet. Prick top. Bake in 400° oven 35 to 45 minutes. Serve with hot Cheese Sauce.                                  6 *servings.*

**Savory Tuna Filling:** Brown onion in butter. Blend in flour, salt, marjoram, thyme and pepper. Gradually add cream. Cook, stirring constantly, until thickened. Remove from heat. Stir in tuna, parsley and egg.

**Cheese Sauce:** Melt butter in saucepan. Blend in flour. Gradually add evaporated milk and water. Cook, stirring constantly, until thickened. Add cheese; stir until melted. Add a little of the hot cheese sauce to beaten egg yolks, stirring constantly. Add egg mixture to sauce. Heat 2 minutes. Stir in salt, pepper and cooked and drained mixed vegetables.

*Weights and measures:* One pound cheese, shredded, equals 4 cups.
*Bit of information:* American cheese is a form of Cheddar cheese.

# Jiffy Crab Meat Eleanor

| | |
|---|---|
| ¼ cup butter | ¼ cup chopped ripe olives |
| 1 4-ounce can (⅔ cup) mushroom stems and pieces | ¼ cup chopped pimiento |
| 1 small green pepper, cut in ¼-inch strips | 2 tablespoons chopped parsley |
| ¼ cup toasted slivered almonds | Dash Tabasco |
| 1 teaspoon grated lemon peel | ¼ teaspoon salt |
| 2 10½-ounce cans condensed cream of celery soup | Dash black pepper |
| ½ teaspoon celery salt | 2 6½-ounce cans (1½ cups) crab meat, flaked |
| | 3 cups hot cooked rice |

Melt butter in large skillet. Add remaining ingredients except rice. Stir thoroughly. Cover; cook gently 25 to 30 minutes. Serve over rice. *6 to 8 servings.*

# Lobster Thermidor

| | |
|---|---|
| 4 lobster tails, 6 to 8 ounces each | 1 teaspoon salt |
| ¼ cup butter | ½ teaspoon celery salt |
| ¼ cup flour | ⅛ teaspoon cayenne pepper |
| 1 cup milk | 2 egg yolks, slightly beaten |
| 1 cup cream | 2 teaspoons lemon juice |
| ¼ teaspoon dry mustard | ¼ cup sherry wine |
| ½ teaspoon grated onion | Parmesan cheese |
| | Paprika |

Cook lobster tails in boiling water to cover, 9 minutes for 6-ounce or 11 minutes for 8-ounce tails. Plunge into cold water to cool. Cut away thin undershells and remove meat, keeping outer shells intact. Cut meat in ½-inch pieces. Melt butter, add flour and stir to make a smooth paste. Gradually add milk, stirring constantly; cook until thickened. Stir in cream, mustard, onion, salt, celery salt and cayenne pepper. Blend a little of the hot sauce with egg yolks, then stir back into remaining sauce. Cook until thickened. Add lemon juice, sherry and lobster meat. Chill until serving time, if desired. Fill shells with lobster mixture, sprinkle with Parmesan cheese and paprika. Place in shallow baking dish. Bake in 375° oven 30 minutes. *4 servings.*

*Gourmet trick:* To successfully add eggs to a hot sauce, stir some of hot sauce into slightly beaten eggs. Then stir eggs into sauce.

# Savory Baked Fish

| | |
|---|---|
| 2 pounds cod fillets, fresh or frozen | ¼ cup butter |
| 3 tablespoons butter, melted | ¼ cup flour |
| ½ teaspoon salt | ½ teaspoon salt |
| Dash pepper | Dash pepper |
| 1 small onion, chopped | ¼ teaspoon oregano |
| ¼ cup chopped celery | 1 cup canned whole tomatoes |
| | 1 cup buttermilk |

Thaw frozen fillets. Cut cod in serving size pieces. Dip in melted butter. Season with ½ teaspoon salt and pepper. Arrange in shallow baking pan. Cook onion and celery in butter until tender, about 10 minutes. Stir in flour and seasonings. Gradually add tomatoes and buttermilk. Simmer 10 minutes, stirring constantly. Pour sauce over cod. Bake in 350° oven 45 minutes or until fish flakes easily when tested with a fork.     6 *servings.*

**Variation:** Use halibut, perch or whitefish in place of cod.

# Dolmades American Style
## (Cabbage Bundles In Tangy Golden Cream)

| | |
|---|---|
| **CABBAGE BUNDLES:** | ½ teaspoon basil |
| 12 large cabbage leaves | 2 cups shredded Cheddar cheese |
| ½ cup chopped onion | |
| ½ cup butter, melted | **TANGY GOLDEN CREAM:** |
| 2 pints frozen oysters, thawed and drained | 2 cups dairy sour cream |
| 2 cups cooked rice | 2 cups shredded Cheddar cheese |
| 2 teaspoons salt | 2 tablespoons lemon juice |

**Cabbage Bundles:** Parboil cabbage leaves 10 minutes; drain. Cook onion in melted butter until tender but not brown; remove onion. In remaining butter heat oysters until edges curl. Mix rice, salt, basil and cheese together. Blend onion, oysters and melted butter into cheese-rice mixture. Put about ⅓ cup of this mixture into each cabbage leaf. Roll and secure with wooden picks. Place in buttered oblong baking dish; cover with half of sauce. Bake in 375° oven 15 minutes. Top with remaining sauce. Serve immediately.     6 *servings.*

**Tangy Golden Cream:** In saucepan, blend together sour cream and cheese. Stirring constantly, warm over low heat until cheese melts; stir in lemon juice.     *Makes about 2 cups sauce.*

# Shrimp a La Ming

| | |
|---|---|
| 6 tablespoons butter | 1 16- or 17-ounce can (2 cups) |
| ¼ cup finely minced onion | mixed Chinese vegetables, |
| 6 tablespoons flour | well drained |
| 2 cups milk | 1 cup chopped celery |
| 1½ teaspoons soy sauce | Dash salt |
| 2 4½-ounce cans shrimp, or | Dash pepper |
| 2 cups cooked shrimp, cut in | 3 cups cooked rice OR |
| half lengthwise | 1 1-pound 4-ounce OR 1 16- or |
| | 17-ounce can (2½ or 2 cups) |
| | Chinese noodles |

Melt butter in saucepan over low heat; add onion and cook until transparent, but do not brown. Blend in flour. Add milk slowly, stirring constantly. Cook until sauce is smooth and thickened. Add soy sauce, shrimp, Chinese vegetables and uncooked celery. Season with salt and pepper. Pour into baking dish. Bake in 350° oven 25 to 30 minutes until thoroughly heated, but not until celery is soft. Serve with hot fluffy rice or Chinese noodles.

*6 servings.*

Note: Soy sauce may be increased to 1 tablespoon if more pronounced flavor is desired.

# Tuna Suey

| | |
|---|---|
| ¼ cup butter | 1 1-pound 4-ounce can (2½ |
| 1 cup sliced fresh mushrooms | cups) mixed Chinese |
| (about ¼ pound) OR | vegetables, well drained |
| ½ cup canned sliced | ¼ cup julienne strips green |
| mushrooms | pepper |
| ¼ cup sliced onion | 1 cup chopped celery |
| 5 tablespoons flour | ¼ cup sliced ripe olives |
| 2½ cups milk | Dash salt |
| 2 tablespoons soy sauce | Dash pepper |
| 1 6½- or 7-ounce can (1 cup) | Chow mein noodles OR |
| tuna, drained and flaked | Steamed rice OR |
| | Buttered toast cups |

Melt butter in skillet, add mushrooms and onion. Cook until onion is transparent. Blend in flour. Add milk, stirring constantly. Cook until sauce is smooth and thickened. Add soy sauce, tuna, Chinese vegetables, green pepper, celery and olives; season with salt and pepper. Heat to serving temperature, but do not cook. Serve at once over heated noodles, steamed rice or in hot buttered toast cups.

*6 servings.*

# Lobster and Crab Meat Casserole

¼ cup butter
5 tablespoons flour
1 teaspoon salt
Dash white pepper
¼ teaspoon paprika
3 cups milk
2 egg yolks, slightly beaten
¼ teaspoon Worcestershire
   sauce
1 tablespoon sherry wine

1 tablespoon lemon juice
½ pound fresh mushrooms,
   cooked and drained
2 10½-ounce packages frozen
   lobster tails
2 6½-ounce cans (2 cups)
   crab meat
2 hard cooked eggs
¼ cup sliced stuffed olives
1 cup crushed potato chips

Melt butter, add flour and seasonings; cook until bubbly. Add milk. Cook, stirring constantly, until sauce thickens. Reduce heat; cook 5 minutes. Stir a little hot sauce into egg yolks. Mix well; stir into remaining sauce. Cook 1 minute. Add Worcestershire sauce, wine, lemon juice and mushrooms. Cook lobster tails according to directions on package. Remove from shell, cut meat in chunks. Flake crab meat; remove membrane. Slice eggs. In a 2-quart casserole place half of lobster and crab meat. Add eggs and olives. Pour half of sauce over eggs. Add remaining lobster and crab meat; add remaining sauce. Sprinkle with potato chips. Bake in 325° oven 25 to 30 minutes.     8 *servings.*

# Individual Crab Meat Souffles

3 cups flaked crab meat
½ cup finely chopped celery
3 tablespoons lemon juice
Dash salt
Dash freshly ground pepper
¼ cup margarine
¼ cup flour

1½ cups milk
1 teaspoon salt
Dash cayenne pepper
½ pound process American
   cheese, sliced
6 eggs, separated

Combine crab meat, celery, lemon juice, dash of salt and pepper; divide evenly among 8 individual ungreased casseroles or baking shells. Make a sauce with margarine, flour, milk, 1 teaspoon salt and cayenne pepper. When thickened and smooth add cheese; stir until cheese is melted. Remove from heat and add the slightly beaten yolks of the eggs; mix well. Slightly cool mixture, then pour it slowly onto stiffly beaten whites of eggs, cutting and folding mixture thoroughly together. Pour sauce over crab meat in casseroles. Bake in 300° oven 40 to 45 minutes. Serve at once.

8 *servings.*

# Poached Eggs on Wild Rice—
# Western Sauce

**RICE:**
¾ cup wild rice
1½ teaspoons salt
1½ quarts water
**WESTERN SAUCE:**
1 teaspoon salt
⅛ teaspoon ground pepper
1 tablespoon paprika
1 tablespoon sugar
½ clove garlic or ½ teaspoon
garlic salt

1 cup catsup
1 medium onion, finely chopped
⅓ cup water
3 tablespoons white vinegar
1 tablespoon Worcestershire
sauce
¼ cup butter or margarine
**EGGS:**
8 poached eggs, drained
Parsley

**Rice:** Wash rice. Add rice to boiling salted water in 3-quart saucepan. Cover tightly. Simmer 30 to 40 minutes. Drain rice in a strainer and run hot water through it until water runs clear. To keep hot and fluffy, return rice to lightly greased saucepan. Leave cover ajar and place in warm oven until ready to serve.
*Makes about 3 cups cooked rice.*

**Western Sauce:** Blend salt, pepper, paprika and sugar. Add remaining ingredients. Heat to boiling. Cover; simmer 20 minutes.
*Makes about 2¼ cups sauce.*

**To serve:** Arrange poached eggs on hot rice. Top with Western Sauce or serve sauce separately. Garnish with parsley. 4 *servings.*

Note: On the matter of poached eggs, tastes vary from very soft to firm. Allow 1 to 2 minutes at simmering temperature for the former and up to 5 to 6 minutes for the latter.

# Savory Scrambled Eggs

¼ cup butter or margarine
6 eggs, slightly beaten
⅓ cup milk
¼ teaspoon salt

Dash pepper
1 3-ounce package cream
cheese, cut in pieces

Melt butter in skillet over low heat. Combine eggs, milk and seasonings; pour into skillet. Cook very slowly, stirring constantly, until eggs begin to thicken. Add cream cheese. Continue cooking very slowly, stirring occasionally, until cheese is blended in and eggs are cooked. 4 *servings.*

# Baked Eggs Au Gratin with Nippy Cheese Sauce

8 thin slices bread
⅓ cup melted butter
8 eggs
Dash salt
Dash pepper
NIPPY CHEESE SAUCE:
¼ cup butter

¼ cup flour
½ teaspoon salt
Dash pepper
1 teaspoon dry mustard
2 cups milk
1 cup (¼ pound) shredded
 sharp Cheddar cheese

Cut crusts from bread. Brush bread on both sides with butter. Press slices into 3-inch muffin cups or custard cups. Toast in 375° oven 5 to 10 minutes or until very lightly browned. Reduce heat to 350°. Break egg into center of each toast cup. Season with salt and pepper. Bake eggs to firmness desired. (Medium eggs take 15 to 20 minutes.) Remove to plates. Top with Nippy Cheese Sauce. 8 *servings.*

**Nippy Cheese Sauce:** Melt butter in saucepan over low heat; blend in flour and seasonings. Add milk, stirring constantly; cook until sauce is smooth and thickened. Add cheese and stir until cheese melts.

# Egg Fondue

½ cup butter or margarine
3 tablespoons flour
½ teaspoon salt
½ teaspoon ground pepper
2 to 2¼ cups milk
5 egg yolks, slightly beaten

¾ cup freshly grated Parmesan
 cheese
Bite-size pieces of apple
 sections, celery and carrot
 diagonals, green pepper
 strips and French bread

Melt butter in heavy saucepan over low heat. Add flour and stir until frothy. Add salt, pepper and 2 cups milk all at once. Cook, stirring constantly, until thickened throughout. Pour a small amount of sauce into egg yolks, stirring constantly. Pour this egg mixture into remaining sauce; cook stirring until thickened, about 2 minutes. DO NOT BOIL. Add cheese. If too thick, add more milk but do not exceed ¼ cup. Consistency should be thick enough to coat the bite-size food dipped into it.

*Makes about 1 quart or 8 to 10 servings.*

# Creamy Poached Eggs

1 10-ounce can frozen cream of
  shrimp soup
¼ cup milk
Dash Tabasco
¼ teaspoon curry powder OR
  thyme

4 eggs
4 waffles
Water cress
Pickled crab apples

Heat soup in 8-inch skillet. Add milk and seasonings; stir occasionally. When smooth and simmering, break eggs gently into soup. Cover pan and simmer until egg white is set or about 5 minutes. Place an egg and sauce on each waffle. Garnish each plate with water cress and crab apples.     *4 servings.*

# Danish Egg Casserole

2 tablespoons butter or
  margarine
2 tablespoons flour
1 cup milk
6 hard cooked eggs, chopped
2 tablespoons diced pimiento
¼ cup minced celery
1 cup (⅛ pound) finely crushed
  crackers

¼ cup mayonnaise
½ teaspoon salt
¾ teaspoon garlic salt
½ teaspoon ground pepper
TOPPING:
½ cup cracker crumbs
3 tablespoons melted butter
  or margarine

Melt butter in 2-quart saucepan. Stir in flour; cook over low heat, stirring constantly, until bubbly. Add milk all at once and cook until thickened, stirring continually. Blend sauce and all remaining ingredients except topping. Spread in 1-quart greased shallow casserole. To make topping, mix cracker crumbs with melted butter. Sprinkle over casserole. Bake in 400° oven 20 minutes or until golden brown.     *4 to 6 servings.*

## Swiss Cheese Fondue

2 cups shredded Swiss cheese
1½ tablespoons flour
1 clove garlic
1 cup dry white wine
Dash salt

Dash pepper
Dash nutmeg
French or Vienna bread, cut
   in chunks

Toss together the cheese and flour. Rub a chafing dish or sauce-pan with cut clove of garlic. Pour in wine; heat until bubbles rise to surface. (Never let it boil.) Add cheese mixture—a half cup at a time—stir with fork, letting each amount completely melt before adding another. Stir until mixture bubbles lightly. Add salt, pepper and nutmeg. Keep the fondue bubbling while serving. To serve, dunk bite-size chunks of bread with a crusty edge into the fondue.                    *6 servings.*

## Rice and Cheese Timbales

1 cup cooked rice
1 cup shredded Cheddar cheese
1 cup soft bread crumbs (1 to 2
   slices bread)
½ cup chopped green olives
1 small onion, grated
¼ teaspoon dry mustard
¼ cup melted butter

2 eggs, slightly beaten
¾ cup milk
1 10½-ounce can condensed
   tomato soup
1 tablespoon Worcestershire
   sauce
4 stuffed olives, sliced

Mix all ingredients together except tomato soup, Worcestershire sauce and sliced olives. Spoon mixture into 4 6-ounce custard cups. Place cups in pan containing about 1 inch of hot water. Bake in 325° oven 1 hour or until set in center. Loosen with knife around edges and turn out. Heat soup; add Worcestershire sauce. Serve as sauce for timbales. Garnish with sliced olives.

*4 servings*

## Green Rice Casserole

2 cups cooked rice
1 cup chopped parsley
¼ cup chopped green onion
½ teaspoon salt

¼ cup melted butter
1 egg, slightly beaten
¼ cup chicken bouillon

Combine all ingredients in order given; stir lightly until thoroughly mixed. Place in 1½-quart casserole. Casserole may be made in advance and refrigerated until time to put in oven. Bake in 375° oven 25 to 30 minutes.                    *4 servings.*

# Rice and Vegetables

2 cups water
1 cup rice
1 tablespoon butter or
  margarine
1/8 teaspoon curry powder
1 teaspoon salt
Dash pepper

2 cups mixed fresh vegetables
  (shredded spinach, shredded
  carrots, chopped onion and
  tomatoes cut in small pieces)
1 raw sweet potato, peeled and
  cut in small cubes

Bring water to boiling; add rice and butter. Cover and cook gently 20 minutes, stirring occasionally. Add seasonings and vegetables. Mix well; continue cooking, covered, over low heat about 25 minutes.               6 *servings.*

# Wild Rice and Mushroom Casserole

1 cup wild rice OR
2 16-ounce cans (4 cups) cooked
  wild rice
1/3 cup butter
1/2 pound fresh mushrooms,
  sliced

1 tablespoon chopped onion
2 tablespoons flour
1 cup beef bouillon
1 teaspoon salt
1/8 teaspoon pepper
1/2 cup buttered bread crumbs

Cook rice according to package directions. Melt butter in large skillet; add mushrooms and onion; cook until lightly browned. Add flour and bouillon; cook until thick and smooth, stirring constantly. Add rice and seasonings. Place in greased 1½-quart casserole. Top with buttered crumbs. Bake in 375° oven 25 minutes or until browned.               6 *to* 8 *servings.*

# Tomato-Corn Scramble

6 tablespoons butter
6 tablespoons flour
3/4 teaspoon salt
Dash pepper
2¼ cups milk
1½ cups grated Cheddar cheese

1 12-ounce can (1½ cups)
  kernel corn, drained
3/4 cup catsup
1/8 teaspoon Worcestershire
  sauce
Crisp crackers OR toast
Sweet pickle chips

Melt butter in saucepan. Add flour, salt and pepper. Cook until mixture is smooth and bubbly. Add milk. Cook, stirring constantly, until thickened. Add cheese; stir until melted. Stir in corn, catsup and Worcestershire sauce; cook over low heat 5 minutes. Serve on crackers or toast. Garnish with pickle chips.
                                        6 *servings.*

# Gourmet Macaroni

1 7-ounce package macaroni
¼ cup butter
3 tablespoons flour
1 teaspoon salt
⅛ teaspoon pepper
2½ cups milk
⅓ cup crumbled blue cheese

1 tablespoon parsley flakes
2 tablespoons diced pimiento
1 4-ounce can (⅔ cup)
 mushrooms, drained and
 sliced
¼ cup buttered dry bread
 crumbs

Cook macaroni according to package directions; drain, pour into 1½-quart casserole. Melt butter over low heat; blend in flour and seasonings. Add milk, stirring constantly; cook until sauce is smooth and thickened. Add cheese; stir until melted. Stir in parsley, pimiento and mushrooms. Pour sauce over macaroni in casserole, stirring with a fork. Top with buttered crumbs. Bake in 350° oven 30 minutes.                     6 *servings.*

# Spaghetti Marinara

1½ teaspoons minced garlic
3 tablespoons olive oil
2 1-pound 12-ounce cans (6
 cups) Italian pear-shaped
 tomatoes
1 teaspoon salt

½ teaspoon pepper
3 tablespoons chopped parsley
¼ cup chopped Italian black
 olives
1 pound long spaghetti

Brown garlic lightly in olive oil. Drain liquid from tomatoes; save liquid. Chop tomatoes and add to garlic, blending well. Add liquid from tomatoes, salt and pepper. Bring mixture to boiling. Reduce heat and simmer 1 hour. Add parsley and olives. Continue cooking about 5 minutes longer. Meanwhile, cook spaghetti in boiling salted water until tender. Drain. Arrange cooked spaghetti on platter. Pour hot Marinara Sauce over spaghetti. Serve immediately. Sauce may be prepared ahead of time. 8 *servings.*

*For perfect spaghetti strands:* Put one end in boiling salted water. As spaghetti strands soften, gradually coil them around in kettle until all strands are under water.

# Pancake Hawaiian

2 tablespoons butter or
  margarine
3 eggs
⅛ teaspoon salt
⅓ cup sifted flour
½ cup pineapple juice

Grated peel of ½ lemon
2 teaspoons lemon juice
1 cup crushed pineapple
¼ pound Cheddar cheese,
  shredded (about 1 cup)

Place butter in a 10- to 12-inch skillet and place in 450° oven while pancake ingredients are being mixed. Beat eggs and salt until light and fluffy. Add flour; beat until smooth. Add pineapple juice; blend. Remove skillet from oven and tip back and forth to distribute melted butter over bottom. Pour in batter. Bake in 450° oven 12 minutes or until pancake is delicately browned and edges draw away from pan sides. As pancake is cooking, place lemon peel, lemon juice and crushed pineapple in saucepan over medium heat. When pancake is done, remove from oven and distribute half the cheese over top. Roll pancake. Leave in skillet. Pour pineapple sauce over pancake and sprinkle remaining cheese on top. Place under broiler and broil until cheese melts and just begins to brown. Place on heated serving platter. Adaptable as either entrée or dessert.

*Makes 2 to 4 servings.*

Note: Pancake Hawaiian plus beverage makes a perfect luncheon for two.

# SALADS and SALAD DRESSINGS

TOMATO ARTICHOKE SALAD
VINAIGRETTE SALAD WHEEL
TOSSED SALAD
ITALIAN SALAD BOWL
SOUR CREAM COLE SLAW
POTATO SALAD
MINTED PINEAPPLE SALAD
  WITH LEMON DRESSING
AVOCADO AND CITRUS
  FRUIT SALAD
CHICKEN GRAPE SALAD
CURRIED CHICKEN SALAD
SHRIMP AND PINEAPPLE
  SALAD
SOUTHERN BAKED
  JAMBALAYA SALAD
BAKED CHICKEN SALAD
RING-AROUND SALAD
  SUPREME
LEMON TUNA MOLD
TOMATO SHRIMP ASPIC RING
RED AND WHITE FRUIT
  MOLD

MOLDED CRANBERRY
  RELISH SALAD
STRAWBERRY-SOUR CREAM
  MOLD
LIME-STRAWBERRY
  SURPRISE
GRAPEFRUIT SALAD
SPICED PEACH SALAD
DARK SWEET CHERRY MOLD
GOLDEN SALAD RING
OLD FASHIONED BOILED
  DRESSING
TROPICAL SALAD DRESSING
CELERY SEED DRESSING
WHIPPED FRUIT DRESSING
BUTTERMILK DRESSING
SOUR CREAM FRUIT SALAD
  DRESSING
SOUR CREAM DRESSING
GOURMET SOUR CREAM
  DRESSING

*Illustration:* Italian Salad Bowl (page 135).

# SALADS and Salad Dressings

Various groups of connoisseurs cling to various notions about salads. There are those who say salads must be eaten *before* the main course to be enjoyed to the fullest. An equally dedicated group insists that salads provide the fitting finale and must come *after* the "meat and potatoes" course. Still a third group of gastronomes firmly proceed to eat salads *with* the meal. And just to confound the issue, a whole new realm of main dish salads have made their debut in America which *are* the meal! So take your choice as to when to eat salads . . . but do make your selection frequently from the choice collection given here.

## Tomato Artichoke Salad

**Firm red tomatoes, peeled**
**Leaf lettuce**
**Canned artichoke hearts, drained**

**Water cress**
**French dressing**

For each serving cut a tomato in wedges almost to the stem end. Place on lettuce on a salad plate. Spread the sections apart and place a canned artichoke heart in the center. Garnish with water cress. Serve with French dressing.

# Vinaigrette Salad Wheel

**SALAD:**
1 large head cauliflower
6 to 8 carrots, cut in strips
1 10-ounce package frozen
  asparagus spears
1 1-pound 4-ounce can (2½
  cups) French style green
  beans
1 cup French dressing
Small lettuce leaves OR cups
**VINAIGRETTE DRESSING:**
½ cup salad oil
⅓ cup vinegar

½ teaspoon salt
¼ teaspoon pepper
Dash cayenne pepper
Dash paprika
1 hard cooked egg, chopped
1 tablespoon chopped pimiento
1 tablespoon chopped sweet
  pickle
1 tablespoon chopped onion
1 tablespoon chopped parsley
1 tablespoon chopped green
  pepper
1 tablespoon pickle juice
  (drained from pickles)

**Salad:** Cook cauliflower, carrots and asparagus separately, only until tender; drain well. Drain beans. Place vegetables in separate bowls. Pour ¼ cup French dressing over each. Chill in refrigerator several hours or overnight.

**Vinaigrette Dressing:** Combine all ingredients in a large glass jar; refrigerate.

To serve, place cauliflower in center of large platter. Arrange lettuce leaves around cauliflower; alternate marinated vegetables on lettuce. Pour Vinaigrette Dressing over cauliflower. 8 *servings.*

# Tossed Salad

1 clove garlic
½ teaspoon salt
1 head lettuce
6 green onions, sliced
10 radishes, sliced
¼ green pepper, cut in strips
1 tablespoon chopped parsley

2 tomatoes, cut in wedges
½ cup salad oil
¼ teaspoon pepper
½ teaspoon seasoned salt
2 tablespoons grated Parmesan
  cheese
3 tablespoons wine vinegar

Mash garlic and salt in a wooden salad bowl. Rub in well; remove garlic bits. Break lettuce into bowl. Add green onions, radishes, green pepper, parsley and tomato wedges. Slowly drizzle oil over greens, tossing lightly until each leaf is coated. Sprinkle with pepper, seasoned salt and cheese. Add wine vinegar; toss well.                    8 *to* 10 *servings.*

For tasty tossed salads: Use crisp and dry salad greens.

# Italian Salad Bowl

½ clove garlic
¼ teaspoon prepared mustard
1 teaspoon salt
Few grains pepper

¼ teaspoon Worcestershire
  sauce
1½ tablespoons vinegar
4 tablespoons corn oil
1 quart assorted salad greens

Place garlic in wooden bowl. Add mustard, salt and pepper. Blend thoroughly with fork. Add Worcestershire sauce, vinegar and corn oil. Beat with fork until thoroughly mixed. Add crisp well drained salad greens, broken in bite-size pieces. Toss lightly until greens glisten. Serve at once.     4 *servings.*

Note: Assorted salad greens might include Italian salad greens such as dandelion, chicory, escarole, endive and romaine. Cherry or plum tomatoes may be added for color.

# Sour Cream Cole Slaw

2 teaspoons salt
¼ teaspoon pepper
1 to 1½ tablespoons sugar
½ teaspoon dry mustard

¼ cup lemon juice OR vinegar
1 cup dairy sour cream
6 cups finely shredded cabbage

Stir seasonings and lemon juice into sour cream until well mixed. Add to cabbage; toss lightly. Serve well chilled.     12 *servings.*

# Potato Salad

6 medium potatoes
1 pint Old Fashioned Boiled
  Dressing (page 143)
12 hard cooked eggs, peeled
  and sliced

1 large sweet onion, scraped
  or minced
Salt
Pepper
Paprika
Leaf lettuce

Cook potatoes in skins; drain. Cool just enough to handle easily; peel; slice thinly. Spread boiled dressing over bottom of bowl. Fill bowl with alternating layers of sliced potato, spread of salad dressing, sliced eggs, onion and sprinkling of salt and pepper. Finish with carefully arranged layer of egg slices and sprinkling of paprika. DO NOT STIR. Chill. Just before serving, tuck lettuce around edge of bowl.     6 *to* 8 *servings.*

Note: The secret of superior flavor in potato salad is in using boiled dressing and in putting together while potatoes are warm. They absorb the flavor of the dressing as they cool. Commercial salad dressing may be used instead of the Old Fashioned Boiled Dressing.

# Minted Pineapple Salad
# with
# Lemon Dressing

2 1-pound 4-ounce cans (5 cups) minted pineapple chunks
1 11-ounce can (1¼ cups) mandarin orange segments

Salad greens
Mint OR small green leaves
LEMON DRESSING:
½ fresh lemon with peel
¼ cup sugar

Drain and chill fruit. Arrange on salad greens. Top with lemon dressing. Garnish with mint or small leaves.      6 *servings.*
Dressing: Grind unpeeled lemon; mix with sugar. Allow to stand about 15 minutes before serving.

# Avocado and Citrus Fruit Salad

1 small head lettuce
1 cup grapefruit segments
1 cup orange segments
1 avocado

½ cup sliced celery
¼ teaspoon celery seeds
Celery Seed Dressing

Shred lettuce. Remove membrane from citrus fruits. Peel and dice avocado. Combine ingredients; toss with Celery Seed Dressing (page 143).      6 *servings.*

# Chicken Grape Salad

4½ cups cooked, cubed chicken (¾-inch cubes)
3 cups diced celery (¼-inch pieces)
1 cup red grapes, halved and seeded OR whole green seedless grapes

1½ cups mayonnaise
1½ cups boiled salad dressing
1 tablespoon salt
Crisp lettuce cups
Water cress

Combine cubed chicken, celery and grapes. Stir together mayonnaise, boiled salad dressing and salt until well blended. Add to chicken mixture, tossing together lightly. Keep refrigerated until ready to use. Serve in crisp lettuce cups. Garnish with water cress.

8 *servings.*

# Curried Chicken Salad

1½ cups cooked rice
1 tablespoon vinegar
2 tablespoons salad oil
1 teaspoon salt
¾ teaspoon curry powder
2 cups cubed cooked chicken
1 cup chopped celery

¼ cup chopped green pepper
1½ to 2 cups cooked green peas
¾ cup mayonnaise or salad
  dressing
Lettuce OR
Tomato cups

Mix cooked rice with vinegar, oil, salt and curry powder; refrigerate several hours. Just before serving, mix gently with chicken, celery, green pepper, peas and mayonnaise. Serve on lettuce or as a filling for tomato cups.          5 *to* 6 *servings.*

# Shrimp and Pineapple Salad

1½ pounds fresh shrimp,
  cooked and cleaned
3 tablespoons lemon juice
½ cup chopped green pepper
½ cup finely chopped pimiento
1 13½-ounce can (1½ cups)
  pineapple tidbits, drained

1½ cups diced celery
½ cup blanched, slivered,
  toasted almonds
½ cup mayonnaise
4 or 6 lettuce cups
Ripe olives

Dice shrimp; sprinkle with lemon juice. Add green pepper, pimiento, pineapple, celery, almonds and mayonnaise. Mix together lightly. Serve in lettuce cups. Garnish with olives.

4 *to* 6 *servings.*

# Southern Baked Jambalaya Salad

2 parboiled green peppers
2 firm tomatoes
1 4½-ounce can shrimp,
  jumbo pack
1 cup cooked rice
1 cup cubed Cheddar cheese
1 teaspoon salt
Dash pepper

¼ teaspoon tarragon
Pinch turmeric
Whole shrimp
Parsley
SHRIMP-CHEESE SAUCE:
1 10-ounce can frozen
  condensed shrimp soup
1 cup shredded Cheddar cheese

Drain and halve peppers. Hollow out tomatoes, leaving ¼-inch rim; dice tomato pulp. Mix canned shrimp, rice, cheese, salt, pepper, tarragon, turmeric and diced tomato. Fill green pepper halves and tomatoes. Place in buttered casserole. Pour over Shrimp-Cheese Sauce. Bake in 375° oven 10 minutes. Garnish each "salad" with whole shrimp and parsley.          6 *servings.*
Shrimp-Cheese Sauce: Heat together condensed soup and cheese until cheese melts.

# Baked Chicken Salad

| | |
|---|---|
| 1 3-pound can whole chicken | 1 cup diced celery |
| 2 tablespoons butter | ¼ cup minced green pepper |
| 2 tablespoons flour | 2 teaspoons minced onion |
| ½ teaspoon salt | 4 hard cooked eggs, diced |
| ¼ teaspoon pepper | coarsely |
| Dash cayenne pepper | ½ cup mayonnaise |
| 2 tablespoons lemon juice | 1 4½-ounce package potato |
| ½ teaspoon Worcestershire | chips, crushed |
| sauce | |

Drain chicken; reserve 1 cup broth. Remove chicken from bones. Cut chicken in bite size pieces. Melt butter; add flour and cook until bubbly. Stir in reserved 1 cup broth, salt, pepper, cayenne, lemon juice and Worcestershire sauce. Cook until sauce begins to thicken. Reduce heat; cook sauce 5 minutes allowing mixture to bubble occasionally. Add chicken, celery, green pepper, onion and eggs. Stir in mayonnaise. Turn into 1½-quart casserole. Sprinkle top with potato chips. Bake in 400° oven 15 to 20 minutes. *6 to 8 servings.*

Note: Use remaining broth drained from chicken for soup.

# Ring-Around Salad Supreme

**RING-AROUND LOBSTER SALAD:**

1½ tablespoons (1½ envelopes) unflavored gelatin
¾ cup milk
1 cup creamed cottage cheese
1 cup dairy sour cream
2 tablespoons tarragon vinegar
3 6-ounce cans (3 cups) lobster, drained and diced
3 tablespoons lobster liquor, drained from can
½ cup peeled, diced cucumber
⅓ cup sliced celery
1 teaspoon onion salt
¼ teaspoon salt
Lettuce leaves

**RING-AROUND PINEAPPLE SALAD:**

1 1-pound 4-ounce can (2½ cups) crushed pineapple
1¼ cups pineapple syrup, drained from can
1 3-ounce package lemon-flavored gelatin
3 tablespoons lemon juice
1 cup sliced, fresh green seedless grapes
1 5½-ounce jar chicken, diced
¼ cup shaved Brazil nuts
1 1-pound 4-ounce can (2½ cups) pineapple chunks, drained

Ring-Around Lobster Salad: In a saucepan mix gelatin with milk. Heat just to boiling, stirring constantly to dissolve gelatin. Blend in cottage cheese, sour cream, vinegar, 1 cup lobster meat and lobster liquor, cucumber, celery, onion salt and salt. Pour into 4- or 5-cup ring mold. Refrigerate. When ready to serve, unmold on platter. Fill center with lettuce leaves. Top with remaining lobster meat. *8 to 12 servings.*

**Ring-Around Pineapple Salad:** Drain pineapple; save syrup. Heat syrup to boiling point; add to gelatin. Stir until dissolved. Blend in pineapple, lemon juice, grapes, chicken and Brazil nuts. Pour into 4- or 5-cup ring mold. Refrigerate. When ready to serve, unmold on same platter next to Ring-Around Lobster Salad. Fill center with pineapple chunks. *8 to 12 servings.*

# Lemon Tuna Mold

1 7-ounce can tuna, drained
1½ tablespoons (1½ envelopes) unflavored gelatin
½ cup cold water
1½ cups boiling water
¼ cup lemon juice
½ teaspoon seasoned salt
1 large avocado
¼ cup salad dressing
½ cup diced celery
½ cup diced green pepper
Lettuce
Lemon wedges

Flake tuna. Soften gelatin in cold water, add boiling water; stir until dissolved. Add lemon juice and seasoned salt. Chill. Cut avocado in half lengthwise; remove seed and skin. Cut into medium size cubes. When gelatin mixture is thick, but not firm, add salad dressing, avocado, tuna, celery and green pepper. Mix lightly. Pour into 5-cup fish mold. Chill until firm. Unmold. Garnish with lettuce and lemon wedges. *6 to 8 servings.*

# Tomato Shrimp Aspic Ring

4 cups tomato juice
2 tablespoons (2 envelopes) unflavored gelatin
2 tablespoons lemon juice
Dash salt
Dash pepper
1 cup chopped celery
2 7-ounce cans shrimp, drained, cleaned, coarsely chopped
Lettuce
Salad dressing
Lemon wedges
Scored unpared cucumber slices

Heat 3½ cups tomato juice. Soften gelatin in remaining ½ cup cold tomato juice; dissolve in hot juice. Add lemon juice, salt and pepper. Chill until slightly thickened. Fold in celery and shrimp. Pour into 1½-quart ring mold. Chill until firm. Unmold on lettuce on serving plate. Line center of ring with lettuce; fill with salad dressing. Garnish plate with lemon wedges and cucumber slices. *8 to 10 servings.*

# Red and White Fruit Mold

1 1-pound can (2 cups) fruit
   cocktail
1 (3-ounce) package raspberry
   or strawberry-flavored gelatin
1 (3-ounce) package
   lemon-flavored gelatin

1 cup hot water
1 6-ounce can frozen
   lemonade concentrate
½ cup mayonnaise

Drain fruit cocktail; save syrup. Add water to syrup to make 2 cups liquid. Heat 1 cup to boiling; add raspberry gelatin and stir to dissolve. Add remaining 1 cup liquid. Pour into 6½- or 7-cup mold. Chill until firm. Meanwhile, dissolve lemon gelatin in hot water; add lemonade concentrate. Blend in mayonnaise. Chill until partially set; stir in fruit. Pour over gelatin in mold. Chill until firm.                    9 *to* 12 *servings.*

# Molded Cranberry Relish Salad

1 10½-ounce package frozen
   cranberry relish
1 (3-ounce) package
   cherry-flavored gelatin

1½ cups hot water
Lettuce
Mayonnaise

Thaw cranberry relish 30 minutes at room temperature. Dissolve gelatin in hot water; cool; stir in relish. Pour into molds. Chill until set. Serve on lettuce with mayonnaise.     6 *servings.*

# Strawberry-Sour Cream Mold

1 (3-ounce) package
   strawberry-flavored gelatin
1 tablespoon unflavored gelatin
2 cups boiling water
2 tablespoons lemon juice

2 10-ounce packages frozen
   sliced strawberries, slightly
   thawed
½ teaspoon red food coloring
1 cup dairy sour cream
Garnish as desired

Mix gelatins together. Add boiling water. Stir until dissolved. Add lemon juice, strawberries and juice. Stir until strawberries are completely thawed. Add food coloring to make a bright red color. Chill until partially thickened. Pour about ⅓ mixture into 5-cup ring mold. Spoon sour cream gently on center top of gelatin being careful that cream does not touch sides of mold. Carefully spoon remaining gelatin on top. Chill until thoroughly set. Unmold. Garnish.                    8 *servings.*

# Lime-Strawberry Surprise

1 (3-ounce) package
  lime-flavored gelatin
1 cup hot water
1 9-ounce can (1 cup) crushed
  pineapple
1 tablespoon lemon juice
¾ cup salad dressing

1 8-ounce package cream cheese
½ cup chopped nuts
1 (3-ounce) package
  strawberry-flavored gelatin
2 cups hot water
Frosted grapes
Salad dressing

Dissolve lime gelatin in 1 cup hot water. Drain pineapple; measure syrup; add cold water to make 1 cup. Add with the lemon juice to gelatin. Chill until slightly thickened; add pineapple. Pour into 8-inch square pan. Chill until firm. Gradually add ¾ cup salad dressing to cream cheese, blending until smooth. Add nuts; spread over lime layer. Chill. Dissolve strawberry gelatin in 2 cups hot water. Cool. Pour over cheese mixture. Chill until firm. Cut in squares. Arrange alternating red and green squares on plate. Garnish with frosted grapes. Serve with salad dressing.                                                 6 *servings.*

# Grapefruit Salad

3 grapefruit
2 tablespoons (2 envelopes)
  unflavored gelatin
½ cup cold water
2 cups boiling water
1 cup sugar

1 cup grapefruit liquid and
  cold water
½ cup chopped nuts
1 8-ounce package cream
  cheese (room temperature)
Milk
4 maraschino cherries

Pare grapefruit, section, drain. Sprinkle gelatin over cold water; let soften 5 minutes. Add boiling water and sugar; stir until dissolved. Stir in grapefruit liquid and cold water. Pour half of gelatin in 8-or 9-inch square pan. Chill until consistency of egg whites. Arrange broken or less perfect sections of grapefruit in gelatin; chill until firm. Add nuts to cream cheese and enough water, milk or cream to allow easy spreading. Spread in even layer on firm gelatin. Place remaining perfect sections of grapefruit over cheese, arranging to form a pattern on top of each serving (such as three sections swirled from a well drained maraschino cherry half). Top with remaining partially thickened gelatin. Chill until firm. Cut in squares.                9 *servings.*

Note: If canned grapefruit is used, reduce sugar to ½ cup.

# Spiced Peach Salad

1 1-pound 13-ounce can (3½ cups) peach halves
¼ cup vinegar
1 teaspoon whole cloves
1 4-inch stick cinnamon

1 (3-ounce) package lemon-flavored gelatin
Curly endive
Salad dressing

Drain peaches; save syrup. To syrup, add vinegar, cloves and cinnamon; bring to boil. Add peaches. Simmer 10 minutes. Drain peaches; remove cloves and cinnamon. Measure syrup; add water to make 2 cups, if necessary. Heat to boiling. Add to gelatin; stir until dissolved. Chill until partially set. Put a layer of gelatin into 5-cup ring mold. Add peaches. Pour in remaining gelatin. Chill several hours or overnight. Unmold; garnish with endive. Serve with desired salad dressing.     8 *servings.*

# Dark Sweet Cherry Mold

2 1-pound cans (4 cups) dark sweet cherries
Water
2 (3-ounce) packages cherry-flavored gelatin

1 cup dry red wine
Curly endive OR
Water cress
Sour Cream Dressing

Drain cherries saving syrup. Measure syrup and add enough water to make 2½ cups liquid. Bring to a boil. Add to gelatin, stirring until gelatin is dissolved. Add wine. Set aside to chill until partially thickened. While gelatin is chilling, pit cherries. Fold into thickened gelatin. Pour into 5-cup ring mold. Chill several hours. Unmold and garnish with curly endive or water cress. Serve with Sour Cream Dressing (page 144).   8 *servings.*

# Golden Salad Ring

2 (3-ounce) packages lemon-flavored gelatin
2 cups boiling water
1 16-ounce can (2 cups) crushed pineapple, drained

1½ cups pineapple syrup and water
¾ cup grated raw carrots
Crisp greens
Whipped Fruit Dressing

Dissolve gelatin in boiling water. Cool. Add pineapple, pineapple syrup and water and carrots. Pour into 1¼-quart ring mold. Chill until firm. Unmold on greens. Serve with Whipped Fruit Dressing (page 143).                    10 *servings.*

# Old Fashioned Boiled Dressing

| | |
|---|---|
| 7 tablespoons sugar | ⅛ teaspoon paprika |
| 2 tablespoons flour | 3 eggs or 6 yolks |
| 1 tablespoon dry mustard | ¾ cup water |
| 1 teaspoon salt | ¾ cup vinegar |
| ⅛ teaspoon pepper | 1 tablespoon butter |

Blend dry ingredients (sift if lumpy) in double boiler or heavy saucepan. Add eggs. Mix until smooth. Add water; stir in vinegar. Cook over low heat, stirring constantly, until thickened. Stir in butter. Cool before serving. *Makes 3½ cups.*

# Tropical Salad Dressing

| | |
|---|---|
| ½ cup orange juice | ¼ teaspoon salt |
| ¼ cup lemon juice | 2 tablespoons honey |
| 2 tablespoons sugar | ½ cup salad oil |

Combine juices. Add sugar, salt and honey; stir until dissolved. Blend in oil. Chill. Beat before serving. Serve on variety of fresh fruits. *Makes 1¼ cups.*

# Celery Seed Dressing

| | |
|---|---|
| 6 tablespoons cider vinegar | 1 tablespoon dry mustard |
| 2 tablespoons lemon juice | 1½ teaspoons salt |
| 1½ tablespoons paprika | 4 teaspoons celery seeds |
| ½ cup sugar | 1 cup salad oil |

Put all ingredients except salad oil in mixing bowl. Beat for 2 minutes. Add salad oil, a few drops at a time, beating continuously. Chill. *Makes 1 pint.*

# Whipped Fruit Dressing

| | |
|---|---|
| ½ cup sugar | ½ cup unsweetened pineapple |
| 1 tablespoon flour | juice |
| 1 egg yolk | 1 cup heavy cream, whipped |
| Juice of 1 lemon | |

Combine sugar and flour. Beat egg yolk; blend in sugar mixture. Gradually add fruit juices. Cook in top of double boiler until thick, stirring constantly. Cool; fold in whipped cream.

*Makes 2 cups.*

# Buttermilk Dressing

3 tablespoons flour
¾ teaspoon salt
¼ teaspoon dry mustard
Dash cayenne pepper
3 tablespoons sugar
¾ cup buttermilk

1 egg, slightly beaten
1 tablespoon butter or
 margarine
2 tablespoons lemon juice
¼ cup orange juice

Combine flour, salt, mustard, pepper and sugar. Gradually stir in buttermilk and egg. Cook over hot water, stirring constantly until thickened. Remove from heat. Stir in butter, lemon and orange juices. Chill. *Makes 1¼ cups.*

# Sour Cream Fruit Salad Dressing

1 teaspoon grated orange peel
2 tablespoons orange juice
2 tablespoons lemon juice
1 tablespoon honey

½ teaspoon dry mustard
1 cup dairy sour cream
Dash salt
Dash pepper

Fold orange peel and juice, lemon juice, honey and dry mustard into sour cream. Season with salt and pepper. Chill. Serve on fruit salad. *Makes 1 cup.*

# Sour Cream Dressing

1 cup dairy sour cream
1 tablespoon lemon juice
¼ teaspoon salt

½ teaspoon sugar
4 marshmallows, cut very fine

Mix all ingredients together. Chill. *Makes 1⅓ cups.*

# Gourmet Sour Cream Dressing

2 tablespoons minced onion
3 tablespoons wine vinegar
2 teaspoons sugar
1 teaspoon salt

1 teaspoon prepared mustard
Dash Tabasco
⅛ teaspoon pepper
1 cup dairy sour cream

Combine all ingredients. Chill in refrigerator ½ hour or longer to blend flavors. Serve with vegetable salads, sliced tomatoes or cucumbers and onions. *Makes 1¼ cups.*

# SANDWICHES and SOUPS

JIFFY SUPER SANDWICH
FIRESIDE SANDWICHES
TRIPLE-DECKER SANDWICH
  BAKE
BROILED SALMON-WICH
BEEF-RYE SANDWICH
  SPECIALTY
JUMBO PIZZA SANDWICH
BROWN 'N' SERVE PIZZAS

BEEFEATER SANDWICH
STUFFED HAMBURGERS DE
  LUXE
BEAN CHOWDER
MAIN DISH EGG CHOWDER
SEAFOOD CHOWDER
CORN 'N' CRAB CHOWDER
HEARTY WINTER CHOWDER
TOMATO-CORN CHOWDER

*Illustration:* Corn Chowder (page 150).

# Sandwiches and Soups

Soup and sandwiches have become a happy twosome . . . frequent companions at lunch and supper. Here are excellent recipes for both, to please the most delicate or hearty appetite.

## Jiffy Supper Sandwich

6 slices cooked ham
6 slices cooked chicken
6 slices buttered toast
1 10½-ounce can condensed
    cream of mushroom soup

⅓ cup milk
Grated Parmesan cheese
1 2½-ounce can mushroom
    caps, drained

Arrange a ham slice and chicken slice on each slice of buttered toast in a shallow baking pan. Blend soup with milk and pour over each sandwich. Sprinkle with cheese. Top with mushrooms. Broil until heated through and lightly browned, about 5 minutes.

*6 servings.*

# Fireside Sandwiches

| | |
|---|---|
| 2 cups finely chopped cooked ham | ½ teaspoon horseradish |
| 1 cup shredded sharp Cheddar cheese | 2 tablespoons mayonnaise |
| | 8 sandwich buns, halved |
| 2 teaspoons grated onion | Potato chips |
| 2 teaspoons prepared mustard | Pickles |
| | Sliced tomatoes |

Combine ham, cheese, onion, mustard, horseradish and mayonnaise. Fill split buns with mixture. Wrap sandwiches individually in foil. Heat in 350° oven 20 minutes or over hot coals 10 minutes. Serve hot with potato chips, pickles and sliced tomatoes.

*Makes 8 sandwiches.*

Note: The sandwiches may be prepared and wrapped several hours in advance, then kept in refrigerator until ready to heat and serve.

# Triple-Decker Sandwich Bake

| | |
|---|---|
| 12 slices sandwich bread | 8 slices (8 ounces) Muenster cheese |
| Butter or margarine | |
| 1½ cups chopped cooked shrimp | ½ cup chopped pimiento-stuffed OR ripe olives |
| ½ cup diced celery | |
| ¼ teaspoon instant minced onion | |
| | 3 eggs, slightly beaten |
| 1 tablespoon lemon juice | 2 cups milk |
| 2 tablespoons mayonnaise | Paprika |

Spread 4 slices bread with butter. Place in bottom of 8-inch square baking dish. Toast lightly in 350° oven about 10 minutes. Combine shrimp, celery, onion, lemon juice and mayonnaise. Spoon mixture over toast in baking dish. Spread 4 more bread slices with butter; place over shrimp. Cover bread with cheese slices. Top cheese with chopped olives. Spread remaining bread slices with butter; place on top. Combine eggs and milk. Pour over sandwiches. Sprinkle top with paprika. Bake in 350° oven about 35 minutes. Serve hot. *Makes 4 sandwiches.*

# Broiled Salmon-Wich

| | |
|---|---|
| 1 1-pound can (2 cups) salmon, drained and boned | 1 10½-ounce can cream of mushroom soup |
| 6 slices bread, toasted and buttered | 6 tablespoons grated Parmesan cheese |
| ⅔ cup crumbled blue cheese | Paprika |

Spread salmon on toasted bread; sprinkle with blue cheese. Spoon soup, directly from can, over sandwich. Sprinkle with

Parmesan cheese and paprika. Place under broiler until soup is bubbly and cheese is lightly browned.    *Makes 6 sandwiches.*

## Beef-Rye Sandwich Specialty

1 pound ground beef
½ cup shredded American
  cheese
½ teaspoon salt

⅛ teaspoon pepper
3 tablespoons thinly sliced
  green onions
5 to 7 slices rye bread

Mix together beef, cheese, salt, pepper and onions. Toast rye bread slices on both sides. Spread meat mixture ¼ inch thick on rye bread, spreading well to edges. Broil about 3 inches from heat until browned, 5 to 7 minutes.    *Makes 5 to 7 sandwiches.*

## Jumbo Pizza Sandwich

1 1-pound loaf French or
  Vienna bread
¼ cup sliced ripe olives
⅛ teaspoon pepper
¼ teaspoon ground oregano
¾ teaspoon salt
2 tablespoons finely chopped
  green onion tops OR chives

½ pound (1 cup) ground beef
¼ cup grated Parmesan cheese
1 6-ounce can (¾ cup) tomato
  paste
14 thin slices tomato
8 1-ounce slices processed
  American cheese, cut in half
  diagonally

Cut bread in half lengthwise. Combine olives, pepper, oregano, salt, onion tops, beef, Parmesan cheese and tomato paste. Spread mixture on bread. Arrange 7 tomato slices over meat mixture on each section. Place on cooky sheet. Bake in 400° oven 15 minutes. Overlap 8 cheese triangles on each section. Bake 5 minutes longer. Cut each section into 12 pieces. Serve hot.    *12 servings.*

## Brown 'n' Serve Pizzas

1½-pound package brown 'n
  serve sausage
1 package refrigerator biscuits,
  6 English muffins OR 6
  sandwich buns

½ 6-ounce can (6 tablespoons)
  tomato paste
Oregano
1 cup shredded sharp Cheddar
  cheese

Cut sausages into halves lengthwise. Roll out each biscuit to about 4 inches in diameter, or split and toast English muffins or sandwich buns. Place on baking sheet. Spread surfaces with tomato paste. Top with brown 'n serve sausages. Sprinkle with oregano and cheese. Bake in 450° oven 5 to 7 minutes. Serve hot.    *Makes 10 to 12 individual pizzas.*

# Beefeater Sandwich

| | |
|---|---|
| ⅓ cup mayonnaise | Lettuce leaves |
| 2 teaspoons prepared | 6 thin slices tomato |
| horseradish | 6 slices (3 ounces) roast beef |
| 6 French rolls | 6 thin slices onion |
| 6 slices (3 ounces) corned beef | Butter or margarine |

Mix mayonnaise and horseradish. Split rolls; spread mayonnaise mixture on bottom halves of rolls. Arrange ingredients on bottom half of French rolls in order listed. Spread cut surface of roll tops with butter and top sandwiches. *Makes 6 sandwiches.*

# Stuffed Hamburgers De Luxe

| | |
|---|---|
| 1½ pounds ground beef | 2 tablespoons minced parsley |
| 1½ teaspooons salt | ½ cup shredded sharp Cheddar |
| ¼ teaspoon pepper | cheese |
| ½ teaspoon monosodium | ⅓ cup butter or margarine, |
| glutamate | softened |
| ¼ teaspoon thyme | ¼ teaspoon garlic powder |
| 6 thin slices tomato | 6 hamburger buns |

Mix thoroughly ground beef, salt, pepper, monosodium glutamate and thyme. Form 12 3-inch patties from hamburger mixture. On 6 hamburger patties place tomato slices. Sprinkle with parsley. Cover parsley with cheese. Top with remaining hamburger patties and seal edges. Blend thoroughly butter and garlic powder. Split hamburger buns; spread with garlic butter. Toast under broiler until lightly browned. Broil stuffed hamburger until well browned on both sides. Serve on toasted buns.

*Makes 6 sandwiches.*

# Bean Chowder

| | |
|---|---|
| 1 pound dried lima beans | 2 quarts water |
| 1 medium onion, chopped | 1 quart milk |
| 3 tablespoons butter | 1 tablespoon soy sauce |
| 1 pound ham bone or hock | ½ teaspoon paprika |
| 1 cup chopped celery | Salt |
| 1 medium carrot, sliced | Pepper |

Rinse and drain beans. In large saucepan cook onion in butter until tender. Add beans, ham bone, vegetables and water. Cover; cook slowly until beans and ham are tender, 2 to 2½ hours. Remove fat from ham. Cut ham in small pieces. Force lima bean mixture through sieve or food mill. Stir in milk, seasonings and ham. Heat until hot. Makes about 3 quarts. **12 *servings.***

# Main Dish Egg Chowder

2 cups raw potatoes (1-inch
  cubes)
1 13-ounce can concentrated
  chicken broth
1/3 cup butter or margarine
1/4 cup flour
1 tall can, 14½-ounces,
  evaporated milk diluted
  with 1 can water
1 1-pound can (2 cups) kernel
  corn with liquid
1 1-pound can (2 cups) green
  beans with liquid

1 small onion, sliced and
  separated into rings
1 2-ounce jar pimiento, diced
1/4 teaspoon pepper
1 small bay leaf
3/4 cup cubed Cheddar cheese
  (½-inch cubes)
9 hard cooked eggs, sliced
Salt
Pepper
Assorted crisp bread

Simmer potatoes in chicken broth, covered, until just tender, about 10 minutes. Meanwhile in a 3-quart saucepan, melt butter. Stir in flour. Add milk and water. Increase heat and cook, stirring constantly, until smooth and thickened. Add corn, beans, onion, pimiento, pepper, bay leaf, potatoes and broth. Simmer 15 minutes to blend flavors; remove bay leaf. Add cheese and eggs just before serving. (Six egg slices may be set aside and floated on top of each serving.) Season to taste with salt and pepper. Serve with assorted crisp bread.

*Makes about* 11 *cups—6 servings.*

# Seafood Chowder

½ pound frozen haddock
1/4 cup butter
1/4 cup chopped onion
1/3 cup chopped leek (white
  part only)
2 cups chicken stock
1 cup chopped celery
1 cup diced carrots
1 teaspoon salt
1/8 teaspoon pepper

2 bay leaves
1/4 teaspoon thyme
3 cups milk
1/3 cup flour
1 cup cream
1 6-ounce package frozen crab
  meat, thawed
1 7-ounce can (1 cup) clams
Parsley

Thaw haddock and cut in bite-size pieces. In large saucepan melt butter. Saute onion and leek. Add chicken stock, celery, carrots, salt, pepper, bay leaves, thyme and haddock. Simmer about 30 minutes, or until vegetables and fish are tender. Add 1 cup milk to flour to make a paste. Pour slowly into stock, stirring constantly. Add remaining 2 cups milk and cream. Continue stirring and cook slowly until thick. Stir in crab meat and clams. Serve in large soup bowls garnished with sprigs of parsley.

*6 to 8 servings.*

# Corn 'n' Crab Chowder

| | |
|---|---|
| 2 cups ¼-inch raw potato cubes | 2½ cups milk |
| ¾ cup thin onion slices | 2 17-ounce cans cream style |
| 1½ cups hot water | corn |
| 1½ teaspoons salt | 1 tablespoon minced parsley |
| 1 6½-ounce can crab meat | |

In 3-quart kettle, combine potatoes, onions, water and salt. Bring to boil; cover. Simmer about 10 minutes. Do not drain. Flake crab meat; remove bits of shell. Add crab meat, milk and corn. Simmer until piping hot. At serving time, sprinkle with parsley.                               *6 to 8 servings.*

# Hearty Winter Chowder

| | |
|---|---|
| 3 tablespoons chopped onion | ¼ teaspoon thyme |
| 1 10-ounce package frozen peas | 3 cups milk |
| and carrots, thawed | 1 10¼-ounce can frozen potato |
| ¼ cup butter, melted | soup, thawed |
| 2 tablespoons flour | ½ cup shredded Cheddar |
| 1 teaspoon salt | cheese |
| Dash pepper | 3 frankfurters, sliced diagonally |
| ¼ teaspoon sage | 2 tablespoons butter, melted |

In 2-quart saucepan, cook onion, peas and carrots in melted butter until tender. Remove vegetables and set aside. Blend flour and seasonings into butter. Gradually add 1 cup milk, stirring constantly; cook until mixture thickens. Add remaining milk, cooked vegetables, potato soup and cheese; stir until cheese melts. Brown frankfurter slices in melted butter. Stir all but 2 tablespoons of the slices into chowder. Serve hot; top with frankfurter slices for garnish. Chowder can be frozen.

*4 to 6 servings.*

# Tomato-Corn Chowder

| | |
|---|---|
| 2 slices bacon, diced | ⅛ teaspoon pepper |
| ¼ cup grated onion | 1 cup drained whole kernel corn |
| 2 cups cubed raw potatoes | 2 cups tomato juice |
| 1 cup cold water | ¼ cup flour |
| 1½ teaspoons salt | ½ cup milk |

Cook bacon and onion until bacon is crisp. Add potatoes, water and seasonings. Cover; simmer about 30 minutes or until potatoes are tender. Add corn, tomato juice, and flour which has been mixed with milk. Cook over low heat, stirring occasionally until thickened.                               *6 servings.*

# VEGETABLES

CREOLE LIMA BEANS
BEST EVER BAKED BEANS
HARVEST-STYLE GREEN
  BEANS
GREEN BEANS AMANDINE
GREEN BEANS AND
  MUSHROOMS
BUFFET GREEN BEANS WITH
  BLUE CHEESE
BEETS IN ORANGE SAUCE
GLAZED CARROT COINS
BAKED CARROT STICKS
CHIVE CORN
CORN CASSEROLE
CRISP-TOP CORN WITH
  HERBS
FROZEN PEAS CONTINENTAL
FRENCH PEAS
ARGANTE POTATOES

AU GRATIN POTATO BAKE
POTATOES AU GRATIN
BAKED CREAMED POTATOES
OVEN-BAKED POTATO
TWICE-BAKED POTATOES
CREAM CHEESE CHIVE
  SAUCE FOR BAKED
  POTATOES
SOUR CREAM BACON
  TOPPING FOR BAKED
  POTATOES
ROSEMARY POTATOES
PARMESAN POTATO STICKS
SWEET POTATO PUFFS
SPINACH SUPREME
HERB BAKED TOMATOES
BUTTERED ZUCCHINI
ZUCCHINI STRIPS

*Illustration:* Green Beans Amandine (page 152).

# Vegetables

Thanks to modern food technology, dozens of vegetables are available the year 'round in American markets. It's a wise home-maker who firmly makes a firm resolution to provide her family with a variety of these nourishing foods. There are literally hundreds of recipes for transforming vegetables into elegant dinner or luncheon fare. Here are some especially tempting examples.

## Creole Lima Beans

4 slices bacon, diced
¼ cup grated onion
2 tablespoons flour
½ teaspoon salt
¼ teaspoon pepper
½ teaspoon paprika

1 1-pound 4-ounce can (2½ cups) tomatoes
1 1-pound can (2 cups) lima beans, drained
1 bay leaf

Fry bacon until crisp; add onion and cook until lightly browned. Blend in flour and seasonings. Add tomatoes slowly; cook until thickened. Add lima beans and bay leaf; simmer about 20 minutes. Remove bay leaf.          6 *servings.*

[ 151 ]

# Best Ever Baked Beans

2 pounds navy beans
1 teaspoon baking soda
1 large onion, quartered
½ pound salt pork, sliced or
  cut in chunks
½ cup molasses

½ cup firmly packed brown
  sugar
1 tablespoon salt
2 teaspoons dry mustard
1 11- or 12-ounce bottle chili
  sauce
1 tablespoon mild vinegar

Cover beans with warm water; soak several hours or overnight. Drain; add fresh water to cover and baking soda. Bring to boiling; cook for 10 minutes; drain. Add fresh boiling water to cover and cook gently until skins on beans will crack when blown upon. Drain liquor and save. Pour beans into bean pot; bury onion in beans. Parboil salt pork about 5 minutes; drain and brown slightly. Bury some of pork in beans and arrange some on top. Blend remaining ingredients; pour half over beans; add enough of saved liquor to cover beans. Bake in 250° oven 3 to 4 hours, adding remaining sauce mixture at intervals and more of the liquor, or water as needed.          10 *to* 12 *servings.*

# Harvest-Style Green Beans

1 10-ounce package frozen
  green beans, French style
1 tablespoon butter
1 egg yolk

1 3-ounce package cream
  cheese, softened
1 tablespoon lemon juice
Paprika

Cook beans according to directions on package. Drain well; add butter. Blend egg yolk with cream cheese in small saucepan. Stir in lemon juice. Heat slowly, stirring constantly. Serve over hot beans; sprinkle with paprika. (If sauce thickens on standing, thin with cream.)          4 *servings.*

# Green Beans Amandine

2 1-pound cans French style
  green beans
¼ cup melted butter or
  margarine

½ cup slivered almonds
Spiced crab apples

Heat beans. Melt butter in 8-inch frying pan. Add almonds. Brown lightly 5 minutes. Drain beans. Top immediately with almonds. Garnish with crab apples.          6 *servings.*

# Green Beans and Mushrooms

1 10-ounce package frozen
green beans, French style
1 6-ounce can button
mushrooms

1 tablespoon mushroom
liquid
½ teaspoon salt
2 tablespoons butter

Partially thaw frozen beans until the block is easily separated. Drain mushrooms, reserving 1 tablespoon liquid. Place all ingredients in 1½-quart casserole; cover. Bake in 375° oven 30 minutes. *4 servings.*

# Buffet Green Beans with Blue Cheese

2 10-ounce packages frozen
green beans, French style
¼ cup butter or margarine
3 tablespoons flour
1½ cups milk

3 tablespoons crumbled blue
cheese
½ teaspoon salt
Dash pepper
½ cup soft bread crumbs

Cook beans according to directions on package. Drain. Melt 3 tablespoons butter in saucepan. Stir in flour. Add milk gradually, stirring constantly, until mixture thickens. Stir in blue cheese, salt and pepper. Reduce heat to very low and simmer 5 minutes. Combine sauce with beans. Pour into a 1-quart casserole. Melt remaining 1 tablespoon butter and mix with crumbs. Sprinkle crumbs over beans. Bake in 350° oven until bubbling at edges, about 25 minutes. *6 to 8 servings.*

# Beets in Orange Sauce

1 cup orange juice
⅓ cup seedless raisins
¾ teaspoon salt
¼ cup sugar
2 tablespoons cornstarch

2 tablespoons beet liquid,
drained from can
1 tablespoon lemon juice
1 tablespoon butter
1 1-pound can (2 cups) sliced
or diced red beets, drained

Combine orange juice with raisins; heat to boiling. Mix salt, sugar and cornstarch. Add beet liquid; stir to a smooth paste. Add to orange juice; cook stirring constantly, until thick and clear. Add lemon juice, butter and drained beets. Heat. *4 to 5 servings.*

# Glazed Carrot Coins

**6 medium carrots, cut in coins**
**½ teaspoon salt**
**½ cup water**
**3 tablespoons butter**
**3 tablespoons honey**

Add carrots and salt to water; cover pan tightly. Cook until tender, about 15 minutes; drain. Add butter and honey; heat to serving temperature. Glazed carrots may be placed in a 1-quart casserole and heated in 350° oven. *6 servings.*

# Baked Carrot Sticks

**8 to 10 large carrots**
**¼ cup water**
**½ teaspoon salt**
**¼ cup butter, melted**
**1 tablespoon lemon juice**
**¼ teaspoon salt**
**Dash pepper**

Cut carrots in thin sticks. Place in 1¼-quart casserole. Add water and ½ teaspoon salt. Cover tightly. Bake in 325° oven 1 hour or until tender. Combine remaining ingredients. Add to carrots. *8 servings.*

# Chive Corn

**1 17-ounce can (2 cups) whole kernel sweet corn**
**1 3-ounce package chive cream cheese**
**3 tablespoons cream**

Heat corn; drain thoroughly. Meanwhile slowly heat cream cheese and cream, stirring constantly until smooth. Pour sauce over corn in serving dish. *4 servings.*

# Corn Casserole

**2 10-ounce packages frozen whole kernel corn**
**2 tablespoons chopped pimiento**
**½ teaspoon salt**
**¼ cup butter**

Place frozen blocks of corn in 2-quart casserole. Sprinkle with pimiento and salt. Dot with butter. Cover tightly. Bake in 325° oven 55 to 60 minutes. Before serving, stir lightly to mix in pimiento, salt and butter. *6 to 8 servings.*

# Crisp-Top Corn with Herbs

5 tablespoons butter
1 cup ready-to-use herb
  seasoned stuffing

1 17-ounce can (2 cups) whole
  kernel corn
Parsley

Melt 4 tablespoons butter in skillet; add stuffing. Stir constantly over medium heat until butter is absorbed and dressing is crisp and lightly browned. Heat canned corn in its own liquid. Drain. Add remaining 1 tablespoon butter. Sprinkle stuffing generously over corn. Garnish with parsley. 4 *servings*.

# Frozen Peas Continental

3 bunches green onions
3 tablespoons butter, melted
4 teaspoons flour
1 cup light cream
¼ teaspoon salt
Dash pepper

3 10-ounce packages frozen
  green peas
2 tablespoons butter
¼ cup water
1 teaspoon salt
1 teaspoon sugar

Clean and cut onions in 1-inch lengths. Cook slowly in melted butter 3 to 4 minutes, stirring occasionally. Blend in flour; stir in cream. Cook until smooth and slightly thickened, stirring constantly. Add ¼ teaspoon salt and pepper. Ten minutes before serving time, drop frozen peas into saucepan with 2 tablespoons butter, water, 1 teaspoon salt and sugar. Cover, bring to boil quickly over high heat, reduce heat and simmer until peas are just tender, 5 to 7 minutes. Combine with hot cream sauce. Serve at once. 8 *to* 10 *servings*.

# French Peas

2 10-ounce packages frozen peas
3 tablespoons butter

½ teaspoon salt
1 very large lettuce leaf

Break blocks of peas by tapping on edge of table. Place in 10-inch skillet. Cut butter in 3 portions and add to peas. Sprinkle with salt. Dip lettuce in water; place over peas. Cover skillet tightly. Set over medium heat. Cook peas 8 to 10 minutes. Remove lettuce before serving. 8 *servings*.

# Argante Potatoes

3 large baking potatoes
¼ cup butter, melted
Salt
Pepper

1 cup shredded Swiss cheese
2 tablespoons grated Parmesan
cheese

Pare potatoes; halve lengthwise; then slice crosswise in ⅛-inch slices. Do not wash potatoes after slicing. Lay potatoes in 8- or 9-inch square pan with slices overlapping. Pour over butter. Season with salt and pepper. Bake in 500° oven 20 minutes. Remove from oven and sprinkle with Swiss cheese; then top with Parmesan cheese. Bake another 5 to 7 minutes until cheese is melted and slightly browned. 6 *servings.*

# Au Gratin Potato Bake

2 medium potatoes
1 large onion
Salt
Pepper
¼ pound thinly sliced Swiss
cheese

Prepared mustard
½ cup dry white wine
¼ cup fine bread crumbs
¼ cup grated Parmesan
cheese
¼ cup butter or margarine

Pare potatoes; cut in very thin slices. Peel onion and cut in thin slices. Arrange layer of potatoes in bottom of well greased baking dish. Sprinkle with salt and pepper. Top the layer of potatoes with slices of cheese. Spread mustard lightly over cheese. Put a layer of onion slices on top of cheese. Repeat these layers until the dish is full; press down. Pour wine over all. Sprinkle bread crumbs and Parmesan cheese over top. Dot with butter; cover. Bake in 350° oven 20 minutes. Remove cover and bake 15 or 20 minutes longer. 4 *servings.*

# Potatoes Au Gratin

6 cups sliced potatoes
1 10½-ounce can cream of
mushroom soup
½ cup milk

1 cup shredded sharp Cheddar
cheese
Dash salt
Dash pepper

Cook potatoes in boiling, salted water 6 to 8 minutes or until slightly tender. Combine soup, milk and cheese. In a greased baking dish, alternate layers of potatoes and soup mixture. Season potato layers with salt and pepper. Bake in 350° oven 30 minutes or until potatoes are fork-tender. 8 *servings.*

# Baked Creamed Potatoes

8 medium potatoes, cooked
½ cup diced green pepper
¼ cup butter or margarine
¼ cup flour

1½ teaspoons salt
3 cups milk
4 teaspoons prepared
   horseradish

Slice potatoes into 2-quart casserole in layers, sprinkling each layer with green pepper. Melt butter in saucepan; stir in flour and salt; cook until bubbly. Add milk. Cook, stirring constantly, until mixture thickens; reduce heat and cook 5 minutes. Stir in horseradish. Add to potatoes. Cover casserole. Bake in 325° oven 30 minutes.      8 *servings.*

# Oven-Baked Potatoes

6 medium potatoes
½ cup butter, melted
½ teaspoon salt

Dash pepper
Paprika

Pare potatoes. Put into shallow pan. Pour melted butter over the potatoes. Sprinkle with seasonings. Bake in 350° oven about 1 hour, or until done. Turn occasionally during baking.

     6 *servings.*

# Twice-Baked Potatoes

6 large baking potatoes
Butter or margarine for
   potato skins
½ cup dairy sour cream
3 tablespoons butter or
   margarine
1 egg, well beaten

1 tablespoon chopped spring
   onions
2 slices crisp bacon, crumbled
Salt
Pepper
Grated Parmesan cheese

Rub potatoes with butter and prick skins with fork. Bake in 400° oven until done, about 45 minutes. Cut each potato in half lengthwise and carefully scoop out the potato, setting shells to one side. Mash potatoes while hot with sour cream, 3 tablespoons butter and egg. Beat until fluffy. Stir in onions and bacon. Season with salt and pepper. Spread the shells with butter. Pile mashed potatoes lightly and high into them. Sprinkle with Parmesan cheese. Bake in 350° oven until brown on top. 6 *servings.*

# Cream Cheese Chive Sauce
# for Baked Potatoes

⅓ cup cream
1 8-ounce package cream cheese
1 tablespoon chopped chives
1½ teaspoons lemon juice

½ teaspoon garlic salt
4 to 6 hot baked potatoes
Parsley

Add cream to cream cheese gradually, blending until smooth. Add chives, lemon juice and garlic salt. Mix well. Serve over baked potatoes. Garnish with parsley.           *4 to 6 servings.*

Note: For a thinner sauce, add a little more cream.

# Sour Cream Bacon Topping
# for Baked Potatoes

½ teaspoon salt
1 tablespoon onion juice
Dash pepper

½ teaspoon Worcestershire
  sauce
1 cup dairy sour cream
4 slices crisp bacon, crumbled

Add seasonings to sour cream; mix well. Serve on baked potatoes. Sprinkle with crumbled bacon.

*Makes 1 cup topping, enough for 6 to 8 medium potatoes.*

# Rosemary Potatoes

2 14½-ounce cans small white
  potatoes
¼ cup salad oil

1 teaspoon salt
1 teaspoon rosemary leaves

Drain and cut potatoes in half. Spread in a shallow baking pan, 13 x 9½ x 2 inches. Pour oil over potatoes and sprinkle with salt and rosemary. Broil 2 or 3 inches from heat until lightly browned, about 15 minutes, stirring frequently. *5 to 6 servings.*

# Parmesan Potato Sticks

2 9-ounce packages frozen
  French fries
¼ cup butter, melted

1 teaspoon onion salt
Paprika
½ cup grated Parmesan cheese

Arrange frozen French fries in a single layer in buttered shallow baking pan. Brush with melted butter and sprinkle with onion salt and paprika. Bake in 425° oven 20 to 25 minutes. Remove from oven; sprinkle with Parmesan cheese, shaking pan so potatoes are evenly coated. Serve immediately.           *6 servings.*

# Sweet Potato Puffs

6 medium sweet potatoes,
  pared
1 teaspoon salt

2 tablespoons butter
1 egg, slightly beaten

Cover potatoes with boiling water. Add salt; cook until tender, 25 to 30 minutes. Drain. Add butter; mash. Chill mixture. Stir in egg. Drop by spoonfuls on lightly greased baking sheet. Bake in 375° oven 15 minutes. Puffs may be prepared for oven ahead of time. *6 servings.*

# Spinach Supreme

2 10-ounce packages frozen
  chopped spinach

1 10½-ounce can condensed
  cream of mushroom soup
¼ cup sherry
1 can French fried onion rings

Cut each frozen spinach block into about 12 pieces. Combine with soup (undiluted) and sherry. Spoon into a 1½-quart casserole. Sprinkle onion rings over top. Bake in 350° oven 20 to 30 minutes or until thoroughly heated. *6 servings.*

# Herb Baked Tomatoes

2 large tomatoes
2 tablespoons butter or
  margarine
¼ teaspoon pepper
¼ teaspoon rosemary

¼ teaspoon thyme
⅛ teaspoon oregano
½ teaspoon salt
¼ teaspoon sugar

Cut core from end of tomatoes and slice in half. Place tomato halves in shallow baking pan, cut side up. Make slight depression in the center of each half and place a dot of butter in it. Combine remaining ingredients and sprinkle over tomatoes. Bake in 300° oven 30 minutes. *4 servings.*

# Buttered Zucchini

2 pounds zucchini
¼ cup butter
1 or 2 cloves garlic

Salt
Pepper

Wash zucchini; cut in ½-inch slices. Soak in cold water 15 to 20 minutes. Cook slowly in butter with garlic. Turn occasionally during cooking to brown lightly all over. Cook until just soft; remove garlic. Season with salt and pepper. Serve at once.

*6 servings.*

# Zucchini Strips

1½ pounds zucchini  
1½ tablespoons olive oil  

¾ teaspoon salt  
¼ teaspoon pepper  

Parboil whole zucchini about 10 minutes. Cut in 2-inch strips about the thickness of a pencil. Heat oil in skillet; add zucchini strips, salt and pepper. Cook until tender, about 5 minutes, stirring occasionally.                                    6 *servings.*

# OVER-THE-COALS COOKERY

FRANKFURTERS IN HERBED BUNS

DILLY BARBECUED CHICKEN

BARBECUED RIBS

CHARCOAL GRILLED STEAK

SKEWERED FISH STEAKS

FLANK STEAK PINWHEELS

OLD-FASHIONED HAMBURGERS

GRILLED FRENCH TOAST WITH BACON

GRILLED LIVER WITH BACON, ONIONS AND TOMATOES

GRILLED BACON AND EGG SANDWICHES

CAMPFIRE PICNIC BUNS

GRILLED POTATOES

ROASTED POTATOES

BAKED POTATOES WITH CHEESE

CORN ON THE COB

CHEESE TOMATOES

GRILLED ROQUEFORT TOMATOES

CURRY BUTTERED BREAD

HERB BUTTERED BREAD IN FOIL

POPPY SEED BREAD

ANGELS ON WINGS

HEATED FRUIT PIE

*Illustration:* Charcoal Grilled Steak (page 163).

# Over-the-coals COOKERY

More and more American backyards are giving evidence that the man of the house has succumbed to the gentle nudge of his family to cook out-of-doors . . . at least once in a while. The conviviality that accompanies the cooking and eating out in the fresh air is hard to match elsewhere. A variety of dishes lend themselves to cooking over the coals. Add some of these to your repertoire along with the traditional family favorites.

## Frankfurters in Herbed Buns

1 pound frankfurters
½ cup butter or margarine
½ teaspoon rubbed sage

3 green onions, finely chopped
10 frankfurters buns, split

Place franks on open grill over hot coals. Turn to brown evenly. Blend butter, sage and green onions thoroughly. Spread on buns and place split side down on grill and toast lightly. Serve hot franks in toasted buns. 10 *servings.*

# Dilly Barbecued Chicken

½ cup butter
2 teaspoons salt
1 teaspoon paprika
2 teaspoons dill weed

2 1½- to 2½-pound broiler-fryer
chickens, cut in halves or
quarters

To make sauce, melt butter in saucepan. Add salt, paprika and dill weed; blend well.

To prepare chicken for grilling, break joints by bending (do not cut). Break joints between drumstick and thigh, where thigh joins body, and where wing is attached to breast. Pull leg and wing close to body and use skewers to hold in place. Brush chicken generously with sauce before and during cooking. Grill over hot coals 50 to 60 minutes or until well done, turning frequently. To test for doneness, cut slash in thigh next to bone. There should be no trace of pink. *4 servings.*

# Barbecued Ribs

2 to 3 sides pork spareribs
BARBECUE SAUCE:
1 cup chopped green onion
2 tablespoons butter or
  margarine
2 teaspoons paprika
½ teaspoon pepper
Dash cayenne pepper

2 tablespoons brown sugar
1 tablespoon dry mustard
2 tablespoons Worcestershire
  sauce
⅛ teaspoon Tabasco
½ cup catsup
2 tablespoons vinegar

Simmer spareribs in small amount of water in heavy covered kettle for about 1 hour. Refrigerate until ready to grill. Cut ribs into serving pieces, 2 or 3 rib portions. Grill over glowing coals, brushing with barbecue sauce and turning frequently until tender, about 15 minutes. For brushing on the barbecue sauce, use a long-handled brush or a "swab" made by tying a soft cloth on the end of a long-handled fork.

Barbecue Sauce: Cook green onion in butter until tender, about 5 minutes. Add remaining ingredients. Simmer about 10 minutes, stirring frequently. This is a thick sauce and keeps well in a covered jar in refrigerator. *4 servings.*

Note: If the spareribs are barbecued without the precooking, they will take about an hour. Simmering them first is preferred; they're more moist and better flavored and even in 15 minutes get a zesty barbecue coating. Cooking time is approximate, varying with heat of charcoal and distance of meat from heat.

# Charcoal Grilled Steak

| | |
|---|---|
| 1 Porterhouse steak, 1½ inches thick | Pepper |
| | Garlic salt, optional |
| Salt | Butter |

Slash fat edge of steak at 2-inch intervals. Top off white ash from coals to increase heat. Place steak on grill over hot coals. Grill 8 to 10 minutes on first side; season. Turn. Grill 6 to 8 minutes on second side for medium rare. Season. Top with butter just before serving. Allow ¾ pound of uncooked beef per serving.

# Skewered Fish Steaks

| | |
|---|---|
| 1 pound fish steaks, fresh or frozen, cut in 1½-inch squares | 2 green or red peppers, cut in 8 1½-inch squares |
| ¼ cup French dressing | 1 16- to 17-ounce can (2 cups) onions |

Marinate fish squares in French dressing in refrigerator at least 1 hour. Alternate fish with vegetables on 4 skewers. Grill over hot coals about 20 minutes; baste with French dressing once or twice. Cook on rotisserie or broil skewered fish for indoor cooking.                                                        4 *servings.*

# Flank Steak Pinwheels

| | |
|---|---|
| 2½-pound flank steak | 1 tablespoon Worcestershire sauce |
| Salt | 1 tablespoon brown sugar |
| Pepper | 1 teaspoon dry mustard |
| BARBECUE SAUCE: | 4 drops Tabasco |
| ½ cup catsup | |
| 2 tablespoons chopped onion | |

Diagonally score flank steaks on both sides, forming diamond-shaped pattern in meat. Brush barbecue sauce on top of steaks. Starting at side, roll each steak jelly-roll fashion, fastening at 1 inch intervals with metal skewers. Slice between skewers. Grill "pinwheels" 4 to 5 inches from glowing coals. Grill on one side about 10 minutes; turn and season with salt and pepper. Brush barbecue sauce on top of pinwheels. Grill second side 5 to 6 minutes for rare, about 10 minutes for medium and about 15 minutes for well done.

**Barbecue Sauce:** Combine catsup and remaining ingredients.

8 *servings.*

# Old-Fashioned Hamburgers

1 pound ground beef
2 tablespoons chopped onion
1 teaspoon salt

1 teaspoon Worcestershire
  sauce
1 tablespoon prepared mustard
4 sandwich buns

Mix together ground beef, onion, salt, Worcestershire sauce and mustard. Form into 4 hamburger patties about ½ to ¾ inch thick. Grill over hot coals until done the way you like it. Serve on warm, split and toasted sandwich buns.     *4 servings.*

# Grilled French Toast with Bacon

2 eggs, slightly beaten
⅔ cup milk
½ teaspoon salt
Dash pepper

12 slices bread
12 slices bacon, cut in half
  crosswise
Maple syrup

Combine eggs, milk, salt and pepper in a shallow pie pan. Quickly dip each slice of bread into egg mixture, turning them to coat both sides. Place in a long-handled, hinged wire broiler or toaster and top with 2 half slices of bacon, side by side. Brown both sides of bread over hot coals, toasting the side with bacon last. Serve hot with maple syrup.     *6 servings.*

# Grilled Liver with
# Bacon, Onions and Tomatoes

1¼ pounds calf liver, ½ inch
  thick
2 large Spanish onions
Melted butter

Cooking oil
8 slices bacon
2 or 3 tomatoes

Wash liver; dry on paper towels. Peel onions; slice ½ inch thick. Brush with melted butter. Coat grill with cooking oil. Place liver and onion on grill; cook 5 minutes. Cook bacon on grill 2 minutes. Turn liver and onions; place bacon on liver. Add sliced or quartered unpeeled tomatoes to grill. Cook all 5 minutes.

*4 servings.*

# Grilled Bacon and Egg Sandwiches

8 slices bread
1⅓ tablespoons soft butter or
  margarine
4 hard cooked eggs, sliced
Salt

Pepper
4 slices bacon, cut in half
  crosswise

Butter bread. Arrange sliced eggs on half the bread slices. Sprinkle with salt and pepper. Top with remaining bread slices, butter side down. Place sandwiches in a long-handled, hinged wire broiler or toaster and top with 2 half slices of bacon, side by side. Brown both sides of sandwiches over hot coals, leaving the side with bacon until last. Serve hot.     *4 servings.*

# Campfire Picnic Buns

1 6-ounce package sliced
  bologna
2 cups shredded sharp Cheddar
  cheese
2 teaspoons grated onion

¼ cup pickle relish
1 tablespoon prepared mustard
¼ cup mayonnaise
8 frankfurter buns

Slice bologna in very thin strips. Add cheese, onion, relish, mustard and mayonnaise. Cut buns in half and fill with meat mixture. Wrap each bun in aluminum foil. Heat over hot coals 20 minutes until cheese melts and buns are hot. Serve hot.

    *8 servings.*

# Grilled Potatoes

4 medium potatoes
2 tablespoons coarsely chopped
  onion
Dash salt

Dash pepper
2 tablespoons butter
Shredded cheese

Pare potatoes; slice thin. Place on a large square of heavy duty aluminum foil. Add onion; season with salt and pepper. Dot with butter. Sprinkle with shredded cheese. Seal foil securely. Cook on grill about one hour, turning once.     *4 servings.*

# Roasted Potatoes

**6 baking potatoes**

Insert prongs of a fork once into each potato. Tightly wrap each potato in foil. Place on grill over hot coals, turn frequently during 1½ hours of baking.                              6 *servings.*

# Baked Potatoes with Cheese

**4 medium baking potatoes**          **Salt**
**Cheese spread**

Scrub potatoes; pierce skins all around with fork. Cut in half lengthwise; scoop out heaping tablespoon of raw potato from each half and fill cavity with cheese spread. Sprinkle with salt, put halves together; wrap each securely in heavy duty aluminum foil. Bake over hot coals 1½ hours, turning several times.

4 *servings.*

# Corn on the Cob

Open outer covering of corn to remove silk. Dip corn in water; replace husks. Wrap corn in foil. Cook on grill or in coals 20 to 30 minutes, turning occasionally.

# Cheese Tomatoes

**4 medium tomatoes, washed**          **¼ cup shredded sharp Cheddar**
**   and cut in half**                            **cheese**

Use shallow foil trays or make trays from aluminum foil. Place tomatoes, cut side up, in tray; sprinkle with cheese. Heat on grill 10 minutes.                                    4 *servings.*

# Grilled Roquefort Tomatoes

**3 large tomatoes**                    **3 teaspoons Roquefort OR**
**                                          blue cheese spread**

Cut tomatoes in half crosswise and place each half in center of a square of heavy aluminum foil. Spread ½ teaspoon cheese spread over cut surfaces. Seal foil securely and grill over hot coals for about 5 minutes.                          6 *servings.*

# Curry Buttered Bread

½ cup soft butter               1 1-pound loaf French bread
½ teaspoon curry powder

Blend butter and curry powder. Cut loaf of bread into thick diagonal slices, leaving attached at bottom. Spread with seasoned butter. Wrap loaf in foil. Place in slow oven or over low coals for 5 to 10 minutes or until heated through. Serve from foil.

*6 to 8 servings.*

# Herb Buttered Bread in Foil

1 clove garlic, cut in half       1 teaspoon snipped fresh thyme
½ cup butter or margarine       or pinch of dried whole thyme
2 tablespoons snipped parsley   1 1-pound loaf sliced white
                                   bread

Rub small skillet with cut side of garlic and remove garlic. (If strong garlic flavor is desired, slice and mash garlic clove to a juicy pulp in the skillet.) Add and melt butter. Stir in herbs. Brush each slice of bread with mixture and put back together into original loaf shape. Wrap tightly in foil. Place on grate near the edge where heat is not intense. Turn from side to side to heat evenly. Allow about 30 minutes for thorough heating. Turn foil down from top to form a basket and serve hot.

*Makes 1 loaf herb buttered bread.*

Note: For oven heating allow about 15 minutes in 425° oven.

# Poppy Seed Bread

1 small loaf unsliced white     Melted butter OR
   bread                         garlic butter
                                 Poppy seeds

Cut bread in half lengthwise, almost through to bottom, then crosswise to make eight pieces. Place on double thickness of heavy duty aluminum foil. Brush all cut and outside surfaces with melted butter or garlic butter. Sprinkle top and sides with poppy seeds. Wrap securely in foil. Place on grill 20 to 30 minutes turning occasionally to warm. To serve, pull sections apart.

*4 servings.*

Note: For garlic butter, mix 1 teaspoon garlic salt or 3 or 4 peeled and crushed cloves of garlic with ½ cup butter. Remove crushed garlic before spreading butter on bread.

# Angels on Wings

**12 ⅜-inch slices loaf angel food cake**
**12 marshmallows**

**6 ⅞-ounce milk chocolate bars without nuts, cut in 2-inch squares**

Using a long-handled wire grill, fork or skewer, hold cake slices over coals until toasted on both sides. Toast marshmallows over coals. For each serving, place a square of chocolate on each hot cake slice. Top with 2 hot marshmallows, then place another square of chocolate and another toasted cake slice on top. Press cake slices together.                    *6 servings.*

# Heated Fruit Pie

**1 baked fruit pie**

Overwrap fruit pie in foil. Heat at side of grill where heat is not too intense for 30 minutes.                    *6 servings.*

# QUANTITY COOKERY FOR FIFTY

## MENUS

### MAIN DISHES
Super Swiss Steak
Applesauce Meat Balls
Ham Slices with Orange-Cherry
    Sauce
Barbecued Meat Balls
Veal Lasagna
Macaroni and Cheese

### SALADS
Hot Potato Salad
Tossed Green Salad
Emerald Salad
Wedding Ring Mold
Saucy Blue Cheese Dressing

### BREAD
Barbecued Bread

### DESSERTS
Apple Spice Crumble
Cherry Bubble
Meringues and Peppermint Stick
    Ice Cream with Mocha Sauce
Bridal Cake-Butter Cream Frosting

### BEVERAGES
Nuptial Nectar
Canned Fruit Juice Punch
Orange Sherbet Punch
Reception Chocolate
Coffee
Tea

Meat and Poultry Buying Guide
    and timetable for roasting meat
    quantities for 50 servings.

*Illustrations:* Bridal Cake (page 178), Nuptial Nectar (page 178).

# Quantity Cookery
# for Fifty

You'll rejoice in this section when you are asked to be one of the home-style caterers for the church group or other large gathering. Recipes to implement the menu ideas are included. All "carry" well and are planned to please . . . whatever the age group.

# Feeding a Crowd

### BUFFET DINNERS

**Super Swiss Steak***

Potatoes Au Gratin                    **Buttered Peas and Mushrooms**

**Emerald Salad***

Hot Rolls                                     **Butter**

**Fruit Compote**

**Assorted Cookies**

Coffee*                                       Tea*


**Cold Platter of Sliced Turkey, Salami, Virginia Ham, Cheese**

Crisp Relishes          **Sliced Tomatoes on Bed of Romaine, Dressing**

**Hot Potato Salad***

**Applesauce Meat Balls***

**Punch Bowl Filled with Fresh Fruits in Own Juices**
**(In summer, peaches, pears, sliced oranges, grapefruit, berries,
melon, sweet cherries, bananas, etc. In winter, use some canned
fruit.)**

**Pear Seafoam Salad**

**Barbecued Bread***

**Apple Spice Crumble***

**Coffee***

For the cold platter, buy prepared foods, ready sliced, if you can.
Most of the menu may be prepared a day ahead of time. Don't
put mixture of fresh fruit together more than two hours before
serving.

* Asterisks indicate recipes are included in this book.

## CHURCH SUPPERS

Barbecued Meat Balls*
on
Fluffy Rice

Tossed Green Salad*          French Dressing

Crusty French Bread

Cherry Bubble*

Coffee*


Veal Lasagna*
or
Macaroni and Cheese*

Crisp Green Salad with Oil and Vinegar Dressing

Carrot and Celery Sticks          Black and Green Olives

Bread Sticks and/or Garlic Bread                    Butter

Vanilla Ice Cream or Pineapple Ice

Coffee*          Tea*          Milk


## WEDDING BUFFET

Ham Slices with Orange-Cherry Sauce*

Wedding Ring Mold*

Saucy Blue Cheese Dressing*

Buttered Corn          Relishes and Jelly

Buttered Hot Rolls

Meringues and Peppermint Stick Ice Cream with Mocha Sauce*

Coffee*

\* Asterisks indicate recipes are included in this book.

# Super Swiss Steak

16 pounds round or flank steak
5 tablespoons salt
1 teaspoon pepper
3½ cups flour
1¼ cups shortening

10 onions, sliced
10 carrots, sliced
1 quart diced celery
3 1-pound 12-ounce cans
(10½ cups) tomatoes

Cut steak into 48 portions of about 5 ounces each. Combine salt, pepper and flour. Pound flour mixture well into each side of steak. Brown in hot, melted fat. Add onions, carrots, celery and tomatoes. Cover lightly. Bake in 350° oven 2½ to 3 hours.

*48 servings.*

# Applesauce Meat Balls

7 pounds ground beef
3 pounds ground veal
3 pounds ground pork
6 cups dry bread crumbs
6 cups unsweetened applesauce
1 dozen eggs
6 large onions, chopped
2 teaspoons mace
1½ teaspoons allspice
¼ cup salt

3 tablespoons monosodium
 glutamate
Shortening or butter for
 browning
GRAVY:
2¼ cups flour
½ pound butter
1½ gallons well seasoned
 chicken stock (canned broth
 is good)
1½ tablespoons parsley flakes

Combine ingredients for meat balls. Chill and shape into small balls. Brown all around in shortening or butter. Add to hot gravy and simmer 30 minutes. Freeze these ahead, to save time, or make them a day early.

Gravy: Blend flour into butter melted in saucepan. Add chicken stock and parsley flakes. Cook and stir until thickened.

*48 or more servings.*

# Ham Slices with Orange-Cherry Sauce

1 13-pound round boneless
 ham, fully cooked
2 16- to 17-ounce cans (4 cups)
 pitted tart red cherries
2 cups orange juice
3 tablespoons lemon juice
3 tablespoons cornstarch

½ cup firmly packed brown
 sugar
1 tablespoon grated orange peel
1 teaspoon cinnamon
1 teaspoon whole cloves
⅛ teaspoon salt

Slice ham in 50 slices. Drain syrup from cherries; mix with orange and lemon juices. Gradually add juices to cornstarch in saucepan; add remaining ingredients, except cherries. Cook until sauce is thickened, stirring constantly. Stir in cherries. Pour sauce, hot or cold, over cold ham slices and serve. Makes about 4 cups sauce.

*50 servings.*

# Barbecued Meat Balls

**MEAT BALLS:**
8 pounds ground beef
1 pound (6 cups) instant nonfat
  dry milk
1 quart (4 cups) water
1¼ pounds (2½ quarts) soft
  bread crumbs
1¼ cups (6) eggs, beaten
1½ tablespoons salt
¾ teaspoon pepper
2½ teaspoons monosodium
  glutamate

**BARBECUE SAUCE:**
1 lemon, sliced
4 medium onions, chopped
1½ tablespoons chili powder
¼ cup celery seed
1 cup firmly packed brown
  sugar
1 cup vinegar
3 tablespoons Worcestershire
  sauce
1 teaspoon Tabasco
1 quart (4 cups) catsup
1½ quarts (6 cups) hot water

**Meat Balls:** Mix together ingredients for meat balls. Shape into about 100 meat balls. Place in shallow baking pan, 17 x 26 inches.

**Barbecue Sauce:** Thoroughly mix sauce ingredients. Pour sauce over meat balls. Bake in 325° oven 1 hour and 20 minutes.

*48 servings.*

# Veal Lasagna
# (Veal with Wide Noodles)

**TOMATO SAUCE:**
2 quarts tomato puree
2 6½-pound cans (6 quarts)
  solid pack canned tomatoes
1 quart tomato paste
2 tablespoons oregano
Salt
Pepper

**VEAL:**
10 ounces or 1 quart
  mushrooms, sliced
½ cup butter or margarine
2 quarts cooked, cubed veal
5 pounds uncooked lasagna
  noodles
4 tablespoons cooking oil
10 pounds Mozzarella cheese,
  sliced
2 cups grated Parmesan cheese

**Tomato Sauce:** Combine ingredients for sauce. Cook until mixture has consistency of a medium white sauce.

**Veal:** Cook mushrooms in butter until lightly browned. Add veal and mushrooms to tomato sauce. Cook noodles in boiling salted water 10 minutes. Drain. Grease two baking pans, 12 x 20 x 2 inches, with cooking oil. Put a thin layer of tomato sauce in bottom of pans. Top with a layer of cooked noodles. Add a layer of Mozzarella cheese. Sprinkle with Parmesan cheese. Repeat layers until all ingredients are used, beginning with tomato sauce and ending with Parmesan cheese. Bake in 375° oven 10 minutes, then reduce heat to 350° and bake 20 minutes. *50 servings.*

# Macaroni and Cheese

**CHEESE SAUCE:**
1 pound (2 cups) butter
8 ounces (2 cups) flour, sifted
1½ gallons milk, scalded
2 tablespoons salt
1 pound sharp Cheddar cheese,
  shredded

**MACARONI:**
4 pounds 4 ounces uncooked
  macaroni
3 pounds 2 ounces sharp
  Cheddar cheese, shredded

**Cheese Sauce:** Melt butter; add flour and mix until smooth. Cook 5 minutes, but do not brown. Gradually add scalded milk, stirring constantly. Add salt. Cook until thickened, about 15 minutes. Add cheese and stir with wire whip until cheese is melted and sauce is smooth.

**Macaroni:** Cook macaroni in boiling salted water until tender. Drain. Add macaroni to Cheese Sauce and blend well. Place 7 ounces (⅞ cup) of mixture in each greased shallow casserole dish. Sprinkle 1 ounce shredded cheese over the top of each. Bake in 350° oven about 10 minutes. Remove from oven and place under preheated broiler until cheese is a delicate brown.

*50 servings.*

# Hot Potato Salad

1 cup finely chopped onions
2 1-pint bottles Italian dressing
4 teaspoons salt
2 teaspoons pepper

2½ gallons cooked sliced
  potatoes
2½ cups crisp crumbled cooked
  bacon
Lettuce to line salad bowl

Simmer onions in dressing 5 minutes; add salt and pepper. Pour over potatoes and bacon. Mix lightly. Heat in baking pans in 350° oven 20 minutes.

*48 servings.*

# Tossed Green Salad

3 heads endive
3 medium heads lettuce
3 cups diced celery
3 cups diced green pepper
1 bunch carrots, shredded
3 cups French dressing

1 tablespoon salt
1 dozen tomatoes, cut in
  wedges
3 bunches radishes, sliced or
  made into roses

Wash endive and lettuce; drain well. Place in vegetable drawer of refrigerator to chill. Break crisp greens into salad bowls; add celery, green pepper and carrots. Toss lightly together with dressing and salt. Garnish with tomatoes and sliced radishes or radish roses.

*48 servings.*

# Meringues and Peppermint Stick Ice Cream with Mocha Sauce

**MERINGUES:**
6 egg whites
½ teaspoon salt
2½ cups sugar
2 teaspoons vinegar
1 teaspoon vanilla
Slivered almonds OR
  Silver decorettes

**MOCHA SAUCE:**
3 cups sugar
6 tablespoons cocoa
6 tablespoons instant coffee
6 tablespoons cornstarch
6 cups water
1½ cups butter

**Meringues:** Beat egg whites until frothy; add salt and continue beating until mixture will stand in soft peaks. Add sugar, a tablespoon at a time, alternately with vinegar, beating well after each addition. Continue beating after all sugar has been added until meringue will stand in stiff peaks. Beat in vanilla. Line 2 cooky sheets with heavy unglazed paper. Spoon meringue onto paper in 25 small mounds; make an indentation in center of each with back of spoon; spread to a circle about 3 inches in diameter. Sprinkle edges with slivered almonds or silver decorettes. Bake in 275° oven for about 1 hour or until crisp and lightly browned. Cool before removing from paper. Makes 25 meringues. To serve, fill with a scoop of Peppermint Stick Ice Cream and top with Mocha Sauce.

**Mocha Sauce:** Mix together sugar, cocoa, instant coffee and cornstarch; gradually add water. Cook over low heat until thickened, stirring constantly. Stir in butter until melted. Cool. Makes about 1½ quarts sauce. *50 servings.*

Note: Make Meringue recipe twice to serve 50, unless you have adequate oven space to bake all 50 at once.

For 50 servings you will need 8 quarts (2 gallons) peppermint stick ice cream.

# Butter Cream Frosting

1 pound butter
6 cups sifted confectioners'
  sugar
6 egg whites

2 teaspoons almond extract
Red food coloring
Green food coloring

Cream butter and sugar until light and creamy. Slowly add egg whites. Beat until light and creamy; add extract. Makes enough frosting for 4-tier wedding cake and tinted decorations. To decorate, tint remaining frosting light pink and light green and make tiny rosettes and green stems with leaves.

# Bridal Cake

3/4 cup butter
1 3/4 cups sugar
3 1/2 cups sifted cake flour
3 1/2 teaspoons double action
   baking powder
1/2 teaspoon salt

1 cup milk
1 teaspoon lemon extract
1 teaspoon vanilla
6 egg whites, beaten stiff
Butter Cream Frosting

Cream butter. Add sugar; cream until light and fluffy. Sift together three times flour, baking powder and salt. Add to creamed mixture alternately with milk and flavorings, adding dry ingredients first and last. Fold in egg whites. Turn into greased and floured pan. Bake according to chart below. Frost with Butter Cream Frosting.

| Size of Pan | Depth | Temperature and Time |
|---|---|---|
| 6 inches | 2 inches | 350° for 25 minutes, then increase heat to 375° for 10 minutes. |
| 8 inches | 2 inches | 350° for 25 minutes, then increase heat to 375° for 15 minutes. |
| 10 inches | 2 inches | 325° for 25 minutes, then increase heat to 350° for 25 minutes. |
| 12 inches | 2 inches | 325° for 30 minutes, then increase heat to 350° for 20 minutes. |

One full recipe makes 1 12-inch layer (8 cups batter). One and one-half of the recipe makes 1 10-inch layer (6 cups batter), 1 8-inch layer (4 cups batter) and 1 6-inch layer (2 cups batter).

# Nuptial Nectar

5 cups sugar
5 cups water
5 cups grape juice

2 1/2 cups orange juice
5 quarts chilled ginger ale
6 pints lemon sherbet

Boil together sugar, water, grape juice and orange juice for 2 minutes. Chill thoroughly. To serve, pour 1/2 of fruit juice in punch bowl. Add 1/2 of ginger ale and top with 3 pints of lemon sherbet. Refill with remaining ingredients.     *75 servings.*

# Canned Fruit Juice Punch

1 cup sugar
2 cups water
2 46-ounce cans (11 1/2 cups)
   orange juice
1 46-ounce can (5 3/4 cups)
   pineapple juice

2 1-pint 2-ounce cans (5 cups)
   apricot nectar
1 1/2 cups lemon juice (about
   5 medium lemons)
1 quart ice water

Mix sugar and 2 cups water; bring to boil. Chill. Combine with chilled canned juices, lemon juice and ice water.

*Makes 50 servings of about 1/2 cup each.*

# Orange Sherbet Punch

| | |
|---|---|
| 3 cups boiling water | 1½ cups lemon juice |
| 4 tablespoons tea | 1½ cups pineapple juice |
| 2¼ cups sugar | 3 quarts ginger ale OR ice water |
| 6 cups orange juice | 3 pints orange sherbet |

Steep tea in boiling water 5 minutes; strain. Dissolve sugar in hot tea; cool. Just before serving add chilled fruit juices. Pour into punch bowl; add ginger ale or ice water. Float orange sherbet on top. *Makes 50 small glasses punch.*

# Reception Chocolate

| | |
|---|---|
| 9 squares (9 ounces) | Dash salt |
| unsweetened chocolate | 2 cups whipping cream, |
| 2 cups water | whipped |
| 2 cups sugar | 6 quarts milk |

Add chocolate to water and place over low heat, stirring until chocolate is blended. Add sugar and salt; cook 4 minutes, stirring constantly. Cool. Fold in whipped cream. Place 1 rounding teaspoon of chocolate mixture in each cup; add about ½ cup hot milk. *Makes 50 cups chocolate.*

# Coffee

1 pound coffee (medium grind)    2½ gallons cold water

Tie coffee loosely in double thickness cheese cloth or muslin bag, allowing space for coffee to expand. Heat water to boiling. Place coffee bag into boiling water. Cover kettle and let stand over low heat about 10 minutes or until coffee is as strong as desired. Remove coffee bag before serving. Do not allow coffee to boil. *Makes 50 cups coffee.*

# Tea

1 cup tea    2½ gallons cold water

Tie tea loosely in cheese cloth bag. Heat water to boiling. Add tea to freshly boiling water. Turn off heat. Let steep 3 to 5 minutes. Remove tea bag. Serve at once. *Makes 50 cups tea.*

# Quantity Roasting Guide *(50 servings)*

ROAST MEAT

Place roast(s), fat side up, on rack in an open roasting pan. If roast has bone which forms a natural rack, no rack is necessary. Allow space between roasts. Do not stack roasts on top of each other. If more than one roast is being cooked in the same oven, thermometer is placed in smallest roast. When roast is done, it is removed and thermometer inserted into the roast next in size. This procedure is repeated until all roasts are done. Do not add water; do not cover. Place in a preheated oven. Follow time and temperature chart below:

| Cut | Approximate Weight | Oven Temp. | Reading of Meat Thermometer | Minutes per Lb. | Approximate Roasting Time | Approx. Wt. of Each Serving of Cooked Meat |
|---|---|---|---|---|---|---|
| **BEEF** | | | | | | |
| Standing Rib Roast (7 rib) | 20-25 lbs. | 300° | 125° rare | 11 | 4 hrs. | 2½-3 oz. |
| | | | 140° med. | 12 | 4½ hrs. | |
| | | | 150° well | 13 | 5 hrs. | |
| Rolled Rib | 16-19 lbs. | 300° | 125° rare | 22 | 5¾ hrs. | 2½-3 oz. |
| | | | 140° med. | 23 | 6 hrs. | |
| | | | 150° well | 24 | 6¼ hrs. | |
| Sirloin Butt | 16-19 lbs. | 300° | 125° rare | 22 | 5¾ hrs. | 2½-3 oz. |
| | | | 140° med. | 23 | 6 hrs. | |
| | | | 150° well | 24 | 6¼ hrs. | |
| Round Steaks Cube, Swiss | 16 lbs. | 350° | | | 2½-3 hrs. | |
| Ground Beef for Meat Loaf | 12 lbs. (3 loaves) | 325° | | | 1-1¼ hrs. | |
| **LAMB** | | | | | | |
| Leg, Roast | 19-23 lbs. | 300° | 180° | 30-35 | 3½-4 hrs. | 2½-3 oz. |
| **PORK** | | | | | | |
| Loin Roast, bone-in | 4 (5 lb.) roasts | 350° | 185° | 30 | 3 hrs. | 2½-3 oz. |
| Loin Roast, bone-in | 2 (10 lb.) roasts | 350° | 185° | 18 | 3½ hrs. | 2½-3 oz. |
| Ham, bone-in (whole ham) | 23-28 lbs. | 300° | 160° | 15-18 | 3-3½ hrs. | 2½-3 oz. |
| Ham, bone-in (fully cooked) | 12-15 lbs. | 325° | 160° | 10 | 1¾-2 hrs. | 2½-3 oz. |
| Ham, canned, small | 2 (6 lb.) roasts | 325° | 160° | 15-18 | 1½-2 hrs. | 2½-3 oz. |
| large | 1 (12 lb.) roast | 325° | 160° | 10 | 1½-2 hrs. | 2½-3 oz. |
| **VEAL** | | | | | | |
| Leg, Roast | 8 lb. | 300° | 170° | 25 | 3-3½ hrs. | 2½-3 oz. |

# Directions and Time Table
## for Roasting Poultry

**TO ROAST POULTRY:**

Rinse bird with cold water; pat dry. Rub cavity of bird lightly with salt. Fill wishbone area with stuffing, if used. Fasten neck skin to back with skewer. Fill cavity lightly, if stuffing is used. Push drumsticks under band of skin at tail; or tie them to tail.

Place bird on rack in shallow roasting pan. Brush skin with fat. Place in preheated oven following the time and temperature in chart. If desired, baste or brush occasionally with pan drippings—especially any dry areas. When bird is ⅔ done, cut trussing cord on bridge of skin at drumsticks.

To test doneness, a roast meat thermometer placed in center of the thickest breast muscle should register 195°. Also, to test for doneness, move the drumstick up and down. The joints should yield readily and the meatiest part of drumstick should feel very soft when pressed.

| Poultry | Oven Temperature | Approximate Roasting Time | Reading of Meat Thermometer |
|---|---|---|---|
| **CHICKEN** (ready to cook weight) | | | |
| 1½ to 2 pounds | 325° | 1-1½ hrs. | |
| 2 to 2½ pounds | 325° | 1½-2 hrs. | Use |
| 2½ to 3 pounds | 325° | 2-2½ hrs. | |
| 3 to 4 pounds | 325° | 2½-3 hrs. | drumstick |
| | | | |
| **CAPON** (ready to cook weight) | | | test |
| 6 to 8 pounds | 325° | 3½-4½ hrs. | |
| | | | described |
| **ROCK CORNISH GAME HEN** | | | above |
| 12 to 14 ounces | 400° | 1 hr. | |
| 16 to 18 ounces | 400° | 1¼ hrs. | |
| | | | |
| **TURKEY** (ready to cook weight) | | | |
| 4 to 6 pounds | 325° | 3-3½ hrs. | 195° |
| 6 to 8 pounds | 325° | 3½-4 hrs. | 195° |
| 8 to 12 pounds | 325° | 4-4½ hrs. | 195° |
| 12 to 16 pounds | 325° | 4½-5 hrs. | 195° |
| 16 to 20 pounds | 325° | 5-6½ hrs. | 195° |
| 20 to 24 pounds | 325° | 6½-7½ hrs. | 195° |
| | | | |
| **DUCKLING** (ready to cook weight) | | | Use |
| 4 to 5 pounds | 325° | 2½-3 hrs. | |
| | | | drumstick |
| **GOOSE** (ready to cook weight) | | | |
| 4 to 6 pounds | 325° | 2¾-3 hrs. | test |
| 6 to 8 pounds | 325° | 3-3½ hrs. | |
| 8 to 10 pounds | 325° | 3½-3¾ hrs. | described |
| 10 to 12 pounds | 325° | 3¾-4¼ hrs. | |
| 12 to 14 pounds | 325° | 4-4¾ hrs. | above |

Allow ¼ to ½ hour less for rotisserie cooking.

# Index

Almond-herb Stuffing, 120
Almond Tea Cakes, 64
Angels on Wings, 168
Appetizers and Beverages, 17-30
Appetizers
    Artichoke Antipasto, 23
    Avocado Ham Dip, 27
    Cheese Appetizer Puffs,
    Do-ahead, 19
    Cheese Ball, Party, 22
    Cheese Party Tray, 22
    Cheese Swirls, 21
    Cucumber Dip, Appetizing, 27
    Crab Meat Spread, 20
    Egg Foo Yung, 25
    Eggs, Deviled, 20
    Fruit Curry Dip, 27
    Ham-olive Dip, 26
    Herb Dip, 27
    Kabobs, Cock, 26
    Liver, French Fried, 24
    Marinated Meat, 25
    Meat Balls, Oriental-style, 25
    Orange Cup, Fresh, 23
    Rumaki, 24
    Sesame Cheese Log, 21
    Sharp Cheddar Spread, 20
    Shrimp Cocktail, Red-rock, 17
    Shrimp Puffs, 19
    Smoked Egg Dip, 24
    Snow Cap Mold, 23
    West Indies Dip, 26
Appetizing Cucumber Dip, 27
Apple
    Caramel, 87
    Cider Cake, 49
    Dutch Pie, 71
    Pie with Warm Cheddar
    Cheese Sauce, 10
    Slices, 88
    Spice Crumble, 176
    Upside-down Cake, 50
Applesauce Cake, 49
Applesauce Meat Balls, 172
Apricot Squares, 59
Argante Potatoes, 156
Artichoke Antipasto, 23
Au gratin Potato Bake, 156
Autumn Pear Pie, 71
Avocado and Citrus Fruit
    Salad, 136
Avocado Ham Dip, 27

"Babka" Yeast Raisin Coffee
    Cake, 28
Baked Alaska Raspberry
    Fluff Pie, 76

Baked Carrot Sticks, 154
Baked Chicken Salad, 138
Baked Creamed Potatoes, 157
Baked Eggs Au gratin with
    Nippy Cheese Sauce, 127
Baked Ham with Cumberland
    Sauce, 108
Baked Ham Slice with Apricot
    Glaze, 110
Baked Ice Cream Pie, 76
Baked Potatoes with Cheese, 166
Bambinos, 18
Banana-nut Bread, 34
Barbeque Sauce, 98
Barbecued
    Beef on Buns, 101
    Bread, 176
    Chicken, Dilly, 162
    Flank Steak Pinwheels, 163
    Lamb Shanks, 112
    Lemon Beef Loaves, 101
    Meat Balls, 173
    Ribs, 162
Basic Coffee Cake Dough, 45
Basket Cake, 7
Bean Chowder, 148
Beans
    Baked, 152
    Green, Amadine, 152
    Green, and Mushrooms, 153
    Green, Harvest Style, 152
    Green, with Blue Cheese, 153
    Lima, Creole, 151
Beef
    and Broccoli Skillet Dinner, 99
    and Egg Scramble, 102
    Balls in Onion Soup, 102
    City Chicken Style, 96
    Corned, Cereal Flake
    Casserole, 103
    Corned, Hash with Shirred
    Eggs, 103
    Flank Steak Pinwheels, 163
    Frozen Meat Sauce, 100
    Grecian with Cheese Noodles, 96
    Hamburger-Cream Cheese
    Casserole, 101
    Hamburgers, Old-fashioned, 164
    Helene, 103
    Kick-off Burgers, 102
    Loaves, Lemon Barbecued, 101
    Meat Balls, Barbecued, 173
    Roast, Standing Rib, 93
    Pot Roast, Sweet Sour, 94
    Pot Roast with Vegetables, 94
    Rye Sandwich Specialty, 147
    Sauerbraten, 95

Sausage-stuffed Birds in
  Barbecue Sauce, 98
Steak, Charcoal Grilled, 163
Steak, Chopped Round and
  Fresh Mushrooms in Sour
  Cream, 98
Steak, Swiss Savory, 94
Steak, Swiss Super, 172
Stew, Italian Style, 95
Stroganoff, 97
Sukiyaki, 97
Zucchini Casserole, 99
Beefeater Sandwich, 148
Beets in Orange Sauce, 153
Best Ever Baked Beans, 152
Beverages
  Canned Fruit Juice Punch, 178
  Cinnamon Sparkle Punch, 28
  Coffee, 179
  Fruit Juice Shrub, 28
  Heavenly Nectar Punch, 29
  Hot Buttered Tomato Juice, 28
  Hot Mulled Pineapple Juice, 29
  Milk Punch, 30
  Nuptial Nectar, 178
  Orange-pineapple Punch, 29
  Orange Sherbet Punch, 179
  Party Punch, 30
  Passion Punch, 29
  Reception Chocolate, 179
  Rhubarb Shrub, 28
  Tea, 179
  Teenagers Swingin' Swizzle
    Punch, 30
  Tomato Cream Frosty, 30
Bitter-sweet Fudge Frosting, 8
Breads (Yeast, Quick, & Ways
  With Bread) 31-46
Breads
  Bambinos, 18
  Banana-nut Bread, 34
  Barbecued, 176
  Biscuits, Cheese, 32
  Cinnamon "Whizzes," 44
  Coffee Cake Dough, Basic, 45
  Coffee Crescents, 42
  Corn Bread or Sticks, 33
  Cottage Cheese Spirals, 42
  Currant Scones, 34
  Curry Buttered, 167
  Flat, 34
  French Toast, Grilled with
    Bacon, 164
  French Toast, Wine, 46
  Garlic Bread Slices, Broiled, 46
  Herb Buttered in Foil, 167
  Herb or Garlic French, 46
  Holiday Fruit, 44
  Italian, 43
  Muffins, Cranberry, 32

Muffins, Molasses Bran, 32
Muffins, Spoonbread, 33
Muffins, Tiny Corn, 33
Mustard, 46
Pastry Boats, 18
Popovers, 31
Poppy Seed, 167
Roll Glazes, 41
Rolls, Corn Meal, 41
Rolls, Hot, 40
Rolls, Miniature Pan, 39
Rolls, Pecan, 45
Swedish Tea Ring, 45
Waffles, Pecan with Peach
  Sauce, 35
Bridal Cake, 178
Broiled Garlic Bread Slices, 46
Broiled Salmon-wich, 146
Brown 'n Serve Pizzas, 147
Brownies
  Fudge-topped, 58
  Pecan, 57
  Two-tone, 58
Brunch Cake, 35
Buffet Green Beans with
  Blue Cheese, 153
Butter Cream Frosting, 177
Buttermilk Dressing, 144
Butter Toffee, 91
Buttered Zucchini, 159

Cake
  Apple Cider, 49
  Apple Upside-down, 50
  Applesauce, 49
  Basket, 7
  Bridal, 178
  Chocolate Marble, 52
  Cocoa Pound, 52
  Crumb, 51
  Date, Frosty, 47
  Fudge Sauce, 53
  Marigold, 53
  Orange Loaf, 48
  Party, 48
  Pineapple Upside-down, 48
  Sour Cream Spice, 52
  Springtime Chiffon, 54
  Strawberry Pound Cake Ring, 50
  Torte, Elegant, 54
  Torte, Othello, 55
  Walnut Honey, 51
Cakes, Cookies and Pies, 47-78
Campfire Picnic Buns, 165
Candy
  Choco-mint Balls, 90
  Chocolate No-Bake Clusters, 90
  Divinity Fudge, 90
  Fudge, Million Dollar, 89
  Lemon Coconut Creams, 92

Orange Coconut Creams, 92
Orange Sugared Walnuts, 92
Pralines, Louisiana Cream, 91
Spiced Pecans or Walnuts, 92
Toffee, Butter, 91
Canned Fruit Juice Punch, 178
Caramel Pecan Pie, 77
Casseroles
 Beef-Zucchini, 99
 Chicken and Rice, 116
 Chicken Cashew Casserole, 116
 Chicken Salad, Baked, 138
 Corn, 154
 Corned Beef, Cereal Flake, 103
 Corned Beef Hash with
  Shirred Eggs, 103
 Dolmades American Style, 123
 Egg, Danish, 128
 Hamburger-Cream Cheese, 101
 Jambalaya Salad, Southern
  Baked, 137
 Lobster and Crab Meat, 125
 Macaroni and Cheese, 174
 Macaroni, Gourmet, 131
 Pork Chop-Rhubarb, 104
 Rice, Green, 129
 Rice, Wild, and Mushrooms, 130
 Veal en Casserole, 114
 Veal Lasagna, 173
Celery Seed Dressing, 143
Celestial Chicken, 117
Cereal Flake Blueberry Kuchen, 38
Cereal Flake Corned Beef
 Casserole, 103
Charcoal Grilled Steak, 163
Cheese and Fruit, 89
Cheese Biscuits, 32
Cheese Party Tray, 22
Cheese Swirls, 21
Cheese Tomatoes, 166
Cherries Jubilee, 86
Cherry Bubble, 176
Cherry Orange Coffee Cake, 38
Chicken
 a la Romano, 117
 and Curried Rice, One Bowl, 118
 and Rice Casserole, 116
 Barbecued, Dilly, 162
 Cashew Casserole, 116
 Celestial, 117
 Ginger Glazed, 115
 Grape Salad, 136
 Lickin' Good Pork Chops, 105
 Loaf, 114
 Orange Kissed, 116
 Oven-Fried, 115
 Oven-Fried with Sauce
  Variations, 115
 Pork Divinity, 106
 Salad, Baked, 138

Salad, Curried, 137
 Tropicale, 118
Chiffon Dessert Waffles with
 Frozen Strawberries and
 Whipped Cream, 81
Chili Con Carne, 100
Chinese Almond Cakes, 65
Chinese Pork Chops, 104
Chive Corn, 154
Choco-mint Balls, 90
Chocolate
 Cake, Cocoa Pound, 52
 Cake, Fudge Sauce, 53
 Cake, Marble, 52
 Cake, Rum Refrigerator, 87
 Chip Cookies, Oatmeal, 61
 Cookies, Drop, 60
 Cookies, Fudge Nut, 65
 Cookies, Nut, 60
 Frosting, Fudge, 8
 Fudge, Bitter-Sweet, 8
 Fudge, Million Dollar, 89
 Mint Balls, 90
 No-Bake Clusters, 90
 Pie, Almond Dream, 72
 Pie, Cream Mint, 72
 Pie, Fudge, 72
 Reception, 179
Chopped Round Steak and Fresh
 Mushrooms in Sour Cream, 98
Chowder
 Bean, 148
 Corn 'n Crab, 150
 Egg, Main Dish, 149
 Hearty Winter, 150
 Seafood, 149
 Tomato-corn, 150
Cinnamon Sparkle Punch, 28
Cinnamon "whizzes," 44
City Chicken-Beef Style, 96
Cock Kabobs, 25
Cocoa Pound Cake, 52
Coconut
 Kisses, 60
 Lemon Cookies, 62
 Tart Shells with Strawberry
  Parfait Filling, 67
Coffee, 179
Coffee Cake
 "Babka" Yeast Raisin, 28
 Basic Dough, 45
 Brunch, 35
 Cereal Flake Blueberry
  Kuchen, 38
 Cherry Orange, 38
 Fruit Filled, 37
 Layered, 36
 Peach Kuchen, 39
 Sausage-Apple, 38
 Sweet, 37

186 *Index*

Yum Yum, 36
Coffee Crescents, 42
Cole Slaw, Sour Cream, 135
Confetti Topped Cream Pie, 73
Cookies
  Almond Tea Cakes, 64
  Apricot Squares, 59
  Brownies, Fudge-Topped, 58
  Brownies, Pecan, 57
  Brownies, Two-toned, 58
  Coconut Kisses, 60
  Chinese Almond Cakes, 65
  Chocolate Drop, 60
  Chocolate Nut, 60
  Diamond Dainties, 63
  Dream Bars, 57
  Dutch Almond, 66
  Early American Ginger
    Cutouts, 62
  Empire Biscuits, 65
  Fudge Nut, 65
  Gumdrop Oatmeal, 61
  Krullers, 66
  Lemon Coconut, 62
  Mincemeat Squares, 64
  Molasses, Crisp, 63
  Molasses, Snaps, 62
  Oatmeal, Chocolate Chip, 61
  Oatmeal, Old-Fashioned, 61
  Pecan or Almond Crescents, 63
  Toffee Nut Bars, 59
  Toffee Squares, 59
Corn
  and Tomato Scramble, 130
  Bread or Sticks, 33
  Casserole, 154
  Chive, 154
  Crisp-top with Herbs, 155
  'n Crab Chowder, 150
  on the Cob, 166
Corned Beef Hash with
  Shirred Eggs, 103
Cottage Blintzes, 85
Cottage Cheese Spirals, 42
Corn Meal Rolls, 41
Crab
  and Lobster Casserole, 125
  corn 'n Crab Chowder, 150
  Jiffy Eleanor, 122
  Meat Spread, 20
  Souffles, Individual, 125
Cracker Torte Confetti, 83
Cranberry Muffins, 32
Cranberry-Orange Stuffing for
  Roast Chicken, 120
Cream Cheese Chive Sauce for
  Baked Potatoes, 158
Cream Puffs with Chocolate Chip
  Cream Filling, 81

Creamed Turkey with Lemon-
  Buttered Noodles, 119
Creamy Cheese Cake, 85
Creamy Planked Pork, 107
Creamy Poached Eggs, 128
Creme de Cacao Bavarian, 79
Creole Lima Beans, 151
Crisp Molasses Cookies, 63
Crisp-Top Corn with Herbs, 155
Crumb Cake, 51
Currant Scones, 34
Curried Chicken Salad, 137
Curried Fruit, 89
Curry Buttered Bread, 167

Danish Egg Casserole, 128
Dark Sweet Cherry Mold, 142
Delectable Turkey Hash, 120
Desserts — Candies and
  Confections, 79-92
Desserts
  Angels on Wings, 168
  Apple Caramel, 87
  Apple Slices, 88
  Apple Spice Crumble, 176
  Cheese and Fruit, 89
  Cherries Jubilee, 86
  Cherry Bubble, 176
  Chiffon Dessert Waffles with
    Frozen Strawberries and
    Whipped Cream, 81
  Chocolate Rum Refrigerator
    Cake, 87
  Cottage Blintzes, 85
  Cracker Torte Confetti, 83
  Cream Puffs with Chocolate
    Chip Cream Filling, 81
  Creamy Cheese Cake, 85
  Creme de Cacao Bavarian, 79
  Curried Fruit, 89
  Donut Cartwheels, 80
  Frozen Hawaiian Cream, 80
  Ice Cream and Fruit
    Compote, 83
  Ice Cream Party Loaf, 82
  Individual Alaskas, 84
  Lime or Lemon Sherbet, 82
  Meringues and Peppermint
    Stick Ice Cream with Mocha
    Sauce, 177
  Peaches Delightful, 88
  Pina Schooner, 80
  Pineapple Cheese Cake, 84
  Raspberry Cream Torte, 87
  Rum Torte, 86
  Sherbet Ring with
    Strawberries, 82
Deviled Eggs, 20
Diamond Dainties, 63
Dilly Barbecued Chicken, 162

Directions and Time Table for Roasting Poultry, 181
Divinity Fudge, 90
Do-ahead Cheese Appetizer Puffs, 19
Dolmades American Style, 123
Donut Cartwheels, 80
Dream Bars, 57
Dutch Almond Cookies, 66
Dutch Apple Pie, 71

Early American Ginger Cutouts, 62
Egg
  and Beef Scramble, 102
  Baked Au gratin with Nippy Cheese Sauce, 127
  Danish Casserole, 128
  Deviled, 20
  Dip, Smoked, 26
  Fondue, 127
  Foo Yung, 24
  Main Dish Chowder, 149
  Poached, Creamy, 128
  Poached on Wild Rice — Western Sauce, 126
  Scrambled, Savory, 126
Eggplant with Meat Sauce, 100
Elegant Torte, 54
Emerald Salad, 175
Empire Biscuits, 65

Feeding a Crowd
  Buffet, 170
  Church Supper, 171
  Wedding Buffet, 171
Fireside Sandwiches, 146
Fish
  Baked, Savory, 123
  Steaks, Skewered, 163
Flank Steak Pinwheels, 163
Flat Bread, 34
Fluffy Icing, 56
Fondue
  Egg, 127
  Swiss Cheese, 129
Frankfurters in Herbed Buns, 161
French Fried Liver, 26
French Peas, 155
Fresh Orange Cup, 23
Frosting
  Bitter-Sweet Fudge, 8
  Butter Cream, 177
  Fluffy Icing, 56
  Fudge, 56
  Lemon Butter, 55
  Orange Butter Cream, 56
  Royale, 57
  Thin Confectioners' Sugar Icing, 56

Vanilla Cream Cheese, 55
Frosty Date Cake, 47
Frozen
  Hawaiian Cream, 80
  Ice Cream Party Loaf, 82
  Meat Sauce, 100
  Peas Continental, 155
  Pie, Lemon, 75
  Pie, Peppermint Ice Cream with Chocolate Crust, 75
  Pie, Pumpkin "Peace Pipe" with Caramelized Almonds, 76
  Pina Schooner, 80
  Sherbet, Lime or Lemon, 82
  Sherbet Ring with Strawberries, 82
Fruit Curry Dip, 27
Fruit Filled Coffee Cake, 37
Fruit Juice Shrub, 28
Fudge Frosting, 56
Fudge Nut Cookies, 65
Fudge Sauce Cake, 53
Fudge-Topped Brownies, 58

Ginger Glazed Chicken, 115
Gingersnap Crust, 68
Glazed Carrot Coins, 154
Glazed Ham Balls in Noodle Ring, 109
Golden Glazed Ham, 109
Golden Salad Ring, 142
Gourmet Macaroni, 131
Gourmet Pork Chops, 105
Gourmet Sour Cream Dressing, 144
Grapefruit Salad, 141
Grecian Beef with Cheese Noodles, 96
Green Beans Amadine, 152
Green Beans and Mushrooms, 153
Green Rice Casserole, 129
Grilled Bacon and Egg Sandwiches, 165
Grilled French Toast with Bacon, 164
Grilled Liver with Bacon, Onions and Tomatoes, 164
Grilled Potatoes, 165
Grilled Roquefort Tomatoes, 166
Gumdrop Oatmeal Cookies, 61

Ham
  and Asparagus Rolls with Cheese Sauce, 110
  Baked, with Cumberland Sauce, 108
  Glazed Balls in Noodle Ring, 109
  Golden Glazed, 109
  Olive Dip, 25

Slice, Baked with Apricot
Glaze, 110
Slices, with Orange-Cherry
Sauce, 173
Hamburger-Cream Cheese
Casserole, 101
Harvest-Style Green Beans, 152
Hearty Winter Chowder, 55
Heated Fruit Pie, 168
Heavenly Nectar Punch, 29
Herb Baked Tomatoes, 159
Herb Buttered Bread in Foil, 167
Herb Dip, 27
Herb or Garlic French Bread, 46
Holiday Fruit Bread, 44
Honeymoon Lemon Meringue
Pie, 74
Hot Buttered Tomato Juice, 28
Hot Mulled Pineapple Juice, 29
Hot Potato Salad, 174
Hot Rolls, 40

Ice Cream and Fruit Compote, 83
Ice Cream Party Loaf, 82
Individual Alaskas, 84
Individual Crab Meat Souffles, 125
Indonesian Sausage, 111
Irish Coffee Pie, 77
Italian Bread, 43
Italian Salad Bowl, 135
Italian Style Beef Stew, 95

Jiffy Crab Meat Eleanor, 122
Jiffy Supper Sandwich, 145
Jumbo Pizza Sandwich, 147

Kick-off Burgers, 102
Krullers, 66

Lamb
and Bean Whirls, 112
Barbecued Lamb Shanks, 112
Chops, Sweet 'n Sour, 112
Rotisserie Rolled Leg of, 113
Shish Kabob with Pilaff, 111
Lattice Cherry Pie, 71
Layered Coffee Cake, 36
Lemon Barbecued Beef
Loaves, 101
Lemon Butter Frosting, 55
Lemon Coconut Cookies, 62
Lemon Coconut Creams, 92
Lemon-Cranberry Meringue
Pie, 74
Lemon Fluff Pie, 78
Lemon Tuna Mold, 139
Lime or Lemon Sherbet, 82
Lime-Strawberry Surprise, 141
Lobster
and Crab Meat Casserole, 125

Ring-Around Salad
Supreme, 138
Thermidor, 122
Louisiana Cream Pralines, 91

Macaroni
and Cheese, 174
Gourmet, 131
Maikai Spareribs, 108
Main Dishes, 93-132
Main Dish Egg Chowder, 149
Mandarin Orange Cream Pie, 73
Marigold Cake, 53
Marinated Meat, 24
Meat
Balls, Applesauce, 172
Balls in Onion Soup, 102
Grilled Liver with Bacon,
Onions and Tomatoes, 164
Menus
General, 7-16
Quantity, 170-71
Meringues and Peppermint
Stick Ice Cream with Mocha
Sauce, 177
Milk Punch, 30
Million Dollar Fudge, 89
Mincemeat Squares, 64
Miniature Pan Rolls, 39
Minted Pineapple Salad with
Lemon Dressing, 136
Molasses Bran Muffins, 32
Molasses Snaps, 62
Molded Cranberry Relish
Salad, 140
Muffins
Corn, Tiny, 33
Cranberry, 32
Molasses Bran Muffins, 32
Spoonbread, 33
Mustard Bread, 46

Noodles
Creamed Turkey with
Lemon Buttered, 119
Grecian Beef with Cheese, 96
Nuptial Nectar, 178

Oatmeal
Cookies, Chocolate Chip, 61
Cookies, Gumdrop, 61
Cookies, Old Fashioned, 61
Old Fashioned Boiled
Dressing, 143
Old Fashioned Hamburgers, 164
Old Fashioned Oatmeal
Cookies, 61
One-Bowl Chicken and Curried
Rice, 118
Orange Butter Cream Frosting, 56

Orange Coconut Creams, 92
Orange Kissed Chicken, 116
Orange Loaf Cake, 48
Orange-Pineapple Punch, 29
Orange Sherbet Punch, 179
Orange Sugared Walnuts, 92
Oriental-Style Meat Balls, 24
Othello Torte, 55
Oven-Baked Potatoes, 157
Oven-Fried Chicken, 115
Oven-Fried Chicken with Sauce
    Variations, 115
Over-the-Coals Cookery, 161-68

Pancake Hawaiian, 132
Parmesan Potato Sticks, 158
Party Cake, 48
Party Cheese Ball, 22
Party Punch, 30
Passion Punch, 29
Pastry Boats, 18
Pastry for 8- or 9-inch Pie Shell, 67
Pastry for 10-inch Pie Shell, 68
Pastry for 2-Crust Pie, 67
Peach Kuchen, 39
Peaches Delightful, 88
Pecan Brownies, 57
Pecan or Almond Crescents, 63
Pecan Rolls, 45
Pecan Waffles with Peach Sauce, 35
Peppermint Ice Cream Pie with
    Chocolate Crust, 75
Pies
    Apple Pie with Warm Cheddar
        Cheese Sauce, 10
    Autumn Pear, 71
    Baked Alaska Raspberry
        Fluff, 76
    Baked Ice Cream, 76
    Caramel Pecan, 77
    Chocolate Almond Dream, 72
    Chocolate Cream Mint, 72
    Chocolate Fudge, 72
    Coconut Tart Shells with
        Strawberry Parfait
        Filling, 69
    Confetti Topped Cream, 73
    Dutch Apple, 71
    Frozen Lemon, 75
    Frozen Pumpkin "Peace
        Pipe," 76
    Gingersnap Crust, 68
    Graham Cracker Crust,
        8-inch, 68
    Graham Cracker Crust,
        9-inch, 68
    Heated Fruit, 168
    Honeymoon Lemon
        Meringue, 74
    Irish Coffee, 77

Lattice Cherry, 71
Lemon-Cranberry Meringue, 74
Lemon Fluff, 78
Mandarin Orange Cream, 73
Pastry for 8- or 9-inch
    Pie Shell, 67
Pastry for 10-inch Pie Shell, 68
Pastry for 2-Crust Pie, 67
Peppermint Ice Cream with
    Chocolate Crust, 75
Rice and Peach Ginger, 70
Sparkling Red Cherry, 70
Strawberry Glace, 69
Pina Schooner, 80
Pineapple
    and Shrimp Salad, 137
    Cheese Cake, 84
    Minted, Salad with Lemon
        Dressing, 136
    Ring-Around Salad
        Supreme, 138
    Upside-Down Cake, 48
Poached Eggs on Wild Rice —
    Western Sauce, 126
Popovers, 31
Poppy Seed Bread, 167
Pork
    Barbecued Ribs, 162
    Chicken Lickin' Good
        Chops, 105
    Chicken-Pork Divinity, 106
    Chop-Rhubarb Casserole, 104
    Chops, Chinese, 104
    Chops, Gourmet, 105
    Chops with Caper Sauce, 104
    Creamy Planked, 107
    Indonesian Sausage, 111
    'n Potatoes, 105
    South Sea Island Treat, 106
    Spareribs, Maikai, 108
    Spareribs — Tangy Plum
        Glaze, 107
Pot Roast with Vegetables, 94
Potato Salad, 135
Potatoes
    Argante, 156
    Au gratin, 156
    Au gratin Bake, 156
    Baked Creamed, 157
    Baked with Cheese, 166
    Cream Cheese Chive Sauce
        for Baked, 158
    Grilled, 165
    Hot Salad, 174
    Oven-Baked, 157
    Parmesan Sticks, 158
    Roasted, 166
    Rosemary, 158
    Sour Cream Bacon Topping
        for Baked, 158

Sweet, Puffs, 159
Twice-Baked, 157
Pretzel-Fried Turkey, 118

Quantity Cookery for
Fifty, 169-79
Quantity
Beverages
Canned Fruit Juice
Punch, 178
Coffee, 179
Nuptial Nectar, 178
Orange Sherbet Punch, 179
Reception Chocolate, 179
Tea, 179
Breads
Barbecued, 176
Cake
Bridal, 178
Casseroles
Macaroni and Cheese, 174
Veal Lasagna, 173
Desserts
Apple Spice Crumble, 176
Cherry Bubble, 176
Meringues and Peppermint
Stick Ice Cream with
Mocha Sauce, 177
Frosting
Butter Cream, 177
Meats
Applesauce Meat Balls, 172
Barbecued Meat Balls, 173
Ham Slices with Orange-
Cherry Sauce, 173
Super Swiss Steak, 172
Menu
Feeding a crowd
Buffet, 170
Church Supper, 171
Wedding Buffet, 171
Roasting Guide, 180
Salad Dressings
Saucy Blue Cheese, 175
Salads
Emerald, 175
Hot Potato, 174
Tossed Green, 174
Wedding Ring Mold, 175

Raspberry Cream Torte, 87
Reception Chocolate, 179
Red and White Fruit Mold, 140
Red-Rock Shrimp Cocktail, 17
Rhubarb Shrub, 28
Rice
and Cheese Timbales, 129
and Chicken Casserole, 116
and Peach Ginger Pie, 70
and Vegetables, 130

Green Casserole, 129
White, 97
Wild, and Mushroom
Casserole, 130
Wild, with Poached Eggs,
Western Sauce, 126
Ring-Around Salad Supreme, 138
Roasted Potatoes, 166
Roll Glazes, 41
Rolls
Coffee Crescents, 42
Corn Meal, 41
Cottage Cheese Spirals, 42
Hot Rolls, Standard Sweet
Dough, 40
Miniature Pan, 39
Pecan, 45
Rosemary Potatoes, 158
Rotisserie Rolled Leg of Lamb, 113
Royale Frosting, 57
Rum Torte, 86
Rumaki, 26


Salads and Salad Dressings,
133-44
Salad Dressings
Buttermilk, 144
Celery Seed, 143
Gourmet Sour Cream, 144
Old Fashioned Boiled, 143
Saucy Blue Cheese, 175
Sour Cream, 144
Sour Cream Fruit, 144
Tropical, 143
Whipped Fruit, 143
Salads
Avocado and Citrus Fruit
Salad, 136
Chicken, Baked, 138
Chicken, Curried, 137
Chicken Grape, 136
Dark Sweet Cherry Mold, 142
Emerald, 175
Golden Ring, 142
Grapefruit, 141
Hot Potato, 174
Italian Bowl, 135
Lemon Tuna Mold, 139
Lime-Strawberry Surprise, 141
Minted Pineapple with Lemon
Dressing, 136
Molded Cranberry Relish, 140
Potato, 135
Red and White Fruit Mold, 140
Ring-Around Supreme, 138
Shrimp and Pineapple, 137
Sour Cream Cole Slaw, 135
Southern Baked Jambalaya, 137
Spiced Peach, 142

Strawberry-Sour Cream
  Mold, 140
Tomato Artichoke, 133
Tomato Shrimp Aspic Ring, 139
Tossed, 134
Tossed Green, 174
Vinaigrette Salad Wheel, 134
Wedding Ring Mold, 175
Sandwiches and Soups, 145-50
Sandwiches
  Beefeater, 148
  Beef-Rye Specialty, 147
  Broiled Salmon-wich, 146
  Brown 'n Serve Pizzas, 147
  Campfire Picnic Buns, 165
  Fireside, 146
  Frankfurters in Herbed
    Buns, 161
  Grilled Bacon and Egg, 165
  Hamburgers, Old Fashioned, 165
  Hamburgers, Stuffed Deluxe, 148
  Jiffy Supper, 145
  Jumbo Pizza, 147
  Triple-Decker Sandwich
    Bake, 146
Saucy Blue Cheese Dressing, 175
Sauerbraten, 95
Sausage-Apple Coffee Cake, 38
Sausage-Stuffed Beef Birds in
  Barbecue Sauce, 98
Savory Baked Fish, 123
Savory Scrambled Eggs, 126
Savory Swiss Steak, 94
Seafood Chowder, 149
Sesame Cheese Log, 21
Sharp Cheddar Spread, 20
Sherbet Ring with Strawberries, 82
Shish Kabob with Pilaff, 111
Shrimp
  A La Ming, 124
  and Pineapple Salad, 137
  Puffs, 19
  Southern Baked Jambalaya
    Salad, 137
  Tomato Aspic Ring, 139
Skewered Fish Steaks, 163
Smoked Egg Dip, 26
Smothered Turkey with
  Potatoes, 119
Snow Cap Mold, 23
Soups
  Bean Chowder, 148
  Corn 'n Crab Chowder, 150
  Hearty Winter Chowder, 55
  Main Dish Egg Chowder, 149
  Seafood Chowder, 149
  Tomato-Corn Chowder, 150
Sour Cream Bacon Topping for
  Baked Potatoes, 158

Sour Cream Cole Slaw, 135
Sour Cream Dressing, 144
Sour Cream Fruit Salad
  Dressing, 144
Sour Cream Spice Cake, 52
South Sea Island Treat, 106
Southern Baked Jambalaya
  Salad, 137
Spaghetti and Meat Sauce, 100
Spaghetti Marinara, 131
Spareribs — Tangy Plum
  Glaze, 107
Sparkling Red Cherry Pie, 70
Spiced Peach Salad, 142
Spiced Pecans or Walnuts, 92
Spinach Supreme, 159
Spoonbread Muffins, 33
Springtime Chiffon Cake, 54
Standing Rib Roast of Beef, 93
Strawberry Pie Glace, 69
Strawberry Pound Cake Ring, 50
Strawberry-Sour Cream Mold, 140
Stuffed Hamburgers Deluxe, 148
Stuffing
  Almond-Herb, 120
  Cranberry-Orange for Roast
    Chicken, 120
Sukiyaki, 97
Super Swiss Steak, 172
Swedish Tea Ring, 45
Sweet Coffee Cake, 37
Sweet 'n Sour Lamb Chops, 112
Sweet Potato Puffs, 159
Sweet Sour Pot Roast, 94
Swiss Cheese Fondue, 129

Tea, 179
Teenagers Swingin' Swizzle
  Punch, 30
Thin Confectioners' Sugar
  Icing, 56
Tiny Corn Muffins, 33
Toffee
  Nut Bars, 59
  Squares, 59
Tomato Artichoke Salad, 133
Tomato-Corn Chowder, 150
Tomato-Corn Scramble, 130
Tomato Cream Frosty, 30
Tomato Shrimp Aspic Ring, 139
Tossed Green Salad, 174
Tossed Salad, 134
Triple-Decker Sandwich Bake, 146
Tropical Salad Dressing, 143
Tuna
  Lemon Mold, 139
  Savory Tuna Roll, 121
  Suey, 124

Turkey
  Creamed with Lemon-
    Buttered Noodles, 119
  Hash, Delectable, 120
  Pretzel-Fried, 118
  Smothered with Potatoes, 119
Twice-Baked Potatoes, 157
Two-Tone Brownies, 58

Vanilla Cream Cheese Frosting, 55
Veal
  Divine, 114
  en Casserole, 114
  Lasagna, 173
  Paprika with Buttered
    Noodles, 113
Vegetables, 151-60
  Bean Green Amandine, 152
  Beans, Baked, Best Ever, 152
  Green, Harvest Style, 152
  Beans, Green with Blue
    Cheese, 153
  Beans, Green and
    Mushrooms, 153
  Beans, Lima, Creole, 151
  Beets in Orange Sauce, 153
  Broccoli and Beef Skillet
    Dinner, 99
  Carrot Coins, Glazed, 154
  Carrot Sticks, Baked, 154
  Corn Casserole, 154
  Corn, Chive, 154
  Corn, Crisp-Top with Herbs, 155
  Corn on the Cob, 166
  Eggplant with Meat Sauce, 100
  Peas, French, 155

  Peas, Frozen Continental, 155
  Potato Bake, Au gratin, 156
  Potato Sticks, Parmesan, 158
  Potatoes, Argante, 156
  Potatoes, Au gratin, 156
  Potatoes, Baked Creamed, 157
  Potatoes Baked, with
    Cheese, 166
  Potatoes, Grilled, 165
  Potatoes, Oven-Baked, 157
  Potatoes, Roasted, 166
  Potatoes, Rosemary, 158
  Potatoes, Twice-Baked, 157
  Spinach Supreme, 159
  Sweet Potato Puffs, 159
  Tomatoes, Cheese, 166
  Tomatoes, Grilled
    Roquefort, 166
  Tomatoes, Herb Baked, 159
  Zucchini, Buttered, 159
  Zucchini Strips, 160
Vinaigrette Salad Wheel, 134

Walnut Honey Cake, 51
Wedding Ring Mold, 175
West Indies Dip, 25
Whipped Fruit Dressing, 143
Wild Rice and Mushroom
  Casserole, 130
Wine French Toast, 46
Yum Yum Coffee Cake, 36

Zucchini, Beef Casserole, 99
Zucchini, Buttered, 159
Zucchini Strips, 160